Minoritarian Liberalism

Minoritarian Liberalism

A Travesti Life in a Brazilian Favela

MOISÉS LINO E SILVA

The University of Chicago Press   Chicago and London

The University of Chicago Press, Chicago 60637
The University of Chicago Press, Ltd., London
© 2022 by The University of Chicago
All rights reserved. No part of this book may be used or reproduced in any manner whatsoever without written permission, except in the case of brief quotations in critical articles and reviews. For more information, contact the University of Chicago Press, 1427 E. 60th St., Chicago, IL 60637.
Published 2022
Printed in the United States of America

31 30 29 28 27 26 25 24 23 22   1 2 3 4 5

ISBN-13: 978-0-226-81825-2 (cloth)
ISBN-13: 978-0-226-81827-6 (paper)
ISBN-13: 978-0-226-81826-9 (e-book)
DOI: https://doi.org/10.7208/chicago/9780226818269.001.0001

Library of Congress Cataloging-in-Publication Data

Names: Silva, Moises Lino e, author.
Title: Minoritarian liberalism : a travesti life in a Brazilian favela / Moisés Lino e Silva.
Description: Chicago : University of Chicago Press, 2022. | Includes bibliographical references and index.
Identifiers: LCCN 2021036569 | ISBN 9780226818252 (cloth) | ISBN 9780226818276 (paperback) | ISBN 9780226818269 (ebook)
Subjects: LCSH: Transgender people—Brazil—Rio de Janeiro. | Rocinha (Rio de Janeiro, Brazil)—Social conditions.
Classification: LCC F2646.4.R63 S55 2022 | DDC 981/.53—dc23
LC record available at https://lccn.loc.gov/2021036569

♾ This paper meets the requirements of ANSI/NISO Z39.48-1992 (Permanence of Paper).

To Natasha Kellem Bündchen

Contents

Preface ix

	Introduction	1
1	Through Pleasures and Pain	25
2	Laws of the Hillside	44
3	Northeastern Hinterlands	65
4	Queer Kids and the Favela Closet	90
5	Encountering Demons and Deities	113
6	Roman Slavery	143
7	As If There Is No Tomorrow	173

Epilogue 189   Acknowledgments 199   Notes 201
References 223   Index 233

Preface

Natasha liked to talk to strangers.[1] At random, she would approach people in the street and start a conversation. Her preference was for men. That's how our friendship started way back in 2009. She came up and started talking to me. At the time, I was twenty-eight and had been living in Favela da Rocinha, one of the largest slums in Rio de Janeiro, Brazil, to conduct ethnographic research. "Eu adoro dar um it!" (I love to give an it!), she would tell me, laughing. It took me a while to understand what she meant by the expression "to give an it." Another friend of mine in the *favela* volunteered to explain. "To 'give an it' is to take liberties with other people," he told me. "In this case, to give actually means to take. You take the necessary freedom to do something you want to do." I inattentively wrote about the situation in my field notes. I did not realize at that moment how intricate the topic of "liberties" would prove to be in the favela. I scribbled: "Natasha likes to go around chatting and blowing kisses at men. She is 'giving an it.' She derives freedom from situations in which I imagined she had none, given all the oppression, prejudice, and challenges she faces as a *travesti*[2] living in the slum."

I still keep a picture of Natasha taken in 2010. Seven people—four women and three men—pose in front of a black-and-white tiled wall, like pieces in a game of chess. We were at the Bar & Mar, a decaying nightclub in the West Zone of Rio de Janeiro, and no one knew exactly how the night would end. Who would fuck whom? Who would kiss whom? Who would pay whom? In her black, pointy high heels, Natasha is the tallest one in the photo. Her strapless, metallic dress is glued to her slender body, giving her a golden glow. She has no breasts, but she looks very feminine, with smooth hair and delicately applied makeup. Her black smoky eyes draw attention. In her right hand, she holds a glass of whiskey. Natasha didn't like to drink, but that night, she'd made an exception. She'd accepted an invitation to share a fancy bottle of Johnnie Walker Red Label with the young, muscular man standing behind her in the photograph. He wears a tight white T-shirt and blue jeans with white shoes. His bulging biceps wrap around her waist, and his knee peeks out from in between her legs. Natasha responds with a slight smile. She's enjoying the manly arms wrapped around her. Those were glorious times for us.

When I started my research in Rocinha, I had minimal knowledge of daily life in favelas. I believe the same would be true for most middle-class Brazilians, like myself. I had never lived in Rio, either. My previous experiences with favelas had been mainly through the media, either watching the news or depictions through movies such as *City of God*,[3] which uses a documentary-style language to portray extreme violence as the "real" face of favelas. During my years studying anthropology, I brought some nuance to this knowledge through readings on social justice, development, liberalism, and other important themes in urban studies. However, nothing quite prepared me for the situations I experienced when I moved to Favela da Rocinha.

While living in the favela, I had initially expected to witness and register contemporary processes of oppression using ethnographic methods. I assumed that the scarcity of freedom in the lives of the Brazilian urban poor would be an important topic for in-depth anthropological analysis. Above all, I hoped that an exposé on the lack of liberties in Brazilian favelas could help to bring change to the unfortunate situation I anticipated to encounter. However, it only took me a couple of weeks of fieldwork to start noticing that there was no scarcity of freedoms in the favela in an absolute sense. Instead, day after day, I began to notice different expressions and practices of freedom in the slum. The problem seemed to be that most of these favela freedoms were not the same freedoms that I already knew, and those which liberal supporters cherished. Some of them were very unfamiliar to me and probably unfamiliar to others who had never set foot in a favela. Contrary to what I had anticipated, the research process for this book allowed me to witness liberties where I least expected them to exist, and to understand their importance for those who lived by them.

In late 2012, unexpectedly, I lost contact with Natasha. It took me a couple of months to encounter Natasha again. In a sense, we only actually reconnected after I was able to understand more about my normative prejudices and about her liberalism; the pleasures and pain that a "liberated" (*liberada*) life in the favela implied for my friend. What are the multiple forms that liberalism assumes in Brazil? What are the relationships among different forms of power that create the conditions of possibility for people living in the slums of Rio—not only for the elites—to desire and experience freedom? What do the intersections between "neighborhoods of urban relegation"[4] and "queer forms of life" tell us about contemporary operations of liberation? What happens when we take seriously the possibility that liberalism can be inflected by subjects considered deviant in terms of gender and sexuality, subaltern in terms of class, and marginal in terms of power?

The word *liberalism* derives from the Latin *liber*, with a deep history that can be traced back to the Greco-Roman empires.[5] The normative definition of liberalism evoked in this book springs from events in European history, such as the Glorious Revolution (1688), the French Revolution (1789), and ideas derived from "contractualist" philosophy, mainly through the work of John Locke.[6] The core argument of this mode of Eurocentric liberalism is that individual liberties should be protected against abuses of the sovereign, who should have enough power to avoid the potential chaos inherent to the "state of nature" ("the war of all against all") but not enough power to become a tyrant. In normative liberalism, "society" should be organized to protect core values such as private property and individual autonomy. Formerly a European project, this mode of liberalism can now be found in most territories around the globe.[7] It has aligned itself with both left and right political currents, and over the centuries it has ambiguously contributed to projects such as colonialism and slavery.[8] Nowadays, liberalism finds its highest expression in the United States, where it is a fundamental value of the American Constitution.

This book presents a challenge to the stability of normative liberalism. It does so not through an aloof philosophical argument but through the use of grounded ethnographic theory. In practice, normative liberalism has promoted the freedom of privileged subjects, those entitled to "rights" (usually white, adult, heteronormative, and bourgeois people), at the expense of other minorities (such as children, travestis, Amerindians, Black people, and slum dwellers). A typical response to these inequalities has been to campaign for the "inclusion" of minorities into liberalism; in other words, the universalization of Eurocentric liberties.[9] A queer anthropology of liberalism should take issue with such aspiration.

My fieldwork focused on questions of *liberdade* and how it was practiced in the life of favela dwellers. In Portuguese, the official language in Brazil, the word *liberdade* encompasses the meanings of both freedom

PREFACE

and liberty, without distinction. Meanwhile, *liberalismo* has acquired a much more "economic" dimension in Brazil, as a possible shorthand for *neoliberalismo*. As I was preparing this book, I was aware that "liberalism" has a complicated history in relation to questions of freedom, especially for marginalized subjects. It was a conscious decision to mobilize such a signifier as part of the analytical framework I propose. My use of the word is not meant to straightforwardly translate *liberalismo* into "liberalism," nor simply to reaffirm the established Eurocentric connotations that the word expresses in English. I choose to translate a marginalized politics of freedom under the heading of "liberalism" as an effort to introduce difference to the established meanings of the word in English. As a move toward the decolonization of liberalism, I intend to make such a familiar concept strange. In doing so, I wish to express an appreciation for the minoritarian[10] modes of liberdade (freedom and liberty) that I witnessed in Favela da Rocinha, postulating them on a par with one of the most cherished concepts of the Western philosophical tradition. As such, I argue for an understanding of liberalism much more aligned with a politics of liberation than has been the case otherwise.

Minorities are not excluded from the liberal project in an absolute sense. Liberalism presupposes the existence of the "unfree."[11] Nevertheless, subjects historically marginalized in normative liberalism also respond to their dislocated condition. One way they do so is through a process that queer theorist José Esteban Muñoz would call "disidentification," creative strategies through which minoritarian populations engage with dominant forces to produce their own truths. What also happens is that some truths regarding liberalism tend to be rendered invisible because they do not conform to core (Eurocentric) liberal values. *Minoritarian liberalisms* are not necessarily individualistic and focused on private property, for example. Acts of disidentification offer the conditions of possibility for "a disempowered politics or positionality [of freedom, I would add] that has been rendered unthinkable by the dominant culture."[12]

In my research for this book, long-term fieldwork and ethnographic methods have proven to be critical tools that allowed me not just to witness the existence of minoritarian modes of liberalism in a Brazilian favela but also to understand that these liberalisms operate according to their own theories. Rather than struggling to preserve Eurocentric meanings of liberalism so as to disqualify experiences of freedom in the life of minorities as something other than liberalism (as *libertinism*, for example), my proposal is that, in the company of Natasha Kellem and other queer friends from the favelas, the power and stability of normative liberalism should be challenged.

Introduction

I think there are more secrets, more possible freedoms, and more inventions in our future than we can imagine . . . MICHEL FOUCAULT, *TECHNOLOGIES OF THE SELF*

The European colonization of what is now known as the Federative Republic of Brazil started around 1500, with the Portuguese invasion of indigenous land in South America.[1] Alongside atrocities such as the pillage of native resources and the slave trade, Eurocentric concerns with Christianization, the commodification of land, and the assurance of royal sovereignty were introduced as part of the colonial project, evolving through different regimes of governmentality. In an extensive analysis of the origins and aftermath of the "colonial encounter" in Brazil, the ethnologist João Pacheco de Oliveira demonstrates that questions over the appropriate "management" of the (post)colonized populations in Latin America have mutated under different "alterity regimes"—forms of dealing with otherness—over the centuries.[2]

But from the time of the Enlightenment in Europe, other questions came to the fore, concerning issues of liberty: What (if anything) could justify, legally and morally, the exploitation of Amerindian and Black peoples? Could the abused populations in nascent Brazil be considered "subjects" of the Portuguese Crown? What should be the legal limits, if any, of colonial power? Slavery brought about extensive ontological debates regarding the humanity (and, consequently, rights) of the enslaved Amerindian and Black populations. In Brazil, liberty was a prominent cause for social movements struggling toward the independence of the country as early as the eighteenth century, even if such efforts would only later lead to the formal declaration of Brazil's independence in 1822 and the so-called Proclamation of the Republic (Proclamação da República) in 1889.[3]

At least two overlapping genealogies must be recounted regarding the effects of colonialism and liberalism when it comes to the emergence of favelas, particularly those located in Rio de Janeiro. The formal abolition of slavery in Brazil only took place in 1888. Nevertheless, this historical event alone does not do justice to the complexities of the different processes for obtaining freedom taking place side by side with the horrors of enslavement. Even before 1888, freedom could be secured through individual manumission and, after 1871, also through birth.[4] During the slavery period, resistance and rebellions against colonial powers were frequent, as was to be expected. In some cases, these movements led to the formation of hidden, but de facto free, maroon communities—made up of "runaway" Africans and their descendants.

As the freed Black population started to grow in the latter half of the nineteenth century, housing became a significant issue. Previously, enslaved subjects were mainly incorporated into farms and into the domestic sphere of white owners in urban centers, but once liberated, more and more Black people looked for better opportunities in the city, which lacked adequate housing.[5] Historical data post-abolition suggests that the Black population in Rio de Janeiro lived mostly in collective "substandard" housing called *cortiços*. When fears of "freed slave" rebellions started to grow, the local government started to repress the proliferation of new cortiços and to demolish existing ones. Licia do Prado Valladares, for instance, discusses how Francisco Franco Pereira Passos, the mayor of Rio from 1902 to 1906, started in 1904 to demolish large cortiços in the central zone of the city. The Black population of Rio, along with other poor classes, were left with no affordable housing option. Some of them started to occupy the least desirable areas of the city, such as the steep hillsides and distant suburbs, turning these into their homes.[6] This is how favelas started.

A second favela genealogy, which continues to operate as a powerful "origin narrative" of Brazilian slums, refers to a rebellion that took place in response to the newly created Brazilian Republic of 1889. What became known as the Canudos War (Guerra de Canudos) generated certain conditions of possibility for the "invention" of favelas both as physical sites and as an ideological construct.[7]

To tell the short version of the events: Around the turn of the twentieth century (1896–97), a peasant group from the Brazilian Northeast took over a very impoverished area in the dry hinterlands of the state of Bahia. This political movement followed a charismatic and religious figure, known as Antônio Conselheiro. Under his leadership, the small town of Canudos rapidly grew, attracting more and more migrants to form a new "nation." Large farm owners in the region, together with the Catholic Church, tried their best to halt the movement. Tensions rose to the point that the Brazilian army was required to intervene in the situation. What looked like an easy task, however, turned into a series of defeats for the Republic. It took four different expeditions to vanquish the rebels—a significant moral and material cost for the Brazilian state at that point.[8] The conscription of soldiers for those battles drew on recruits from several locations, including Rio de Janeiro, the federal capital during those years. These men were promised a series of benefits upon their victorious return to Rio, including housing. But as they returned, hundreds of soldiers discovered that the government's promises were empty. As a form of protest—and still in need of housing—they occupied a hill centrally located in Rio de Janeiro. Today, this area is known as Morro da Providência; at the time, it became known as Favela Hill (Morro da Favela).[9]

Canudos then became more than a short-lived experiment: it became a physical and discursive territory for freedom, one that was violently repressed by the state, but that also left a heritage of possibilities. According to Euclides da Cunha, who wrote one of the best-known literary descriptions of the Canudos War,[10] Canudos came to represent liberty vis-à-vis the Brazilian state, the possibility of the poor to control rights to the land and to their own labor, and to challenge compulsory federal tax payments. It would come to influence the birth of favelas as territories where the poor could not only carve out a space to live, but also to resist and claim a certain freedom from the nation-state.[11]

Ever since, there have been several junctions in Brazilian history in which favela dwellers were implicated in wider liberal debates. In the early 1950s, for example, the Communist Party (Partido Comunista) in Brazil tried to garner more influence and support among the urban poor in Rio, mainly through their "popular democratic committees" (*comitês populares democráticos*). These had a deep impact on the political organization of at least two favelas in Rio de Janeiro: Morro do Borel and Morro do Turano. In 1952 these committees fostered the organization of the first "Residents' Association" in Morro do Borel (Associação dos Favelados do Morro do Borel). Among the leftist liberal plans of the Communist Party at that time, there were proposals to change the names of these two favelas: Borel would become known as Independence Hill (Morro da Independência) and Turano as Liberty Hill (Morro da Liberdade). Obviously, with the rapid change in the political scene and the right-wing military coup a few years later (1964), those plans were never implemented.[12]

During the Brazilian military dictatorship (1964–85), a "tutelary regime" emerged with the objective of managing certain populations of the country, as was the case with Amerindians. What was presented as a form of state "protection" and "pacification" of minoritarian groups also constituted a denial of indigenous autonomy and an opportunity to control their territories.[13] Military policies would also impact favela dwellers, leading to political demobilization and violent favela removals. Even during the nefarious period of dictatorship, however, Brazilians witnessed the emergence of liberal campaigns. The Brazilian Democratic Movement (Movimento Democrático Brasileiro), for instance, had a liberal rhetoric based on anti-authoritarianism, and, at different moments, items such as the protection of Universal Human Rights were also part of their agenda.

Other institutions, such as religious organizations, are also part of the liberal history of the favelas. The 1980s were the height of Catholic social movements in Brazil. Liberation theology brought great inspiration for collective amelioration projects in Favela da Rocinha in that decade.[14] It carried the promise of the liberation of the oppressed through political consciousness and self-organized collective action (*mutirões*).[15] Nevertheless, initiatives of Catholic groups working toward liberating the urban poor from structural violence were almost nonexistent in the favela by the time of my fieldwork.

In 1990 Fernando Collor de Mello, the first openly neoliberal president post-dictatorship, was elected. The national mood changed. From the 1990s, there has been an explosion in the number of Evangelicals in Brazil, a country mainly colonized by Portuguese Catholics.[16] The rise of Neo-Pentecostal Evangelical churches, along with the implementation of neoliberal state policies, led to the popularization of more individualistic possibilities for liberation in the life of the urban poor.[17]

Pacheco de Oliveira asserts that different colonial mechanisms of power continue to operate in Brazil today, bringing different forms of control (and promises of liberation, I would suggest) to the daily life of Amerindian and Black populations—alongside other urban poor residents, particularly favela dwellers.[18] With the end of the military regime, increasing inequalities were not effectively addressed during the re-democratization process,[19] eliciting a renewed fear on the part of the elites toward poor and Black Brazilians. Kidnappings and robberies, panic over favela dwellers' empowerment through drug trafficking, and scenes of "urban wars" started to dominate the public agenda, newspapers, and TV programs. A response to all these variables was a growing defense of neoliberal governance,[20] with more policing and even fewer benefits to the working classes.[21]

In the first decades of the twenty-first century, well after the end of the Brazilian military government in 1985, extremely oppressive state policies would reemerge in Rio de Janeiro—this time to curtail the autonomy of favela dwellers under the same banner of "pacification," previously used during the military dictatorship.[22] Through all these historical events, and since colonization, liberal concerns and the assertion of control have walked hand in hand in Brazil.

Internal Outsiders

Debates on urban poverty have touched upon questions over agency, autonomy, and freedom in the life of slum dwellers and other populations living in what has come to be known as favelas, barrios, or ghettos. There have been extensive arguments regarding the enduring "habits" and "culture" that limit the life experiences of the poor in areas like the slums of Latin America. The supposed existence of a "culture of poverty" would make it difficult (if not impossible) for slum dwellers to escape their own condition, partly because the poor may get so used to their lifeways that they resist change.[23] Meanwhile, under the framing of "structural violence," others had been debating over the social mechanisms of oppression that turned poverty into some sort of entrapment.[24]

Familiarizing myself with this literature before starting my fieldwork in Favela da Rocinha impacted (but did not determine) my initial understanding of favelas as territories plagued not just by a lack of material resources, but also a lack of freedom. In a sense, this book is a contribution to some of these long-standing debates. It presents a theory of liberalism based on the daily life experiences of Brazilian favela dwellers. I offer a mode of reconceptualizing "liberalism" that challenges normative conceptions of poverty and oppression, as well as the boundaries between the free and the unfree.

Consider this passage from *Development as Freedom*, a treatise on the need for "development" by the philosopher and economist Amartya Sen, which presumes that poverty, along with undemocratic political systems, are the major sources of "unfreedom" in the world today. Sen argues:

Sometimes the lack of substantive freedoms relates directly to economic poverty, which robs people of the freedom to satisfy hunger, or to achieve sufficient nutrition, or to obtain remedies for treatable illnesses, or the opportunity to be adequately clothed or sheltered, or to enjoy clean water or sanitary facilities. In other cases, the unfreedom links closely to the lack of public facilities and social care, such as the absence of epidemiological programs, or of organized arrangements for health care or educational facilities, or of effective institutions for the maintenance of local peace and order. In still other cases, the violation of freedom results directly from a denial of political and civil liberties by authoritarian regimes and from imposed restrictions on the freedom to participate in the social, political and economic life of the community.[25]

Since the 1990s, generations of scholars have been trying to expose challenges like these, generated by oppressive social structures, but without necessarily falling into the same trap as the "culture of poverty" approach: blaming the poor for a supposed resistance to change, that is, blaming the "victim" for their situation.[26] Most of these works on "structural violence" were marked by an explicit "call to action,"[27] so that these studies also aspired to be instrumental for social transformation.

Medical anthropologist Paul Farmer states with confident brevity in *Infections and Inequalities*: ". . . poverty is the great limiting factor of freedom."[28] Similar arguments can be found in the most diverse academic fields. In fact, the philosopher Matt Whitt has argued that poverty necessarily constitutes a state of unfreedom in modern states. In the author's rationale: "The state's promise of actualized freedom can only be fulfilled in relation to a group of internal 'outsiders' to whom that freedom cannot extend."[29] For Whitt, the "poor" were, by definition, a group of "internal outsiders" with limited access to freedom. When I elaborated a project to research the operations of liberalism in Brazilian favelas, the intention was, at first, to understand a form of life excluded from liberdade (freedoms and liberties).

In my wanderings with Natasha, however, I came across liberalisms that were not created for the elites to protect other elites. Favela residents have their own mode of liberal politics, which in some favelas is more distinct than in others.[30] Some dwellers in Rocinha were more concerned with obtaining a radical form of liberdade, at any cost. As part of my field research, I was once talking to a student in the Basic English class that I taught in the slum. He was a former drug trafficker and got fired up, telling me about his experiences: "Let's get hold of guns! Fucking crazy. For us, it was like that, freedom, jail, or death!" Other favela residents, however, were more skeptical about the authentic possibility of acquiring liberdade through violence and were more confident in the power of Jesus, with great faith and desire for spiritual liberation. I started to trace all these different experiences in the favela, even when they seemed unusual to me. Through this grounded approach, and through the lenses of minoritarian modes of liberalism, this book contributes to an understanding of urban life in Latin America.

The Colonial Apparatus

After my first experiences in the favela, I came to suspect that there was a problem with my original research framework. Namely, it was based on assumptions that were themselves a product of normative liberalism. Was there something constitutive of liberalism, at least as I understood it, that prescribed certain freedoms as the norm while denying other possibilities? Was it necessarily a problem that favela dwellers seemed to lack the liberal freedoms valued by those in "developed" countries in Europe and North America? The colonial dimension of the "universal freedom" project started to become more evident. It bothered me, just as it had others before me. An appreciation of life in Favela da Rocinha demanded a more explicit decolonial attitude.

Just a few lines before those cited in the epigraph to this introduction, Michel Foucault expresses his concerns regarding universalisms: "What I am afraid of about humanism is that it presents a certain form of our ethics as a universal model for any kind of freedom."[31] The French historian and philosopher formulated this critique during an interview in which he had been asked to comment on the relationship between processes of "normalization" and the "concept of man." If humanism normalizes a particularly located "human" as a universal character, it sounded plausible to me that normative liberalism did the same in relation to always already located experiences of freedom and liberty. For instance, Article 1 of the Universal Declaration of Human Rights (UDHR) states: "All human beings are born free and equal in dignity and rights."[32] What humans? What rights? What freedoms?

As I reflected upon the emergence of liberalism in Brazil, Elizabeth Povinelli's work called my attention and helped me to conceptualize liberalism not as a form of power simply opposed to colonialism, but as a fundamental part of the colonial apparatus. She asks: "In secular states, we are free to worship any god we choose. But can we choose not to worship freedom? In this way, freedom is the Law of law; it distributes the values of truth and falsity, good and evil, without being subject to them."[33]

The work of Saba Mahmood corroborates this (post)colonial critique.

INTRODUCTION

Deeply engaged with political theory, Mahmood argues that liberalism often presents itself as a colonial artifact in the experiences of "non-Western" populations.[34] Mahmood questions the expectation that there must be a universal innate desire for freedom in all forms of human life by demonstrating, ethnographically, that the agency of pious Muslim women in Egypt should not be limited to what she calls "normative liberal assumptions."[35] She explains that one of the consequences of the Enlightenment and humanism, most of all in its secular inflection, has been the establishment of a certain normative ideal that "the most legitimate source of authorization for a person's opinions, actions, and beliefs must be his or her self." This sense of "self-authorization," Mahmood argues, has been proposed as a foundational form of freedom for any "civilization," one that is not just supposed to be universally cherished, but also institutionally established. As Povinelli also observes, this situation would lead to different effects, for example, making "freedom from social relations seem natural and desirable."[36]

Similarly, Dipesh Chakrabarty, another important postcolonial theorist, argues that "the phenomenon of 'political modernity'—namely, the rule by modern institutions of the state, bureaucracy, and capitalist enterprise—is impossible to *think* of anywhere in the world without invoking certain categories and concepts, the genealogies of which go deep into the intellectual and even theological traditions of Europe."[37] If the Eurocentric, white, liberal project has extended itself from the age of Enlightenment to the present, it is toward the operations of a more recent variation of liberalism, known as neoliberalism, that a vast amount of more contemporary critique has been geared.

Whereas the roots of liberalism derive from classic European thought, the source of neoliberalism springs mostly from North America.[38] In this regard, for example, the sociologist Loïc Wacquant states: "Neoliberalism is 'a transnational project,' originating in the United States and spread by a new dominant class, seeking the top-down reorganization of the relationships between market, state, and citizenship."[39] I will not try to summarize here the vast literature focused on the critical examination of neoliberalism. It suffices to say that, in anthropology, Mathieu Hilgers identifies at least three "modes" of engagement with neoliberal phenomena:[40] neoliberalism as culture (examining neoliberal shared symbols, beliefs, and practice),[41] neoliberalism as a system (aiming at identifying enduring neoliberal structures and constitutive relationships),[42] and neoliberalism as governmentality (inspired by a Foucauldian analysis of power regimes).[43]

In most of these debates, there seems to be little disagreement that (neo)liberalism is part of a colonial project of domination. For as much as life in Brazilian favelas may prove to be difficult, universal (neo)liberal prescriptions such as individualism, privatization, and more police power have caused even further harm.[44] The decolonization of liberalism, therefore—and of my own research agenda—presented themselves as crucial endeavors.

Anthropology and Decolonization

The understanding that liberalism is an artifact of colonialism is not the same as saying that the actual operations of the concept must be taken for granted. Despite her critical analysis on the effects of liberalism, Povinelli has also acknowledged that in practical terms "an equally cogent critique might point out that no matter the ultimate reality of freedom as a state of being, its authority has been constitutive of a variety of social goods for a variety of subjugated social groups. Homosexuals, colonial subjects, women, and indigenous worlds: all have seemed to benefit from their struggle for freedom."[45] Although this might be true, an anthropological unwillingness (or incapacity) to ethnographically conceive of liberalism beyond its Eurocentric matrix may corroborate liberalism's colonial effects.

William Mazzarella addresses a similar point, but from a different angle. In his writings on politics and populism, the author argues that given recent challenges to our liberal assumptions—brought about mainly by the rise of authoritarian, fascist-leaning governments in several countries during the 2010s—constructs such as "the liberal state" and the "the liberal subject" demand, more than ever, critical examination. Mazzarella states:

The founding principle of anthropology is that nothing about the social is self-evident. Too often, however, this radical suspension of certainty in our many ethnographic elsewheres has been sustained by a stable foil: some figuring of "the liberal state," "the liberal subject," and so on. Now that the liberal settlement is under populist pressure, this intellectual bargain is no longer sustainable.[46]

In a provocative review article entitled "The Case for Letting Anthropology Burn," Ryan Jobson seems to agree with Mazzarella. Jobson argues that, as a colonial discourse, "liberal humanism" has proved insufficient to counter the dangers of climate disasters and the rise of authoritarian governance. He proposes: "By abandoning the universal liberal subject as a stable foil for a renewed project of cultural critique, the field of anthropology cannot presume a coherent human subject as its point of departure but must adopt a radical humanism as its political horizon."[47]

To abandon the anthropologist's faith in the "universal liberal subject as a stable foil," I suggest introducing instability to such a "compulsory" form of liberalism. This demands that we dedicate still more ethnographic attention to contemporary liberal operations. We might realize, for example, that liberalism has been creatively maneuvered by the very subjects that, at first sight, were most criticized for not adopting it. There are emergent forms of liberalism that do not follow what colonization has imposed as "the Law of law." Recognizing the existence and legitimacy of "non-normative" liberalisms could allow anthropology to serve in favor of decolonization. The main problem does not lie with liberal desires and dreams per se, but with the historical processes of domination, slavery, and normalization to which *all possibilities* of liberalism seem to have been historically subjected.

The decolonization of liberalism could prove to be a paramount step toward an "anthropology for liberation."[48] As Savannah Shange would put it regarding Black politics, we need an abolitionist strategy. "Abolition is not a synonym for resistance; it encompasses the ways in which Black people and our accomplices work within, against, and beyond the state in the service of collective liberation. As an analytic, abolition demands specificity—the very kinds of granularity that ethnography offers."[49] This book puts forward such an ethnography of decolonial liberalism as a viable anthropological contribution to political struggles toward freedom. In doing so, it acknowledges the historical roots and struggles for liberation that emerge from Black politics at the same time that, ethnographically, it recognizes that the challenges faced by queer slum dwellers are intertwined with multiple forms of oppression and colonial heritage. In that sense, I assume that an "anthropology for liberation" must necessarily be abolitionist, and it must confront several different power dimensions, particularly those that naturalize a particular mode of liberalism as *the norm*.

The anthropologist and activist Faye Harrison has argued for the decolonization of anthropology building on the concept of "double consciousness" developed by W. E. B. Du Bois.[50] In the context of more and more anthropologists who are conducting fieldwork "at home" or in groups with whom they have some kind of shared political interests, Harrison argues, "anthropologists with *multiple* consciousness and vision are rooted in some combination and interpenetration of national, racial, sexual, or class oppressions." She further explains that "this form of critical consciousness emerges from the tension in between, on the one hand, membership in a Western society, a Western-dominated profession, or a relatively privileged class or social category, and, on the other hand, belonging to, or having an organic relationship with an oppressed social category or people."[51]

I carry privileges of race and class in Brazil, and I have grappled with what these privileges afforded to me—what they have meant to me as a person and as an ethnographer. However, as a Brazilian migrant in Europe and the United States, I have at times experienced an intense dislocation of my racial and class privileges. Given these territorial differences, it was common for me to transition into a non-white (or brown) and relatively poor migrant status outside of Brazil. Both in Brazil and abroad, however, my non-heteronormative sexuality always added a dimension of oppression to my existence. Indeed, as much as I've benefited from privilege during my life, normative liberalism has also failed me, mostly as a queer person. Meanwhile, though my suffering as a migrant abroad wasn't deserving of much empathy in Rocinha, not being heterosexual was critical to facilitating my relationship with Natasha and others in the favela. My ethnographic experiences with queer friends from the slum have been an inspiration for the particular mode of decolonial anthropology I present here.[52]

Conceptual Scheme

For the purposes of my argument, "liberalism" will be understood as any set of ideas, desires, or practices in favor of freedom and liberty,[53] regardless of their conformity with more established Western philosophical traditions. Inspired by Mahmood, I will further qualify as "normative liberalism" what others have considered to be the standard and universalizing mode of liberalism derived from European and North American history, philosophy, and political theory since the Enlightenment—a dominant set of modes of freedom based on the prescription of individualism, autonomy, private property, and, at the same time, dependence on state protection, as its trademark. The term *neoliberalism* will be treated as a variant of normative liberalism.

Throughout the book, I engage with the concept of minoritarian liberalisms, which refers to alternative liberal modes that operate through processes of "disidentification"[54] with the norms imposed by the dominant modalities of liberalism. The argument draws from the work of the queer theorist José Esteban Muñoz, which offers insights into the intricate relations through which minoritarian experiences emerge, particularly in queer communities. I argue that it is mainly through a process of "disidentification" with normative liberalism that urban "peripheric" populations from the Brazilian favelas produce their minoritarian freedoms. Minoritarian liberalism is always relational—it is not simply an alternative, but something that emerges "within, against, and beyond"[55] the domination and limited (often bleak) possibilities that normative liberalism brings to the life of "subaltern" populations. The ethnographic theory I present in this book derives mainly from the specific minoritarian modes of liberalism operating in the life of Natasha Kellem and other queer friends that I met while living in Rio de Janeiro.

Terms such as *minorities* and *minoritarian* are associated with the philosophy of Deleuze and Guattari.[56] I use them to refer to groups whose politics are not based on a colonializing ethos—in other words, they do not aim at imposing their own standards as a universal rule. Furthermore, from a normative perspective, minoritarian groups hold a potential considered "subversive." In this case, minorities are not defined through proportions, but according to their particular positionality of power. Favela residents in Rocinha may outnumber residents of the upper-middle-class neighborhood of nearby São Conrado while remaining minorities.[57] As a self-identified travesti, Natasha is considered minoritarian in relation to other gender-normative groups. Black Brazilians are minoritarian in relation to white Brazilians.[58] By the same token, favela liberalisms tend to be (not all) minoritarian in relation to the normative liberalism typical of the "formal" city.

The concept of "minoritarian literature," as discussed in the book *Kafka: Toward a Minor Literature*, helps to further clarify my argument. In a revealing passage, Deleuze and Guattari observe:

The three characteristics of minor literature are the deterritorialization of language, the connection of the individual to a political immediacy, and the collective arrangement of enunciation. We might as well say that minor no longer designates specific literatures but the revolutionary conditions of every literature within the heart of what is called great (or established) literature.[59]

I use the concept of minoritarian liberalisms as an umbrella term to refer to all of the virtual and actual alternative conditions of liberalism beyond the normative type: favela liberalism, queer liberalism, peasant liberalism, maroon liberalism, to cite a few. In this sense, if some modes of liberalism are intimately allied to normative liberalism, other experiences of freedoms and liberties seem more revolutionary. Can we take other people's freedoms seriously as freedoms without resorting to a normative apparatus? At various points during my fieldwork, I failed. Trekking the paths of freedom proposed by others is not easy. We are all limited by our assumptions. Anthropology offers an opportunity to slow down and question our certainties regarding liberalism, but it does not give us clear answers. In this ethnography, I have my friends from Brazilian favelas to thank for their willingness to help us understand and conceptualize minoritarian liberalisms.

For the sake of my argument, as it will become evident in the next sections and chapters, I propose that there are at least three characteristics that are present in minoritarian modes of liberalism: the deterritorialization of established freedoms and liberties; the understanding of liberalism as part of a collective mode (instead of an individual ethos) of politics more independent of the nation-state; and the transformation of the conditions of possibility for liberation.

The Deterritorialization of Liberalism

According to Eric Hobsbawm, the historical process of electing some (elite) freedoms as more important than others can be seen at least since the French Revolution.[60] *Minoritarian Liberalism* focuses on the ethnographic analysis of how processes of liberal (de)territorialization work. The heterogeneous territorial relations in the city of Rio de Janeiro, in which the nation-state operates differently in favelas and in the "formal" city, offer a distinctive position from which to think about the deterritorialization of liberalism, proposing alternative concepts of freedom and liberty in response to the North American and European repertoire.

Apart from Deleuze and Guattari's oeuvre,[61] I refer to the work of the philosopher Manuel DeLanda as it comes to defining concepts such as deterritorialization and territorialization:

In the first place, processes of territorialization are processes that define or sharpen the spatial boundaries of actual territories. Territorialization, on the other hand, also refers to non-spatial processes that increase the internal homogeneity of an assemblage, such as the sorting processes which exclude a certain category of people from membership of an organization, or the segregation processes which increase the ethnic or racial homogeneity of a neighborhood. Any process which either destabilizes spatial boundaries or increases internal heterogeneity is considered deterritorializing.[62]

As we will see, limitations on freedoms and liberties in the life of favela dwellers don't happen only through direct mechanisms of unfreedom—such as impoverishment, police violence, and other forms of explicit social exclusion. The lack of freedom in favelas depends, to a great extent, on operations internal to the concept of liberalism itself. Normative liberalism territorializes because it renders unthinkable alternative possibilities of freedom. I argue that, recently, even queer liberation has come to signify the normalization of queer life through *normative liberalism*—instead of the deterritorialization of liberalism by queer experiences.[63]

When Natasha's sexual freedoms are disqualified and erased as "deviance"—or *libertinagem* in Portuguese—the importance of "disidentification" as a political form of minoritarian politics becomes evident. *Libertinagem* translates as "libertinism" in English, except that the use of the term is not necessarily archaic in Brazil.[64] Natasha's rejection of normative understandings of sexuality, gender, and also freedom is what helps her continued existence as a travesti, which is an identity category that doesn't translate well into the English term "transvestite," either.[65] By paying attention to these conceptual slippages and alternative experiences of queer favela dwellers, this book considers other modes of liberalism and demonstrates the potential that these alternative liberalisms hold when understood as part of minoritarian politics.

While understudied, the ethnographic engagement with freedoms that escape normative liberalism is not something entirely absent in anthropology. Often considered foundational figures of the discipline, both Franz Boas and Bronisław Malinowski dedicated themselves to the study of what they referred at the time as "freedom in primitive society."[66] After them, anthropologists Paul Riesman, Eric Wolf, Peter Loizos, James Laidlaw, and Caroline Humphrey have all considered the concept of freedom in a variety of "non-Western" contexts. Riesman proposed to understand the operations of freedom among the Fulani of West Africa, and Laidlaw among the Jain in India, for example.[67] In turn, Caroline Humphrey's essay "Alternative Freedoms" explores how some people in Russia, with whom she had been working for years, referred to ideas similar to what liberals understand as freedom.[68] Through a conceptual genealogy, Humphrey unravels two examples of "alternative freedoms," *svoboda* and *mir*:

The Russian word most commonly used to translate the English "freedom" is *svoboda*, which today can be broadly construed as liberty or political freedom. Yet in medieval times, svoboda, which is based on the root *svoi* (self, ours), seems to have meant something rather different, that is, the security and well-being that result from living

INTRODUCTION

amongst one's own people. Svoboda (freedom) first of all was the agglomeration of practices of our own way of life, most fundamentally contrasted with those of alien people and enemies. It suggests an image of a social kind of freedom, one that was not centred on the singular individual.[69]

In addition to *svoboda*, Humphrey describes the Russian concept of freedom as *mir*:

Mir has the meaning of the universe, all humanity, the world, or any given world, and in the past, it also referred to the rural commune, the "social world" of the peasant. Mir points to the well-being naturally present between all persons, communities, and their environment. It gives rise not to a concept, but to a feeling (*oschuschenie*) of freedom, which is given by self-realisation in an entire universe conceived as a whole. So the freedom arising from mir has an adverbial quality. To live (how)? Freely. If svoboda freedom is based on the political construction of a bounded society (that of the free), mir by contrast can be directed outwards limitlessly. It is no accident that the Soviet spacecraft is called *Mir*.[70]

Humphrey's work exemplifies an engagement with freedom that does not try to reduce the concept itself to other known anthropological concepts, such as agency or resistance.[71] In addition, Humphrey also acknowledges that not all freedoms are necessarily derived from a normative form of liberalism. As such, her observations question the definition of liberalism as a solely Western and capitalist practice.

My work, similarly, goes against the tendency within anthropology to infer the operations of liberalism through other concepts, by instead directly investigating the politics of liberdade (freedoms and liberties) as an ethnographic project. Avoiding the topic would not do justice to the experiences of my friends in Rocinha, who framed important aspects of their life through the semantic field of liberalism. To take one example, when one of my neighbors in the favela noticed that, as an "outsider," I was afraid of the heavily armed traffickers selling drugs and controlling the area near our house, he remarked: "Rocinha is one of the most liberal favelas [*uma das favelas mais liberais*] in Rio. Nobody will bother you. Don't worry!" I smiled, curious to understand a world in which drug dealers, and not just the police, hold the use of force and are also the guarantors of liberties.[72]

Thus, while I share the concerns of Mahmood and Povinelli regarding the colonial effects of normative liberalism, in this ethnography, I recount what I learned from people in the slum about different situations in which alternative liberalisms emerge in their daily lives. Some

INTRODUCTION

were people perfectly aware of their subaltern situation, exploitation, and oppression, but who, at the same time, believed in liberation. I argue that a possible strategy to counter colonialism is to take seriously the experiences of freedom and liberty that are too often rendered invisible or dismissed as mere reproductions of a colonial liberal discourse. If one of the most evident effects of normative liberalism is that it tends to control the conditions of possibility for freedom (as "the Law of law"), what happens when we learn from unconventional freedoms that exist in "peripheric" territories like Brazilian favelas?

Alternative forms of liberdade, which emerged during my ethnographic research, are derived from active processes of deterritorialization and disidentification with normative liberalism. Inspired by Humphrey, my goal has been to uncover different definitions that often escape through the cracks of normative liberalism. The book asks: Are liberal values only considered legitimate when they align with European and North American standards? Or can people living other forms of life, with other freedoms, stretch and diversify our current understandings of liberalism? I suggest that alternative possibilities emerge from juxtaposing historically dominant modes of liberalism with other modes that are often rendered invisible. In doing so, we can also challenge some of the colonial effects of normative liberalism.

A Queer Collective Mode

The literature on the relationship between gender and liberalism tend to assume that the latter is always an ally to the feminist cause.[73] Among the voices that question this assumption, Carole Pateman turns to classic doctrines to expose the implications of liberal contractualism for current understandings of gender relations. In classic liberalism, Hobbes conceptualized the "state of nature" as an imaginary condition (with very real consequences) of a past in which the war of all against all was the only rule. According to this narrative, human beings would have lived in such a state of chaos before the foundation of civil society.[74] Although Locke and Rousseau present a more positive picture than the Hobbesian "state of nature," for these philosophers the "contract" was a necessity introduced as an instrument for governance and to assure private property rights and liberty. In normative liberalism, these achievements are only possible through the rule of law. Outside of the rule of law, only fear, violence, and brute force can exist.[75]

For Pateman, the effects of the "social contract" are far from dead. Instead, as the image of "the dead hand of the past"[76] suggests, contractualism continues to operate in contemporary life—requiring obedience on the part of minorities in exchange for protection received from dominant groups. For instance, Pateman suggests that through a social contract, such as marriage, women are expected to trade obedience to men in exchange for the latter's protection. As such, the author challenges the assumption that civil freedom, as proposed in normative liberalism, can de facto promote the liberation of those to whom I have been referring as "minorities." She states, "Civil freedom is a masculine attribute and depends upon patriarchal right . . . sexual difference is political difference; sexual difference is the difference between freedom and subjection."[77] The universalization of freedom, which is part of the normative liberal agenda, doesn't promote the elimination of disparities. On the contrary, Pateman demonstrates how the liberal narrative has been used to support the creation, maintenance, and domestication of inequalities.

As a travesti living in a favela in Rio de Janeiro, Natasha endured the effects of normative liberalism through multiple mechanisms. For the elites in Rio de Janeiro, favelas signal unruliness, predation, and lack of respect for private property rights and civility—in other words, the absence of law, a contemporary "state of nature." Travestis, in particular, are considered to be among the most dangerous, unruly, and abject members of favela communities.[78] The dangerous travesti living in a lawless land epitomizes the fears of normative liberals toward those unwilling to submit to dominant norms of gender, sexuality, and, I would add, capitalist projects of individualism and privatization.

Even forms of liberalism that seem to embrace otherwise marginalized identities, like lesbian, gay, bisexual, trans, and queer ones (LGBTQ), still maintain some boundaries between what is considered acceptable and what is not. David Eng presents contemporary queer liberalism in the United States as a form of empowerment of certain LGBTQ people, which happens economically—through an increasingly conspicuous and mass-mediated consumer lifestyle—and politically—through the legal protection of queer rights to individuality.[79] Eng writes:

Simply put, queer liberalism articulates a contemporary confluence of the political and economic spheres that forms the basis for the liberal inclusion of particular gay and lesbian U.S. citizen-subjects petitioning for rights and recognition before the law. While gays and lesbians were once decidedly excluded from the normative structures of gender and kinship, today they are re-inhabiting them in growing numbers and in increasingly public and visible ways.[80]

The liberation of LGBTQ subjects from oppression, violence, and discrimination has been a key item on the political agenda since at least the 1960s.[81] The 1966 Gene Compton's Cafeteria Riots in San Francisco have been recognized as one of the points of departure for transgender activism.[82] Even more prominent within the history of queer liberalism were the Stonewall Riots, conceived in the global LGBTQ imaginary as the source of social movements struggling toward liberation. Since then, I would argue that LGBTQ liberation politics has been de-radicalized and territorialized by normative liberalism to the point that even the Stonewall example becomes alike to a "strategic essentialism"[83]—useful but ultimately insufficient.

Natasha's encounters with daily oppressions and freedoms form a corpus of ethnographic evidence demonstrating that power is not external to freedom.[84] Struggles for freedom in Brazil mobilize, directly and indirectly, the interests of various oppressed groups: the working classes, children, women, LGBTQ people, Amerindians, and the Black population—together with a wide range of intersectional identities that cut across these groups. It is necessary to foreground experiences of freedom and liberty that have been ignored while they take place in the lives of subjects who live in "peripheric" political territories, going beyond experiences at the "home" of liberal values.[85]

Other Conditions of Possibility

My anthropological approach benefits from an understanding of freedom as a practice, along the lines that the philosopher Johanna Oksala proposes: "Freedom is defined and gains meaning only through the concrete operations through which its existence is tested. It emerges through the particular, political, and/or personal struggles that try and test its limits, possibilities or extent."[86] With this in mind, in order to better understand minoritarian liberalisms in the life of favela dwellers in Rio de Janeiro, I took an ethnographic approach that allowed me to trace some of the concrete operations of freedom.

During my fieldwork, I avoided asking direct questions about liberdade. In fact, I didn't conduct many interviews in the favela at all. Instead, I kept a small notebook in my back pocket at all times and a larger notebook at home. I would use the smaller one to take notes during the conversations I had with people, after obtaining oral consent to do so when I first met them. The larger one, I used to write up the experiences of the day. Before going to sleep, I would expand at length on those points from the small notebook that seemed particularly relevant at that moment. Most of the dialogues that I present in this book were first jotted down into the little notebook and then expanded in the larger one. As such, I acknowledge the use of "headnotes" to compose these dialogues. The intention is not to be able to reproduce exchanges with favela dwellers with the precision of a tape recorder. Instead, I aim to present, to the best of my ability, my memories of these conversations. Looking back at my notes, I notice that it was rare for more than three days to pass by without some reference to freedoms and liberties on the part of my interlocutors, unprompted.

When I refer to tracing experiences of liberalism as part of my research, I recognize that an important part of the "tracing" was conducted through the circulation (and performance) of language—that is, following a variety of Portuguese words and phrases (as action—*parole*) related to freedom and liberty, for example: *liberdade, libertação, livre-arbítrio, libertinagem*, among others. As I have mentioned earlier, in Portuguese the distinction made in English between *freedom* and *liberty* is not significant; both can be translated as *liberdade*. For me, as a native Portuguese speaker, what seemed strange was exactly the opposite: the fact that the word *liberty* in English tended to purify the more open-ended meanings of freedom to refer to a Eurocentric political history. As one of the founding values of the United States of America, liberty relates to the classic British liberal concern regarding the protection of individual autonomy, as some sort of protection from unrestrained sovereign power. As such, I assume that the concept of liberty is more likely to operate as a normative liberal concept, whereas freedom is a concept more open to heterogeneous meanings.[87]

When I started to reflect more critically on the importance of certain words for my ethnography, Willard Van Orman Quine helped me to make the research method more explicit: "Little can be done in the way of tracking thought processes except when we can put words to them. For something objective that we can get our teeth into, we must go after the words."[88] In this sense, words, phrases, and language in general were used as a means to understand not only the meanings of liberdade for my friends in Rio de Janeiro, but also their actual practices of liberty and freedom. During my experiences in Rocinha, I considered both speech and their indexical circumstance as part of the same assemblage.[89]

Toward the end of the initial eighteen months of research, I noticed that I had traced different circuits through which practiced meanings and other experiences of freedom and liberty emerged in the lives of my friends. For example, I would often come across the word *libertação* when in the company of neighbors who would take me to their Evangelical churches. On the other hand, my travesti friends in the favela were the ones who more often used the word *liberada*. These different open-ended circuits (assemblages) are part of the complex conditions of possibility for freedom in Rocinha. For instance, someone seeking Evangelical liberation from evil (*libertação*) would likely try to refrain from being sexually liberated (*liberada*). Some modes of freedom were more present in Evangelical churches; others were more accepted at LGBTQ venues.

I find the concept of assemblages useful to refer to the relations established through different concepts and practices of freedom in daily life. I am interested in the emergent relations among different modes of liberdade as constituted through a multiplicity of people, places, words, objects, and events. Explaining the use of the term, Colin McFarlane remarks that an interest in "assemblages" can become a research methodology in which social and cultural processes are understood as relational and necessarily attuned to practice and materiality.[90] Therefore, instead of simply exploring different meanings of liberalism, this research uses ethnographic methods to trace broader assemblages of liberal practices, lived experiences of liberdade, and the material conditions that make them possible.

My ethnographic experiences in Favela da Rocinha demonstrate that, in practice, liberalism operates through interconnected circuits that foster or limit different modes and possibilities to be free. To better understand these multiple possibilities of liberalism, particularly those that could be understood as minoritarian forms of liberalism, I had to partake in a multiplicity of narratives and forms of life in the favela. It was also necessary to understand the control mechanisms implicit in dominant forms of liberalism and to acknowledge processes of disidentification with normative liberalism. Otherwise, I risked confining my ethnographic research to the most dominant and obvious modes of freedom at the expense of minoritarian ones.

Some sites in which I conducted ethnographic work were often assumed to be severed from freedom. This is something that Povinelli also notes when she asks "why some techniques of the self or the social—worlds of religious piety, of kinship, of sexual carnality—are liable to, and disabled by, a characterization of them as unfree?"[91] The possibilities offered in normative liberalism are too often based in either the exclusion of certain practices of freedom or their normalization. Freedom is territorializing in normative liberalism because dominant adult, white (European and North American), capitalist, male, straight, and cisgender values are meant to represent all human possibilities of freedom and liberty, homogeneously.[92]

As a political and ethical project, I suggest that we must go beyond normative liberalism and explore other forms of liberalism. This could be done either by denouncing the ontological impossibility of the universal subject of normative freedom (all of us have embodied and located existences), by creating ever more radically mutant modes of freedom, and/or by interrogating established mechanisms of freedom normalization. To further explore these strategies, we will also be required to critique totalizing narratives, such as Article 1 in the Universal Declaration of Human Rights. We will need to learn more about the queer experiences of those who are not the "universal human"—those who are not white, bourgeois, and heterosexual.

So far, we have been contrasting normative liberalism (mainly in the singular) to minoritarian liberalisms (in the plural). Nevertheless, as Wacquant argues regarding neoliberalism as manifested in different global contexts, including Brazil: "There is not one big-N Neoliberalism but an indefinite number of small-n neoliberalisms born of the ongoing hybridization of neoliberal practices and ideas with local conditions and forms."[93] The same argument could hold for normative liberalisms, in a small-n sense, if we consider that normative liberalism is not actualized under one fixed form; it manifests differently according to changing circumstances, through different claims to universality, and various regulations. However, the distinction I propose between normative liberalism and other minoritarian liberalisms is a conceptual one. Normative liberalism conceives of itself as universal, as a big-N, whereas minoritarian liberalisms imagine and tolerate a multiplicity of other existences. Therefore, the singular form serves to better communicate the will to power embedded in normative liberalism. From a minoritarian perspective, an important political objective is to challenge the supposed universality of normative liberalism(s)—not to prove that there is more than one form of dominant liberalism, but to put forward the claim that liberalisms should always be conceived of as a multiplicity.

The assemblages that this ethnography explores are partly constituted through the relations between different territories: between the Hillside (the favela) and the Asphalt (the formal city), and between the city of Rio de Janeiro (the Hillside plus the Asphalt) and other sites through which my friends from Rocinha circulate, such as the interior of Ceará state and

INTRODUCTION

even Europe. Beyond differences in actual territories, many other distinct spaces are relevant to this ethnography: spaces of fear, pain, and pleasure. As we will see, these are often connected through heterogeneous assemblages of churches, motels, prisons, bars, hospitals, shacks, police stations, and even slaughterhouses.

The Liberation Plot

What would it be like to live another story in relation to state power? The state has been at the core of the normative liberal apparatus since the liberal contract is most frequently invoked as the basis of state legitimacy. How far does liberalism go without the nation-state? How far does the nation-state go in the life of those who live without it, against it, despite it?

From different angles, the following chapters address these questions above. The next pages narrate a series of encounters of Natasha's travesti body with a variety of forms of freedom and oppression. However, this book isn't just about the life story of a "queer individual." The ethnography explores alternative freedoms and liberties in the life of a collective of favela dwellers, some of whom are considered "queer" due to their gender and sexuality, others that are treated as "deviant" simply because they live in favelas. Their experiences often speak of multiple oppressions.

In the first chapters, I recount Natasha's life stories in Rocinha, at the same time that I reflect upon my own immersion in these narratives. After migrating from a small village in Ceará, a state in the interior of Brazil, to the so-called Marvelous City (Rio de Janeiro), Natasha spent several years living in Rocinha. In her hometown, Natasha could not be a liberated transgender woman, as she wanted. She became a (self-identified) travesti in the favela, navigating between the restrictions and possibilities for gender and sexuality afforded by what the slum dwellers referred to as the "laws of the Hillside" (laws of the favela). Natasha's mother, Dona Rosário, was very quick to blame the shantytown lifestyle for Natasha's "excess of freedom." My dear friend flirted with drug traffickers, had sex in public places, and was judged by her family and our Evangelical neighbors.

Chapter 2, "Laws of the Hillside," delves more into the territorial specificities of Rocinha as a slum controlled by powerful drug lords and under the command of a leading trafficker known as the "Owner of the Hillside." I explore the difference between freedoms that are afforded by "laws of the favela" and other "laws of the Asphalt" (laws of the formal city). The chapter puts forward minoritarian forms of liberalism, such as a favela liberalism, and alternative forms of queer liberalism. It also analyzes the role of traffickers as providers of queer freedom and reflects upon how queer experiences in Rio de Janeiro navigate between different territories of freedom and domination.

About one year into my fieldwork in Rocinha, I had an opportunity to travel to Natasha's homeland in the state of Ceará. In the company of some neighbors from the favela, I visited Natasha's family in the Brazilian Northeast, trying to understand some of the reasons why migrants left their homelands to move to Rio de Janeiro. Chapter 3 deepens questions regarding the conditions of possibility for a migrant becoming a favela travesti. The chapter also delves into the violent homophobia and transphobia that shaped Natasha's childhood. At the same time, it focuses on the understanding of peasant experiences in the Brazilian hinterlands, which come together to form a particular mode of minoritarian liberalism, which I call "peasant liberalism." The experiences I lived in between Rio de Janeiro and Ceará helped me to understand how questions of migration, desires for a "modern" life, and the formation of subjectivities are inflected with different modes of freedom.

In chapter 4, "Queer Kids and the Favela Closet," I focus on the emergence of the so-called PAFYC group, or Bonde das Novinhas (the Young Ladies Crew), an openly queer group made up of kids from the favela who considered themselves liberated (*liberadas*). This chapter presents the complexity of the queer scene in the favela and better locates Natasha's experiences within a gamut of "deviant" possibilities. I focus on how the members of the group aggressively pursued freedom through techniques geared toward the cultivation of flexible bodies. I also consider how these embodied expressions of liberdade came in conflict with older generations of queer folks living in Rocinha. As the ethnography shows, for Natasha and her friends, the boundaries between normative liberty and libertinism existed to be flexed, tested, and challenged.

Chapter 5, "Encountering Demons and Deities," explores the intersections of religion, sexuality, and liberty in Rocinha. The ethnographic method of tracing experiences of freedom in quotidian life in the favela exposes fractures and the juxtapositions among Neo-Pentecostal "liberation services," queer liberation, and civil liberties. While normative (secular) liberalism often dismisses religion as a form of oppression only, assuming they are outside of modern politics, I show that religion is an important element in current assemblages of freedoms and liberties, and as such has a profound influence on the governmentality of favela territories. Topics such as drug addiction, sex exploitation, and demoniac possessions all come to light in the contentious relationship between Evangelical exorcisms and Afro-Brazilian possessions. Rather than thinking of religion only as an "anti-liberal" project, this chapter suggests that some religious experiences, such as liberation services in Neo-Pentecostal churches, can be better understood as operating within the multiple folds of normative liberalism.

Chapter 6, "Roman Slavery," explores the assemblages that connect the life of Natasha with other travestis in territories that are geographically removed from Favela da Rocinha. Specifically, I investigate allegations of contemporary transatlantic networks of human trafficking and slavery between Rio de Janeiro and Rome. Relying on my ethnographic encounters with Brazilian sex workers in Italy, this chapter provides a broader panorama of flows of freedom and oppression in the life of queer populations from favelas. The discussion reopens long-standing academic conversations regarding the effects of liberalism on sex work and, notably, offers insights regarding the life experiences of travestis and their desire for sex, money, bodily transformations, kinship (re)connections, and, above all, queer liberation.

The final chapters highlight the differences between a liberal anthropology and an anthropology for liberation. They consider the wider implications of understanding minoritarian liberalisms as political acts and interrogate my own freedom to speak about these issues. In chapter 7, "As If There Is No Tomorrow," narratives come to a close with final scenes of my relationship with Natasha and several other members of the PAFYC crew. In the epilogue, I put together some threads explored in other chapters and offer a closer look into the most recent movements in the assemblages of freedoms and liberties in Favela da Rocinha.

The work of anthropologists can help to unveil liberalism from the ground up, not just in order to analyze and reverse the power dynamics between the freed and the oppressed, but to challenge the logic and the stability of normative, elitist policies. At the same time, the deconstruction of liberalism does not guarantee absolute freedom. I do not deny all the oppression and difficulties faced by slum dwellers in Brazil. This book explores liberal uncertainties and instabilities vis-à-vis the norms, taking seriously the potential creation of "lines of flight," as Deleuze and Guattari would put it,[94] for liberalism. Perhaps the suspension of our certainties and the adoption of long-term (slow) ethnographic research to understand current freedoms and liberties are the best that anthropology can offer in response to the abuses of normative liberalism.[95]

ONE

Through Pleasures and Pain

> What is at stake is not a matter of liberation as opposed to submission—it is a matter of line of flight, escape . . . an exit, outlet. GILLES DELEUZE AND FÉLIX GUATTARI, "WHAT IS A MINOR LITERATURE?"

I first moved to Favela da Rocinha in early 2009, only carrying with me a Crumpler backpack and an egg-yolk-colored suitcase. I lived there until mid-2010. When I concluded this initial period of fieldwork, I went to Scotland to obtain my doctoral degree and, from there, to the United States. Not everyone had the opportunity to move out of the favela; the fact that I did was an obvious privilege. Freedom—including the freedom to move between different spaces—depends on power. Both freedom and power can be destructive, but also productive.[1] To understand the politics of freedoms and liberties in Rocinha, one must be aware of the specific forms of power that are operational both inside and outside of its borders, as well as the forms of power that produce that border. Within Rocinha, drug-trafficking governmentality reigns. A distinct form from the nation-state governmentality, which operates in the "formal" city of Rio de Janeiro. They both act by establishing control over territories and populations, but they do so through different modes of oppression and by allowing different kinds of freedoms. Traffickers are not usually free in territories controlled by the Brazilian state, and the nation-state is not free in territories controlled by traffickers.

The freedom to move between territories was not just a matter of wealth, as might be expected; there were drug dealers in Rocinha with money, but their power did not

CHAPTER ONE

always extend beyond the borders of the favela.[2] As my friend Clarice put it, "And what good is a wealthy trafficker? If they get out of the favela, they are going to be killed! Where's their freedom?" Meanwhile, snitches, also known by the designation of "X-9" in Rocinha, were either killed or forced to leave the favela.[3] A common form of betrayal was for an X-9 to receive money from the police, or a rival faction, to spy on drug-dealing activities in the favela, providing "outsiders" with privileged information. I often worried if traffickers would consider my research as a form of espionage. After the fact, I assume they didn't, considering that I could always leave the favela whenever I wanted, and I was never forced out either.[4]

During my time in Rocinha, I lived in the lowest part of the hill. That area was known as Valão, or literally the "Great Ditch." It was named after the big open sewer that cut through the bottom of the slum and went all the way across to the upper-middle-class neighborhood of São Conrado, on the other side of the main road serving that zone of Rio de Janeiro: the Lagoa-Barra Highway. Water did not flow between the two territories under the same conditions as humans, though. At the end of a long trail, all that dense sewage was discharged into the open green sea, without much purification. The wastewater treatment plant in São Conrado rarely operated. The municipality claimed there was a lack of resources. But the connections permitted between Rocinha and São Conrado were different on the surface of the city. There was always a pair of policemen, wearing gray uniforms and driving light blue battered cars, who monitored the flows between the Hillside (the favela) and the Asphalt (the "formal" city of Rio de Janeiro). They surveilled the rivers of people entering and leaving the shantytown on a daily basis, patting down only those they knew they could bother, given the emasculated power they held at the borders of the favela territory.

These favela frontiers were not difficult to locate. Rio's policemen precisely knew the territorial limits of their activities, and they helped to regulate the boundaries of the slum from the outside, just as traffickers did on the inside. In typical racist fashion, the policemen targeted Black dwellers, or those who looked more "local" than I did.[5] The police never stopped me for a pat-down. Occasionally, they stopped people who looked more *gringo*—or foreign—than I did, investigating backpacks, tote bags, packages, pockets, and wallets. In some cases, they even looked for drugs inside people's underwear. Except for these body searches, the policemen looked bored with their job—they could often be seen chatting and eating deep-fried Brazilian snacks, such as *coxinha* and *pastel*, at the local market at the main pedestrian entry to Rocinha.

The presence of the police at that spot was symbolic, a demonstration of state power required mainly by São Conrado residents, who persistently complained about the "favelization" (*favelização*) of *their* neighborhood. In response, the police tried to prove that they had not given up on their duties to protect the elites.

There were landmarks only known within the favela. At the point where the exposed Valão sewer leaves the slum and hides underneath the asphalt of São Conrado, there was a place called No Limite (literally, At the Limit). I spent weeks mistakenly thinking that when my neighbors arranged to meet "at the limit," they were referring to an actual border to the outside. I was wrong. No Limite was a location internal to the favela, a noisy and cheap clothing store facing the four-lane-wide Lagoa-Barra Highway. To be precise, it sat at the intersection between the street that went all the way down along the bank of Valão and another street parallel to the highway, leading to a small square, Praça Ailton Rosa. It was a point where favela dwellers would assemble before venturing into the "formal" city, close to the limit, but not exactly at the limit. I, too, started to arrange to meet people there, on the sidewalk next to No Limite, the clothing store.

There were also landmarks external to the favela, mostly signaled by vehicle routes. For most outsiders, the closest to Rocinha that they would feel comfortable would be driving by on the highway in a private car; the Brazilian elites tried to avoid public transport at all costs. Still, dwellers of the Asphalt often complained about the "visual pollution" that favelas brought to the city's landscape. One of my closest friends in Rocinha, a mathematics teacher named Auro, explained the geographical relations of the city as if talking me through an equation: "Lagoa Rodrigo de Freitas is the lagoon between Gávea and Ipanema—a favorite region for the elite to live. Barra da Tijuca is also an elite neighborhood but in a different zone. Lagoa is South Zone. Barra is West Zone. Each of these elite areas has their nearby favela areas too. North Zone is different, mostly for the suburban poor." He kept analyzing: "Barra is new money. Lagoa, Ipanema, Leblon, Gávea, these are the areas where the old money is located. The South Zone is home to the most elitist of the elites, like Alto Leblon." I soon realized that most lines connecting these elite areas of Lagoa Rodrigo de Freitas and Barra da Tijuca went along the Lagoa-Barra Highway, which passed right by Rocinha. This highway had been an engineering feat to construct; the road perforated almost two kilometers of hard-rock mountains at the Zuzu Angel Tunnel, making life easier for the wealthy. But then, even more spectacularly, right at the end of the tunnel, it put the elite face-to-face with the favela—one of their greatest fears.

CHAPTER ONE

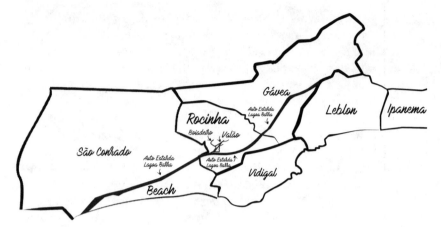

Rocinha and surrounding areas in Rio de Janeiro as drawn by one of my neighbors in the favela. © Daniele Gomes.

Friendship at First Sight

I first met Natasha during a tremendous heat wave. It was April 20, 2009. I was thirsty but wanted something more exciting than plain water, and I had no fridge at home. Luckily, I was invited to go for a walk with Amélia, a very kind middle-aged migrant from Ceará state who lived upstairs from me with Bezerra, the father of her two children. We left the building almost side by side, squeezing through the narrow front gate leading to the alleyway. Amélia's daughter, Maria Beatriz, liked to tease her mother for the generous size of her derriere. We passed by our neighbor Quino's house, and he was there, sitting by the door in his wheelchair, like usual. We continued walking, passing by Dona Irani's sewing workshop, a small space packed with colorful fabric. I waved to her, but despite wearing her new glasses, she didn't see us. We turned right at the end of the alley, then passed by the house of Dona Magali—a short-haired woman who spent most of her days smoking at her front door. We made it to the corner fruit and vegetable store, whose entrance was on Rua do Valão, almost inside the open sewer. During rainy days, the wastewater flowed by a bit clearer, but the risk of flooding was imminent. During hot days, like that one, the flow was slower and more concentrated. The smell of the street changed accordingly.

The store owner, Senhor Jair, stood to the right of the entrance. He was behind a battered counter that held an antique scale, a faulty calculator, a wooden drawer to keep change, and a notebook for writing down customers' debts. He wore a thick gold chain over his abundantly hairy chest and plastic sports sunglasses on top of his bald head. The corner store was tiny—no more than ten square meters. Against the bright green walls, there were boxes and boxes of fruits and vegetables. Some of them were pretty fresh; others were already rotten and covered with flies. While Amélia admired the mangoes, I was drawn to the middle of the store, toward a small table full of watermelon slices. "Which one is the sweetest?" I asked Jair. He slowly came over and helped me choose a slice, as he had done many times before. He weighed the slice and told me the total: 2.50 Brazilian reais, just over the equivalent of one US dollar back then.[6] I declined the plastic bag he offered; I needed that slice of watermelon for immediate consumption.

We found a red motorcycle parked a few steps off the store, obstructing the passage and the entrance to Dona Magali's house. I watched carefully to get past without bumping into it. On the dirty mudguard, one could read: HONDA, THE WINGS OF FREEDOM. "Too much freedom to park a motorcycle that way, disrupting everyone," I complained to Amélia.

She replied: "At least he owns a motorcycle!"

"Freedom as private ownership, one of the foundational values of normative liberalism, emerged within the favela too," I thought. The person who owned a Honda had wings; the manufacturer affirmed. The slogan also mobilized an aspect of freedom related to mobility, freedom of movement.[7] Amélia commented that her oldest son, Moreno, liked motorcycles but didn't know how to ride them, whereas his cousin Ricky was a dexterous pilot. Moreno had olive skin and shiny black hair just like his mother. Motorcycles were not cheap. Neither Ricky nor Moreno worked at that time. Moreno was looking for a formal job at age seventeen. "Do you want to see wicked motorcycles? Go to Cachopa!" Ricky told me, referring to a higher part of the hill, the headquarters of drug trafficking at the time. Yet most traffickers could not ride anywhere outside the slum. Something made no sense to me. Ricky explained: "Inside the favela, they call the shots! What's the matter?" Traffickers wanted to be powerfully free within the favela, since they couldn't be free outside of it? I tried to rationalize it, knowing that rationalizations are more simplistic than lived experiences.

Once I got a few steps past the motorcycle parked outside the fruit store, I stopped again. The more I sweated, the drier my mouth felt. I couldn't wait anymore and decided to bite into the juicy watermelon right there and then. (Amélia was more contained with her luscious pink mangoes and waited until she got home.) A slow whisper came from behind me: "Delicious!" I turned around. The voice was coming from a mouth thickly covered in rouge lipstick. I noticed that she was looking at my lips, too, cool and moist from the fruit I was eating. I smiled at her, and she looked down, as if she wanted a bite of my watermelon. I noticed that she was very thin and quite tall. She was wearing a black tank top, revealing a sculpted abdomen, a pastel pink skirt showing her smooth legs, and high heels, even during the daytime. She had a narrow face with an elongated chin, and pointy ears sticking out through shoulder-length hair. As I followed her enormous dark eyes, she looked up again. Finally, she introduced herself as Natasha, with a mischievous smile. I could not resist and surrendered with a broader grin. I was mesmerized by the game. Her eyes flashed goodbye as I walked away with Amélia. I didn't talk on the way home. Once we were back, sitting on the small couch in front of her television, Amélia decided to break the silence. "You are not to be afraid of Natasha. She is a good person!" my neighbor affirmed, in between bites of sweet mango.

A Libertine Whore

It turned out that Natasha lived not too far away from me. At the time, she shared a "shack" (*barraco*) east of Valão with her friends Vavá, Bira, and Nivaldo, in an alleyway perpendicular to mine. When she fought with them, as she sometimes did, Natasha would move to the apartment that her "blood family" (*família de sangue*) rented. The latter had also been the first roof over her head when Natasha arrived in the favela. As I would come to learn, most of her siblings had migrated to the Brazilian Southeast, leaving the hinterlands of Ceará, a northeastern state in Brazil, one by one for Rio de Janeiro. The eldest of them in Rio was a successful professional cook in a posh restaurant, and he helped finance the travels of the others. Several of Natasha's relatives had settled in Rocinha, the largest favela in the South Zone of Rio, where we lived. Others had moved to Rio das Pedras (literally, River of Stones), one of the largest favelas in the West Zone, where Natasha often went clubbing and cruising for sex.

Natasha was very outspoken. She would affirm in a loud and deep voice: "I am a *travesti*! So what?" Through Don Kulick's research in Brazil, the term *travesti* was added to anthropological parlance in close semantic relation to "Brazilian transgendered prostitutes."[8] Rarely, did Natasha use the term *transgender* (*transgênero*); she much preferred *travesti*. She also denied being a professional prostitute. In one of our first meetings, she told me: "I have quit prostitution, love! It's been a couple of years away from that life!" At that time, she worked as a cleaning lady in a madam's home in Copacabana. "The old woman loves me!" she boasted.

Bad fights broke out when their mother, Dona Rosário, would come from Ceará to spend time with Natasha and her siblings in the favela. I remember one night when Natasha and I returned to Rocinha at dawn from Rio da Pedras. Dona Rosário was at the family home, dozing in a chair, leaning on the small kitchen table. Her thick eyeglasses were still sitting on her face. Upon our arrival, she opened her eyes, looked at us in anger, and started to yell: "You, huh, Clodoaldo! A free man [livre e desimpedido], at the age of getting married, and running after other men? Disgusting! I want to see you married and with a lot of children. Are you listening?" Natasha had a deep hatred toward any mention of Clodoaldo, the male name she had received at birth. All three of us were upset. I wondered if Dona Rosário had an expectation that freedom should be given up in order to raise a family. Natasha's refusal to marry was considered antisocial behavior; it was, in Dona Rosário own words, "disgusting." Under her mother's moral scrutiny, Natasha's liberties were unacceptable.

Natasha pinned up her chemically straightened hair with an elastic band from inside her handbag, then pulled up the neckline of her dress, which had started to slip down to reveal her flat breasts. She screamed back at her mother: "I am terrible indeed! Even God turns his back on me when he looks at me! I'm a demon!" Rosário's red eyes didn't blink. Natasha increased her volume. "Remember that soap opera in which a woman deceived the devil? I'm worse than the devil myself. I am proud of being a libertine [libertina], a whore!" Natasha punctuated the conclusion of her speech with a high-pitched laugh. Dona Rosário did not react with rage. Instead, she smiled, as if awakening from a bad dream. Looking at me, she offered us some black coffee; she had spent the whole night sipping the bitter drink, waiting for her daughter to return home. She even gave me a kiss on the cheek as I left, which Natasha watched with deep anger.

Another time, I was invited to a farewell dinner for Dona Rosário. She had spent a few months in Rocinha at that point, and she was all packed to catch the bus back to her hometown. Her permanent residence was in a small property, in a village not far from the town Guaraciaba do Norte, in Ceará, bordering the state of Piauí. The journey there would take at least three days by bus, almost two thousand miles. She vented to me: "I wish we could all live together! But I own a little piece of land in Ceará and left my other boys behind. It is important to work the soil,

CHAPTER ONE

you know? My sustenance [*sustento*] always came from it. I wish the boys hadn't moved out from that land. I must go! I wasn't born to spend my life doing nothing in a favela." She smiled sadly at each farewell.

Natasha was proud to live in Rio de Janeiro, the Marvelous City, the Cidade Maravilhosa. She was even proud to live in the favela. She used to say that there was space to be different there: "Here I have much more freedom [*liberdade*] to do these things!" She hated the dryness of her hometown. In Ceará, there was no place for Natasha Kellem Bündchen.[9] In Ceará, there could only be Clodoaldo Cortez da Silva. She didn't mind the dryness of the northeastern soil itself; she was bothered by the dryness of the people who lived there, their lack of glamour and imagination. She missed the lube and the frills. In Rio de Janeiro, Natasha often said: "Oh, my pussy is wet!" She was always horny. In Ceará, nobody wanted to hear this. My friend and I enjoyed our adventures in Rio de Janeiro.

The Estrangement

In mid-2012 I temporarily lost contact with Natasha. I was no longer living in the favela. But I returned there at least twice a year, sometimes for short visits and other times for stays of a couple of months. This way, I maintained relationships and tried to keep up-to-date with all the changes in the slum. As I walked around Valão, I relived memories, visited old friends and acquaintances, and shared the latest gossip. In August 2012, I was in Rocinha. This time, the visit carried a special sentimental meaning. I was hoping to reconnect with Natasha. I returned to the exact same area where I had lived before. At every turn, as I walked through the alleyways, I wished to see Natasha's face. Maybe she had not been checking her messages? No internet? Or else she had changed her phone number? I wondered if I would ever see my friend again. I hoped our friendship would survive the distance between us since my previous visit in January that same year.

But Natasha was nowhere to be found. I kept sending her multiple messages, and they all went unanswered. I asked around, but those who claimed to know something about her told me different stories. Some said Natasha had moved houses, due to family matters. Then I learned that she had moved out of Rocinha. Maybe she had taken the bus to the other favela, Rio das Pedras, once and for all? A few people claimed that Natasha had returned to her homeland and no longer lived in Rio de Janeiro. "Back to Ceará? Only if she's dead!" I thought.

Rio das Pedras made more sense. We had taken many trips from Rocinha to Rio das Pedras. I knew that Natasha's family thought that Rio das Pedras was a more "decent" place to live. But I wondered if that was the case. Rocinha was under the domain of a powerful drug-trafficking faction, Amigo dos Amigos (Friends of Friends), or simply A.D.A. Like other major drug factions, such as the Red Command (C.V.) or the Third Command (T.C.), A.D.A. usually recruited their workforce from within their own domains. The cruelties of the drug dealers in Rocinha took place in public. They showed off their rifles and money, and, at times, they made a spectacle out of killing those who defied them. However, Natasha knew the drug traffickers in Rocinha, and they protected her. That was not the case in Rio das Pedras, which was run by a brutal paramilitary group (*milícia*). The paramilitary groups were formed by civil servants—former policemen, firefighters, and retired military—who were seldom residents of the favelas where they ruled. The paramilitaries tried to be invisible in their daily operations, but they seemed to be even crueler in their punishment of those who dared to challenge their power. People and things simply disappeared in Rio das Pedras, often during the night. There was no commotion and no comment.

The next few weeks were agony. I circulated inside and outside the shantytown. I went up and down Rua do Valão several times, leaving word here and there: "Have you seen Natasha?" I asked in desperation. People replied by telling me about their own manifold difficulties. It felt like an endless search. "Did you find the faggot?" my mathematician friend, Auro, asked every single day. He looked down on Natasha. "Isn't she a migrant from Ceará state? Directly from the interior of Brazil? She is a total *matesca*—a critter from the bushes!"[10] Auro laughed, covering his front teeth with his thick fingers, pretending to be surprised at his lack of compassion.

Natasha's closest friends and former roommates—Vavá, Bira, and Nivaldo—were all from the interior of Ceará state. I was also from the interior of the country, but not from the Northeast, from the Brazilian Midwest. I wondered if Auro ever called me a *matesco* too. Auro told me he descended from a famous drug lord family from Rocinha: "Pestana's nephew! My family was respected when I was little. Yes! Even though my mother was terrified of my criminal uncle!" He had been born in Rio and was not sympathetic to migrants, even though his whole family had migrated from the Northeast just a generation ago. Migrants didn't fully know the weight of being a matesco until they had finished crossing the thousands of miles separating their hinterlands from Rocinha. Some would get lost after moving to the Wonderful City.

CHAPTER ONE

Natasha's Whereabouts

Nivaldo told me through an internet chat that he had discovered Natasha's whereabouts. He was a distant cousin of hers and a friend of mine too. I witnessed countless episodes in which Nivaldo was bullied in the favela for being a "cross-eyed fag" (*bicha zarolha*) and I felt terrible about it. Natasha's cousin had been our constant companion in the nights during my fieldwork. But something had happened in the intervening years. He made it clear that he had no interest in meeting Natasha, as they were no longer on speaking terms.

"She's fought with everyone, Moisés!" Nivaldo vented during the internet exchange.

"Everyone?" I asked.

"Yes, she's worse by the day! Crazier!" he remarked.

"Wasn't she living with her brothers?" I asked him.

"It seems that not even her brothers could stand her, my friend . . . They kicked her out!" Nivaldo continued.

"And where did she go?" I asked.

"Bira is the one who knows more about her whereabouts," he replied.

"And where's Bira?" I typed anxiously.

"You are still in Rocinha, right? Stop by our house later on, and he will tell you everything, okay?" Nivaldo assured me.

"Are you still living in the same place?" I checked.

"No, we moved shacks [*barracos*]. Now we live in the alley just behind the one we lived in before," he explained.

"Will Bira be there today?" I asked, with the hope of getting things sorted soon.

"Hmmm . . . Yes, but he only gets home from work after 10 p.m., okay? Ask around Firecracker Alleyway [Beco do Foguete], and you will find our house. Any trouble, you just call my number!" Nivaldo instructed me. I confirmed the meeting and left the chat.

What was Nivaldo saying? Madness? Fights? Natasha was not always on good terms with her blood family but was often affectionate toward them. Was she kicked out of the family home? Did she have food and a place to live? Did the traffickers exile her from the favela? Something strange was in the air. I had spent so long looking for Natasha that I still doubted her friend Bira could have found her before me. I liked him a lot, but he had always been a little strange. He didn't like to talk much. Perhaps he didn't have to talk much to find Natasha? Probably Natasha had contacted him.

Because I was anxious, I worried that I wouldn't be able to find Nivaldo's new place. In fact, it was never easy to find a location in Rocinha, considering that most of them had no formal address. To make matters worse, Beco do Foguete was notorious as a hot spot for drug-dealing operations. For this reason, my Evangelical neighbors refused to circulate there. I had spent a lot of time in the area during my fieldwork, though. Several bars and beauty salons were located in that alleyway, and there was also a candy store near an arcade where I went to access the internet when my home connection wasn't working, which happened often. Still, I knew that it was hard to ask for directions around Beco do Foguete. Confidence was an important skill in favela life. One could never know when bandits would cross your path, or you cross theirs. Bandits were trained to sense fear. The safest thing was to appear like you knew where you were going at all times.

I nervously waited until 10 p.m. on the day I had scheduled to meet Bira. Because Amélia was hosting me at her house at the time, I let her know that I was leaving for an important meeting and would return home late. Feeling tense, I set off for Beco do Foguete. There was an impressive nightlife scene in the favela; ten o'clock was considered early. Lights from all the thousands of shacks went all the way up and down the hill, on every side. The starry-like urban landscape amazed people. There were often blackouts in Rocinha too, but not that night. At the entrance to Beco do Foguete, I recognized a girl sitting near the candy store. I asked her for information. She didn't know of any Bira. "What Bira?"

I described him: "Almond eyes, reddish skin tone, very sleek and short hair. Round face and shy smile. No beard."

She didn't know anything. "Bira?!" she said again, puzzled.

I ventured into an alleyway where I had never been, perpendicular to Beco do Foguete, a short dead end. Somebody was cooking dinner, and the smell of fried beef was intense. I looked up at the favela buildings, noticing that some were at least four stories tall. Too many possibilities. How would I know where to find him? An older lady was sitting at the doorstep of her house. I knew it was dangerous to ask too much, but I decided to risk it and inquired about Bira. She answered with a heavy Carioca (Rio de Janeiro) accent: "Bira? I don't know anyone by that name!" A very pale copper-haired child came out to see what was going on. Across the street, a Black man stuck his head out of a second-story window. The Carioca woman echoed my question: "Someone called Bira?"

Another person responded, sticking her head out of a different window: "Isn't he the one who lives with that other?"

CHAPTER ONE

Unexpectedly, just down the alleyway, from the ground floor of the last house, I saw someone I knew well. "França?" I called out to her.

"Darling! What are you doing lost around here?" she yelled back. França was around fifteen years old and looked more feminine than the last time I'd seen her. It was a profound relief to find an acquaintance in such an unfamiliar area. We chatted a bit and arranged to meet again soon. The nosy neighbors kept watching us through their windows. França told me that Bira was living on the second floor of a building with slate tiles on the façade. "There is no point in calling them from downstairs because the fags don't listen. They play their music at maximum volume at all times! Go up to the second floor and knock hard on the door," my friend advised me. With her directions, I found the right place. I opened the little entrance gate, which was made of flimsy wood, then climbed the steep stairs. I knocked many times until finally the Madonna CD was turned off. Silence.

Nivaldo greeted me. "Girl! You? Come in!" He wore the same thick glasses as before. His skin, dotted with red pimples, and his honey-colored curls were familiar to me. But his smile was slightly different. He seemed more reticent than usual. Was my presence making him uncomfortable? Given my frequent return visits to Rocinha, some dwellers did not even realize that I had moved out of the favela in 2010. During my very first meetings with any of the favela dwellers, back in 2009, I had made a great effort to introduce myself as an anthropologist, in order to explain my research project and obtain their informed consent. "Ethnographer? What is this?" some asked. A few months after these introductions, how many people still remembered that I was conducting research? I wasn't sure if Nivaldo did. Or maybe it was just that he was concerned about Natasha?

He asked me to sit on the old couch, then explained that Bira was taking off his work uniform and would tell me all about Natasha when he was finished. Nivaldo turned the music up again and didn't say much more. I waited, in internal turmoil, until Bira appeared through the bedroom door wearing a white T-shirt and flip-flops. He seemed less shy than usual and asked about my life. But I didn't have time to tell him much. Bira, sensing my anxiety, began to tell me about Natasha. I realized that Nivaldo, Bira, and I all knew that the subject was much more than a research question to me. Bira confirmed my fears: Natasha was not well. The tightness in my chest turned into pain. He explained everything he knew regarding her situation, which he found out through a phone call from her. Bira gave me precise instructions on how to get to where she was staying. But he refused to look for her with me. The conversation ended in a long embrace.

A Brazilian-Gringo, Boy-Fag Anthropologist

There were different analyses among Rocinha residents regarding my fieldwork and my position in the favela. Roy Wagner would call these "reverse-anthropologies," the efforts made to understand, explain, and theorize anthropologists like me.[11] During my first days in Rocinha, I soon got to know my neighbor Carcará. He listened attentively to my initial explanations and then asked: "So, you are an anthropologist?" I confirmed. "And you said you live here in the alleyway?" he continued.

"That is right," I replied.

"You are an anthropologist, and you live here in the favela?" He sounded a bit puzzled.

"I moved here not long ago," I told him.

"And don't you know that anthropologists don't have to live in the slum?" Carcará posed the question, doubting that I could possibly be an anthropologist.

"What do you mean?" I asked for clarification.

"Don't you have money to live elsewhere?" he insisted.

"Maybe. Okay . . . Yes," I replied awkwardly.

"A Brazilian anthropologist who comes to live in the slum! That doesn't make sense!" he affirmed, exasperated.

"An anthropologist has to live with people—" I tried to explain and was interrupted.

"Gringos are the ones who have this habit of living in the favela. Brazilians want distance from the favelas," Carcará informed me.

"All Brazilians?" I challenged him.

"Brazilian anthropologists live in Gávea, Leblon, São Conrado . . ." he continued.

"And how do they do research?" I asked him.

"Hey! You don't know? You schedule a time at the Association [the Rocinha Residents' Association], or at some school . . . You find some contacts in the favela in advance. Those contacts will find people for you to interview. It is easy! Don't you know that? It's even better if you have some research cash to give away!" he told me with an ironic smile on his face.

"But I don't think it would be good just to conduct interviews," I insisted.

"I see . . ." Carcará paused and seemed deep in thought.

"I would like to live here for at least a year," I continued.

"Really? And where are you coming from again?" He sounded even more suspicious.

CHAPTER ONE

"I'm from Goiás state," I told him.
"Are you moving from Goiás here?" he asked, surprised.
"I'm doing my doctorate in Scotland," I replied.
"Where? In Gringolandia?" he said, and laughed.
"Yes, in Europe," I told him.
"Oh, I knew it! I knew that something was out of place. You are a Brazilian-gringo! Now it is all explained," he told me, concluding the conversation.[12]

Carcará and I would come to have many other exchanges on questions of nationality and gringo behavior. He would become one of my good friends in Rocinha, with a particular fascination with things from abroad, including foreigners themselves: Americans, Dutch, Spanish, Italians, French, Swiss, and others that we encountered in Rocinha during the years of my research. Most of these foreigners were volunteers in the favela. In the anthropological categorization of Rocinha residents, gringos would be at the opposite extreme of those considered "natives" of the place, called *cria*, or the "children of the Hillside."

The radical cultural difference introduced by gringos, however, was not necessarily the most troubling relation of alterity in Rocinha. Foreign nationals were considered so different from most others in the favela that, ironically, there was more tolerance toward them. They were not expected to know much about slums—or about anything, really. They aroused a mix of curiosity, infantilization, and sometimes admiration. Even traffickers were more flexible with them. The more concerning problem for Rocinha residents were the arrogant bourgeois Brazilians—residents of the Asphalt.

Paizinha was Ricky's aunt and one of my neighbors. After getting married and giving birth to two girls, she decided to pursue her dream of getting a college degree in education. Her job as a Portuguese language teacher helped with the costs of raising a family. She reported with rage the fear that the Brazilian elites had of favelas. These were people who lived very close, sometimes right across the highway from Rocinha. "Selfish! They are only concerned about themselves!" Paizinha explained that people from São Conrado approached favela dwellers only when they needed something from them: "Drugs, maids, or prostitutes!" There was something else that the elites looked for in the favela. Auro liked to point out, "They want the freedom they don't have in the Asphalt! Many of these little bourgeois people come here not only to buy but to abuse drugs without any trouble. They wander around, thinking that here they are *free*! Ridiculous." He recognized and condemned the fact that the so-called bourgeoisie (*burguesia*) desired the freedoms

THROUGH PLEASURES AND PAIN

of the favela, particularly the time and space to consume drugs, without having to worry about police repression. At the same time, as I noted before, the elites were also very concerned with maintaining their distance and a rigid division between the Hillside and the Asphalt. The word *favelado* had long become a curse, even within the favela community itself. The distinction between bourgeois and favelado was necessary to produce different territories and different subjects of freedom.

What about me? I was a strange phenomenon in Rocinha; the anthropologist from Goiás state who studied in Scotland and lived in the favela. I did not easily fit within the favela categories of difference. Classificatory efforts sometimes had me more as bourgeois, sometimes closer to a backward migrant, at other times an outsider to be exploited. The only person that I suspect ever thought I was a person born and raised in the favela (*cria do morro*) was a German tourist who visited Rocinha as part of a commercial tourist enterprise called Favela Tours. As his group walked down the alleyway where I lived, he pointed his camera close to my face and, without asking for my consent, simply captured my image. He then left proudly, with his record of a "native."

A queer bourgeois person, like me, was likely to be called a "homosexual," "gay," or a "boy-fag." By contrast, the use of the term *gay* had little force among my friends in Rocinha. To be "gay" was more of an Asphalt possibility than a favela one, and the word *gay* itself was an anglicism with undertones of globalization and bourgeois status.[13] In the favela context, a potential synonym for gay would be *bicha-boy burguesa*.[14] The term *bicha* on its own was a different story, more affectionate if used among friends. Other common terms were *marica* and *viado*, instead of gay, or *trava* and *trans*, instead of travesti. Commonly, among my travesti friends in Rocinha, cisgender male queer folks were qualified as "boy-fags." The fact that the word *boy* was kept in English even when the term was used in Portuguese (*bicha-boy*) guaranteed yet another level of differentiation; it was slightly pejorative, perhaps as a critique of privilege. Travestis talked about "being-pussy" (*ser-buceta*), being female, but not in the sense of "being a pussy," nor in the anatomical-biologizing sense of the term. Being a travesti and a member of the bourgeoisie at the same time was almost an impossibility in Rio de Janeiro.

A Virus, *the* Virus

"Go see the *bicha!* Go now," Bira had told me affectionately, before closing the door of his home. I walked slowly down the stairs, consternated.

CHAPTER ONE

I made my way through Beco do Foguete, fearful of missing the entrance, which would lead me safely to the right destination. Natasha was living just past a small sewer, a tributary to the larger one where she used to live before, in the lower eastern part of the favela known as Raiz. I should find her living with her friend Vavá.

"Natashaaa!" I started calling. I should be close to her, but no one seemed to hear me. What I did not know was that I was calling for someone who could not answer; Natasha was too feverish to get up. I was close to giving up but, finally, Vavá appeared in a small window. He gestured for me to wait. I thought back to more than a year ago, when Vavá had spent weeks in the emergency section of Miguel Couto hospital in 2011.[15] At first, Vavá claimed he only had hepatitis. But then he caught the flu, which turned into pneumonia. That is when he was admitted to the intensive care unit. Photographs of a swollen, yellow-skinned Vavá circulated on the internet amongst our mutual friends. "This fag is going to die!" Armando, the director of a non-governmental organization (NGO) where I volunteered in Rocinha, commented after seeing some of the images. Indeed, he had almost died. But instead he was diagnosed with HIV. Soon, doctors started treating him with antiretrovirals.[16] Vavá was sent home and had been doing much better after that initial phase. It turned out that he was the only person who had the strength and willingness to take care of our mutual friend Natasha.

Vavá came down to unlock the narrow gate, then led me into a small studio. He had placed Natasha's bed right in the middle of the room, center stage. Everything else had been pushed against the surrounding walls. During my visit, Vavá continued standing to afford us more space. He invited me to sit on the bed beside Natasha. I could finally look into her eyes. "What is wrong with you, my friend?" I asked her in a soft voice.

"Some flu, a common virosis," she whispered.

"And you went to the doctor, Natasha?" I asked, raising my voice slightly.

"I did," she affirmed.

"And what did they say?" I asked.

"Virosis," she said timidly.

"Just that? Virosis?" I confirmed, slightly exasperated.

"It's a virosis! It's nothing!" she answered, raising her tone and trying to put an end to the conversation.

"What is the difference between a virus, *the* virus, and any other virosis?" I thought. Natasha wore a beige satin nightgown that was a shade paler than her skin. She was swollen and suspicious of me. I realized that Natasha had spent weeks lying on this sweaty piece of foam. Her mother was not there. Her siblings were not there. None of her blood relatives seemed to care enough. But Vavá was there. He understood the situation. The only tie that had survived was this friendship. What could I do? There was none of the laughter of our previous encounters. It had been so hard to find Natasha. It was even harder to encounter her in such a state, damp with fever. At least she was finally in front of me. Was it all in vain? Or worse, did our encounter highlight, even more, the differences between us? I could freely move, travel, and talk, and she could no longer get off of a smelly mattress.

Breaking the Anthropological Pact

Anthropologists tend to understand the act of *going* somewhere else, *moving* to the field, *traveling* for fieldwork, as constitutive of their research efforts—whereas people in their studies do not always have the same opportunities for mobility, or else are simply assumed not to have them.[17] I knew that I was more than a researcher at that moment, but something about my freedom of movement disturbed me in that encounter. Was I unintentionally reaffirming my own freedom? Natasha was so ill. The fever-induced chill made her recoil from my touch. She crossed her arms together to keep her chest protected. She was shaking. Sometimes, her hands rubbed her swollen neck, like a self-soothing gesture. Who else could comfort her? Vavá helped as best as he could; he fed and washed her. For intimate warmth, however, Natasha could only count on herself. Soon, I would have to travel and leave her behind again.

Still, she was kind to me. Maybe a little more alive in my presence. But she was far from the person I had known. The Natasha I knew liked to have a laugh with her friends. Sometimes I would run into someone after having just seen Natasha, and they would tell me, "There's lipstick on your face!" Natasha's red kisses. Now, her lips were cracked and almost invisible. Her mouth didn't speak much. Maybe it was better not to say anything? It seemed painful for her to explain herself in the face of illness; even when she tried to speak, she didn't tell me much. I thought of our lost future. How many times had Natasha joked that she would be my wife someday? Even though she knew that I was about to get married to someone else already.

Faced with such an unexpected encounter, she might have felt the marked pain of what had changed between us. Had I caused her even more discomfort? I wanted to believe that any encounter would be better than sheer absence. Maybe we could go back to the days when we were both more certain of our future. Natasha's voice resurfaced. She would say that it was nothing; nothing was happening. It was all going to pass. Perhaps she wished to be the same her in front of the same me. If I were the same self from other times, I would have trusted her. Maybe I had changed more than I realized.

I used to laugh with Natasha and admire her courage at the same time. I liked Natasha's sense of humor, even if she was too eccentric for some people. I usually preferred the possible world in which Natasha's extravagant stories were real. We inhabited the same narratives full of sexual possibilities, humorous events, and beautiful men. It was a better world for both of us. We also had serious disagreements, which partly derived from her complexities as a person. I was combative against racist attitudes on her part, for example. A certain genealogy of Brazilian favelas mobilizes a minoritarian sense of Black freedom, which, I argue, can also be understood as a form of *maroon liberalism*.[18] Regardless, favelas became home to people of different races. Some of them were explicitly racist. It really troubled me.

That day, I failed to take her seriously. I didn't believe she had a common virosis, as she insisted. I thought she was HIV positive. I didn't seriously consider that everything would be all right. Instead, I searched for a biological explanation, some kind of medical truth that could save Natasha's life. I examined the lumps on her body, looked for clues, tried to diagnose her symptoms. I wanted to take my friend to the hospital. That was something I could do; I had money to pay for a taxi. I could free her from that stuffy, warm, sickening room.

She declined it all. In the face of her resistance, I turned to Vavá. But he also refused to go against Natasha's will. "What are you going to do? Are you going to force her to go?" he asked. I forgot for a moment that not all movement leads to freedom. After all, slavery depended on a series of forced movements. So how did the anthropologist who wanted to understand the complexities of freedom end up suggesting that a friend of his should be taken by force to the hospital? I appreciated Foucault's writings regarding the pernicious effects of biopower in the production of docile bodies, capable of being "manipulated, shaped, trained."[19] At the same time, I demonstrated an irrational desire to turn Natasha into a docile patient.

Perhaps, right there, I broke my anthropological pact of mutual, respectful understanding with Natasha. It was selfish, my desire to keep her alive at all costs. I could not take Natasha's truth as truth; I couldn't join her in a possible world where she would be fine again. I refuted the ways she chose to explain her disappearance, her weight loss, her high fever. I did not value the narrative of someone who had made an immense effort to speak through pain. I was there, in front of Natasha, but still disconnected from her. It hurts me profoundly to remember it. Most disagreements with Natasha emerged from my own ethnocentric insistence on what I came to understand as implicit normative liberal values, based on my sense of respect toward the rule of law, and a bourgeois sensibility—all of which had little traction in the favela.

If I had listened to Natasha more carefully, perhaps our meeting would not have been so painful. What right has an anthropologist to cause suffering? If I failed as an anthropologist that day, it comforts me to think that I did not fail her as a loving friend, a person who knows that love can be selfish and irrational (or, sometimes, too rational). I now assume that redemption had always been there, in the truths offered by the moribund interlocutor herself. Minoritarian subjects have their freedoms, theories, and experiences persistently erased by more powerful modes of truth and knowledge production—such as the medical sciences.[20] I didn't consider that Natasha could free herself from that serious condition without medical help. Nevertheless, some of her conceptions of freedom had been different from mine all along. I write this ethnography to try to fix some of my initial mistakes.

Who's to Blame?

Motorcycles, watermelons, drugs, friends, mattresses, anthropologists, viruses, blood, freedoms. The daily life of Natasha Kellem Bündchen in the favela mobilized all these and more. Some days she had multiple lovers, siblings, and even a mother. On others, she was alone on a mattress smelling of mold. Natasha enjoyed many pleasures and mocked the difficulties of life. She reveled in the joy of being with different men. Sometimes her relationships were silent, and occasionally they were explosive. The mattress where she was trapped had once been a venue for sexual pleasures—a territory of great conquests, the place where Natasha was loved as she wanted, as a woman, on the days she chose to be a woman. To blame Natasha's "libertinism" (deviant freedoms) for contracting a virus would certainly mean defeat in our effort to counter normative liberalism. A different politics of pleasure and liberalism is necessary. Not another set of new or more strict regulations to guarantee freedom, but, as we will see in the next chapters, the realization that a multiplicity of modes of liberalism already exists and these other modes demand recognition.

TWO

Laws of the Hillside

Neoliberalism is conceptualized not as a fixed set of attributes with predetermined outcomes, but as a logic of governing that migrates and is selectively taken up in diverse political contexts. I present an analytics of assemblage over an analytics of structure, and a focus on emerging milieus over the stabilization of a new global order. AIHWA ONG, "NEOLIBERALISM AS A MOBILE TECHNOLOGY"

After a bloody history of violations of Amerindian and Black rights, white Europeans and some of their descendants have become the Brazilian elite. They now occupy most of the prime real estate in the country and accumulate most of its wealth. Ironically, for the urban elites in Rio de Janeiro nowadays, favela dwellers are the ones seen as violators of property rights. Not only that, favela residents seem to pose a daily threat to elite freedoms. After all, the capacity to possess land and to accumulate goods without limitation is one of the most cherished values of normative liberalism. In his seminal work on the topic, Adam Smith considers:

For one very rich man there must be at least five hundred poor, and the affluence of the few supposes the indigence of the many. The affluence of the rich excites the indignation of the poor, who are often both driven by want, and prompted by envy, to invade his possessions. It is only under the shelter of the civil magistrate that the owner of that valuable property, which is acquired by the labor of many years, or perhaps of many successive generations, can sleep a single night in security.[1]

Economic liberalism has long been defined based on a combination of a free-market ideology, rights over private property, and individuality. Apart from the fear that the poor generally bring upon the rich, favelas represent a significant menace to capitalist opportunities for profit based on real estate development, property values, and capital investments. Favela dwellers become enemies to the elites. Beatriz Jaguaribe explains how the particular position of favelas turn into a problem for normative liberal endeavors:

> For inhabitants of large metropolitan areas in Brazil, the fear of urban spaces is tied to the usual threats of rape, robbery, kidnapping. But such forms of violence can occur in any section of the city and are viewed as part of the menacing experience of the streets. Yet within the urban maze, the favelas—as is evidenced by the dramatic drop of real estate prices of houses and apartments located near them—are seen as specific danger zones of violence and poverty.[2]

In particular, slum dwellers challenge liberal values connected to land ownership. The favela logic went very much along the lines of other well-known arguments such as the one posed by Karl Marx: "If every violation of property without distinction, without a more exact definition, is termed theft, will not all private property be theft? By my private ownership do I not exclude every other person from this ownership?"[3] Why has the colonial hijacking of land not been established as a form of theft, but favela dwellers are consistently charged with such accusations?

From the point of view of an elementary school teacher from Rocinha, freedom should not be one-sided: "Freedom starts where another person's freedom ends" (*a liberdade de um começa onde termina a liberdade do outro*). Total freedom for some and misery for the rest is not what Paizinha had in mind. Slum dwellers refute the basis of this liberal contract, of which they have never been considered legitimate signatories. They point out that Brazilian laws are contradictory; they guarantee the universal right to housing and, at the same time, disallow the poor from creating housing where they can actually afford it.[4] Many histories of Brazilian favelas are intimately related to the "illegal" occupation of private land and state-owned property. In turn, the nation-state has responded with repression, expulsion, police violence, and military warfare. There was a crackdown starting in 2008, until around 2014, when an aggressive state policy of favela "occupation" known as Pacificação came into effect. This entailed a military occupation of many favela territories in Rio de Janeiro; scenes of warfare were transmitted live on national TV. In this case, however, the enemies were internal to the nation: favela dwellers. Despite all this oppression, the slum stays alive. The shantytown grows.

Faced with this situation, favela dwellers remember different times.

CHAPTER TWO

"Within the favela, it is the *law of the Hillside* that rules. At first, it was a jungle around here, my son! Whoever came first would just grab land. There, take a piece of land!" Dona Teté, a Black woman and an older resident, told me excitedly. But it's never been easy. It has always been bloody.[5] Forced removals and even arson were common tactics deployed by the elites against favela dwellers.[6] In Portuguese, Rocinha would literally translate as a "small farm." The first inhabitants of the hills upon which Rocinha sits gradually occupied land from an urban farm that delivered produce to the wealthy nearby neighborhoods. Why does the "original sin" of property rights violation persist in the conception of shantytowns but not in the conception of the nation?

Stigma against favela dwellers remains extreme among residents of the so-called formal city (the Asphalt). I once met a resident of São Conrado, the wealthy neighborhood near Rocinha. She used to sit on her balcony, with her long hair, dyed blond, perfectly fixed. This lady would tell me, "When I bought my apartment, this neighborhood was good. My view from the balcony was beautiful! This monstrous slum wasn't there. They invaded it all. Invaded it! That's a crime. It can't be this way!" Why is this a crime against private property? How is it that favela dwellers are seen as criminals when the right to housing is a human right?[7] The residents of the "informal" city are seen as triply guilty before the "formal" city: guilty of not respecting private property rights, guilty of not being civilized, guilty of not being worthy of human rights.

The rule of law fails in favela life. "Slum dogs don't respect the Asphalt law. They don't respect a fucking thing!" my alleyway neighbor Carcará yelled when he was upset. There is no agent to guarantee the human rights of favela residents. Who is the human being of "human" rights? The Rio de Janeiro elite—a sociological concept frequently deployed by my friends in Rocinha—believe in the struggle of the civilized against the savages. Peace against violence. Elites versus slum dwellers. Any purification of Rio de Janeiro's urban complex into simplistic binaries—*formality* against *informality*—only serves the interests of the elites. Gareth Doherty and I have denounced this situation in an article entitled "Formally Informal."[8] Favela residents are an integral part of the fabric of Rio de Janeiro, even if they are often relegated to the most undesirable locations. Bourgeois normative freedoms should not be guaranteed at the expense of so many other rights denied to the residents of Rocinha.

In normative liberalism, humans are universally free, but the freedom of some colonizes the freedom of others. Not everyone agreed to the colonial social contract: Dona Teté barely knew how to sign her name. She never had a chance to learn. Favelas are violent territories; there is no denying that. Violence is not one-sided, however. Many brutalities happen in the name of a social order that was never desired by favela residents. Favela dwellers may violate current understandings of "property rights" and refuse to follow the terms of an unfair social contract, but this is not to say that laws only exist in the Asphalt, that civility only has a place in the Asphalt, that freedoms only exist in the Asphalt. "The absence of the state in the favela is a kind of institutional freedom . . . but people don't want to see it that way!" Renato, a sociology student and favela resident, complained. According to him, the biggest perpetrators of violence in the lives of favela residents were the elites and the liberal rule of law.[9] A lot of violence is perpetrated in the name of freedom—often in defense of more "real freedoms" dictated by the elites. Normative liberalism is particularly aggressive toward favela dwellers.

Ambiguous Relationships

Brazilian favelas are urban territories in an ambiguous relationship with the state because they are at the margins of its formation and, at the same time, at the center of its operations. In a study of urban marginality in Rio de Janeiro, Dulce Pandolfi and Mário Grynszpan argue:

> If, on the one hand, violence is perceived as a defining element of favelas, on the other hand, this violence is not only attributed to poverty, but also to the absence of the state. It should be noted, however, that this absence is not only perceived in the inability to guarantee the rule of law [in the favelas] through the imposition by the state of a monopoly on the legitimate use of violence, but also through almost non-existent investments in infrastructure, sewage, health, education, and public transport. Therefore, the favelas are at the margin of what would constitute the minimum rights of a citizen; it can be said that the favelas are also defined by their social exclusion.[10]

Favelas are considered peripheral territories (even when centrally located), lacking formal rights and normative freedoms. Nevertheless, the narrative would be incomplete if we only referred to what these territories lack. The periphery doesn't exist without the center. Every center is inside and, at the same time, outside the structure of which it is a part.[11] The obvious center of the Marvelous City is not the favela. It was never meant to be the favela. Having said that, without favelas, Rio de Janeiro could not be the city it actually is. Favelas are central to the workings of the normative (neo)liberal state in contemporary politics. Their situation resonates with (neo)liberal operations in a more global perspective:

Neighborhoods of urban relegation—the decaying *favela* in Brazil, the imploding hyperghetto in the United States, the declining *banlieue* in France, and the desolate inner city in Scotland or Holland—turn out to be the prime physical and social space within which the neoliberal penal state is concretely being assembled, tried, and tested.[12]

Normative liberalism operates through processes of territorialization—the homogenization of difference. Ethnographic evidence suggests that the situation in Rio de Janeiro is much more complex than the liberal elites want us to think. Normative liberalism is not the only form of liberalism in operation. Even though this "elite" mode of liberalism does not fulfill its promise of universal freedom, that does not mean that favelas lack freedom in an absolute sense; the modes of liberalism available to favela dwellers are different from the ones in the Asphalt. Put another way, when there is a desire for freedom (which is not something to be taken for granted), there might also happen to be a proliferation of forms of liberalism. In a city like Rio de Janeiro, there are multiple versions of liberalism operating at the same time. Multiple forms of power, with different modes of oppression and affordances of freedom, coexist in everyday life.

The liberal social contract tends to suggest that the nation-state is the sole guarantor of liberties and the legitimate holder of the monopoly on violence; however, the way that governmentality operates in favelas provides a different picture. There, the nation-state is intentionally withdrawing from the provision of equality and universal rights, while intensifying its police powers. These different roles played by the state are not mutually exclusive; they overlap ambiguously. Normative freedom is often violent. State power keeps murdering favela dwellers at a much higher rate than it kills citizens of the Asphalt.[13] When probed, state representatives offer a series of correlated justifications: "Protection from chaos!" "Defense of private property!" "The guarantee of order for progress!" Let us not forget the motto on the Brazilian flag: "Order and Progress." Deaths without weeping?[14] Everyday violence is the most difficult to notice and the hardest to accept. Contractualism attempted to justify centuries ago the need to tolerate the negative effects of state power in the name of liberty.

Raised in the Catholic Church

Despite its importance, the nation-state is not the only source of freedoms and regulations in daily life. Spending time with Natasha's family, I took notes on an episode that took place on July 22, 2009. We passed by the emerald sea at high speed. I was looking out the window of a van used for public transport in the South Zone. That day, the van was flying down Avenida Niemeyer—a reinforced concrete road that hugged the coastline and seemed to float over the water. Moments of free traffic flow like this were rare in the city. The popular route took passengers between Rocinha and the elite neighborhood of Ipanema (made famous in the 1962 song "The Girl from Ipanema" by Antônio Carlos Jobim). The van kept running day and night, taking Rocinha residents to their jobs serving the elites. There were babysitters, waiters, cleaners, teachers, sex workers, drivers, salespeople, drug couriers, cooks, bouncers, and even flight attendants in the van. "Ipanema is the neighborhood of the rich!" Auro told me.

Dona Rosário, Natasha's mother, sat to my right. To my left, I could see the shacks of Favela do Vidigal. I watched the strong waves hitting a large stone jutting out of the sea. It looked like gneiss—a solid foundation for the concrete and brick structures of Vidigal. Dona Rosário kept disrupting my view, moving restlessly in front of the window. We were on our way to Ipanema, seeking medical help for Natasha's little brother. The boy, who wasn't with us and still lived in Ceará, suffered from severe spinal problems. He needed a consultation to be booked for him to see a specialist. "He can't hold his body straight!" the fifty-three-year-old woman told me. Dona Rosário needed my help because she couldn't read or write, which made it difficult to navigate in the Asphalt, and none of her children were willing to accompany her to Ipanema.

Natasha's mother told me that she was worried about Clodoaldo. "Clodoaldo?" I instinctively asked.

"I say Clodoaldo. You say Natasha!" the woman explained. I didn't want to hear about Clodoaldo. "It must be some bad spirit that is with him, that makes him behave like that, and also makes my other son drink too much alcohol!" Dona Rosário lamented.

I turned my eyes away from the sea once again and looked into Dona Rosário's brown eyes. "Don't worry, Natasha seems to be happy just as she is," I replied. As I mentioned, this was 2009, way before Natasha's sickness.

Her mother smiled and continued to complain: "Do you see, Moisés? All my children were raised in the Catholic Church, but they changed a lot when they arrived in that hell called Rocinha!" I didn't comment. I offered her a polite smile, then kept looking out of the window. My eyes followed the white foamy waves. She continued: "You know what? Both Clodoaldo and my drunkard son in Ceará must look for God; to be delivered from their sins." Was she talking about liberation? I took out my pocket notebook. I scribbled some notes and waited for more information from Dona Rosário, but she went silent. Soon after that, we reached our destination, a street near the Hospital Federal de Ipanema.

There were long lines there, as in most public hospitals. We waited. Meanwhile, the overworked staff dealt with documents, files, prescriptions, and hundreds of other patients. We tried different attendants, waiting in different lines. They all told us the same thing: there were no vacancies at that time. The best news Dona Rosário got was the promise that her boy would be taken care of in the future. His first consultation was scheduled for the end of the year. This was much later than we had hoped, but Dona Rosário seemed satisfied.

The return trip to the favela was more pleasant, though less interesting. Dona Rosário told me about her plans to travel to Ceará and bring the sick boy with her to Rio de Janeiro to get treatment. We got off where the van stopped, under the Lagoa-Barra Highway. Dona Rosário held my arm tightly when she was getting down, then kept holding on to it, as we walked into the favela, arm to arm. We stopped by a stationery store where my friend Pedro had been working for years, located near the main entrance to the favela. The place had a coat of a dirty white paint on the walls and spiderwebs on the ceiling, from years of use with no maintenance. No more than three customers could fit inside the store at the same time.

Largo do Boiadeiro was a bustling area. Commerce in Rocinha was intense. There were no serious security concerns in keeping operations going until late at night.[15] I introduced Dona Rosário to Pedro. They were both short in stature. Her head was pretty gray already, with a ponytail. He looked a little younger. As we talked, I realized that both Pedro and Rosário were born in Ceará. They were both Catholics. Pedro was one of the most active members of the Catholic church in Rocinha during the height of liberation theology in the 1980s, with a focus on a more socialist-inspired type of liberation, geared toward the empowerment of the oppressed working classes. I told Pedro that I was Dona Rosário's daughter's friend. "You are my *son's* friend!" she corrected me. Pedro got confused. Dona Rosário noticed and added: "Some complicated issues!" There was a moment of silence.

Pedro and Dona Rosário started to talk about the church, and he remarked on the most beautiful Catholic ceremonies that used to take place in the church of Largo do Boiadeiro. The other Catholic church in the slum was better known, but farther away from my house, up the hill, close to Cachopa—the parish of "Our Lady of Good Travel" (Nossa Senhora da Boa Viagem). Aware of his know-how in liberation theology,

I asked Pedro: "If Dona Rosário wished for the liberation of her children from sin, could the Catholic Church help her, Pedro? Or is that an Evangelical thing?" The question was out of context for the moment, but Rosário understood my intentions, I knew she had been worried about Natasha's liberation. She promptly confirmed her interest in the matter by lowering her chin. Dona Rosário went on to repeat what she had told me several times. "I'm worried about my boys! I wanted them just to be decent people, get married, and take care of their lives," she told us.

Pedro looked at me and answered: "Look, in the Catholic Church, our mission is greater. I am concerned with the liberation of the working class, and people's battle for the land. Everybody wants easy liberation these days. There's no such thing. We also have to carry the Cross, just like Jesus did. Look at the Catholic Cross. Isn't Jesus there? That's to remind us of his suffering." Pedro continued, "Have you seen an Evangelical Cross? Even Jesus has been set free from it! He's not there anymore. Today, everyone wants quick individual liberation. They want everything to be fast and easy!" He added: "Problems are solved with time!" Pedro had told us more than I expected, and more than Rosário wanted to hear. It was almost a sermon. We listened and remained silent. A sermon is a sermon.

A Liberated Faggot

On a different occasion, still in 2009, we were in the apartment that Natasha shared with her blood family. I counted three old single mattresses sharing space with a red two-seater sofa in a small living room. A shelf, covered in cheap plastic decoration, held an expensive sound system and a large flat-screen TV. Next to the window, Natasha struggled in the dim light to finish her makeup. The cheap little mirror, in a fluorescent orange plastic frame, didn't help much. In the next room, her oldest brother, Claudenir, cooked something called Baião de Dois. This was a typical dish from Ceará, made with white rice, cowpea beans (*feijão de corda*), and cheese—all mixed in the same pot. Claudenir invited me to eat with him. Natasha answered on my behalf, telling her brother we didn't have time for dinner. Claudenir was clearly disappointed. He came up close to where we were and looked right at the middle of Natasha's face. "You look awful with that makeup!" Natasha ignored him, while continuing to make quick movements over her face with a sponge covered in shiny powder. "Okay! I'm beautiful now. Shall we go, darling?" she said, and looked at herself one last time, now using a larger mirror attached to the wardrobe in the bedroom, pulling the black Lycra dress a little higher, to show off her ass cheeks.

Natasha's brother followed all our movements in the house from the corner of his eyes. He smiled from time to time. He was quiet but openly sarcastic when speaking. Before we left the house, he added: "Funny . . . in Ceará you weren't like that, right? In Ceará you dressed as a man. Then you came here and lost your shame. Shame on you, man!"

Natasha lost her patience and shouted at him: "Wake up! I wore boy clothes, but I was already a faggot then!" In her high heels, she paraded into the living room and continued, "The difference is that I was an incubated fag. In the favela, I'm a liberated faggot. Fully liberated, my love!" At that point, Natasha stopped talking and just laughed loudly, clapping her hands three times in a row to wrap up her performance. Momentarily without an answer, Claudenir ended up laughing with her, or at her. Natasha found her purse on the shelf, opened the door, and pulled me out of the house.

Soon we were parading hand in hand, among the crowds, down Rua do Valão. We walked with our heads high all the way to the bus stop. Our destination that night was Bar & Mar, an LGBTQ nightclub in Rio das Pedras, the same location where we would end up taking a historical group photo against a black-and-white tiled wall.[16] People looked at us. Some laughed, some waved. But we felt safe. In the favela, a travesti could walk hand in hand with a boy-fag. Once we were on the bus, the scene changed and people looked more aggressively at us. No more hand in hand. We were more vulnerable to aggressions from passengers. When we sat down and relaxed a bit, Natasha mentioned the earlier episode with her brother Claudenir. "In Ceará, people are much more ignorant than Cariocas! Don't mind him!" she apologized to me.

More Freedom in the Favela

The ethnographic tracing of freedoms and liberties often lead me to unexpected observations. Kyle was an Australian surfer, a skinny blond teenager with the tan of someone who enjoyed the sun of Rio de Janeiro. We were both volunteers teaching English at the same NGO in Rocinha, the Friends United School (FUS). Kyle was very shy but seemed to like the liveliness of the favela. Shortly before returning to Australia, he organized a big party at the hostel where he lived in a neighborhood called Flamengo, near the old center of Rio de Janeiro. He told me I could invite whomever I wanted. Everyone involved in the FUS activities would be there, even the students in our Basic English class. I decided to invite Natasha to Kyle's, as my personal guest. She was very hesitant about accepting the invitation. "Do you really think so, sweetie? Is that going to work? Me in this place?" Natasha didn't go to school; she claimed she had no patience for it.

"Of course!" I told her. "It is going to be fabulous!"

On the day of the party, at around 7 p.m., I went to meet Natasha in front of FUS, as we had arranged. She didn't show up. I waited a little longer. Had she changed her mind? I didn't want to be late. I called her cell phone. No response. It was either turned off or out of signal. I decided to run over to her house. I knocked on her varnished wooden door when I got there, almost out of breath. Claudenir answered. "Is Natasha not here?" I asked hurriedly.

He invited me inside. "She's been in the bedroom for a long while, changing her clothes repeatedly!" Claudenir reported. He used the female pronoun *she*, as Natasha had chosen. I was relieved to hear she was at home and getting ready to leave.

As soon as she saw me, she asked in distress: "I better wear pants, right? No dress, not today. Pants are more suitable for this event?" Leaving Rocinha for the Asphalt required more effort than going to Rio da Pedras.

I am not talking only about the effort of getting dressed in a particular way; it was more of a struggle because of her self-doubt. How would she fit into that place? Would she ever fit in? Her insecurity pained me too, but I tried to keep the happy mood alive. "We're late, girl! Let's get this party started. It's going to be glorious!" She smiled grimly as she finished buttoning up a pair of tight jeans. As if to compensate for the pain of not wearing a dress, Natasha asserted herself with her makeup. She put a thick coat of foundation on her face and glitter on her eyelids. Her mouth was dripping with orange-red lipstick. She also chose one of her tallest pair of heels.

As we were leaving, Claudenir looked at her. "Remember when you used to steal my socks to play soccer on the streets of Martinslândia? Look at those shoes of yours! What are those? Don't you have male shoes to put on? Can I lend you a pair?"

She took a deep breath and replied, "Now that my mother has returned to Ceará, the last thing I need is for you to upset me instead of her!" As she passed by Claudenir on our way out the door, she sent him a debauched kiss. We were in a rush to get to Flamengo, but Natasha still tried to walk elegantly over the potholes in the alleyways. She held on to the walls, all the way down the hill. When we finally got to the Asphalt,

CHAPTER TWO

I ordered a taxi to Flamengo. She entered the yellow car gracefully through the back door that I held open for her.

Soon we had arrived at the entrance of Kyle's building. Natasha drank, ate, and talked all night long. At first, she told me that she was enjoying the event, only to confess later: "I don't like rich people's parties! I have more liberty in the favela." To expect freedoms and liberties to exist in privileged parts of cities, in simplistic opposition to an alleged absence of liberalism in favelas, made no sense in Natasha's life. During Kyle's event, this fact became evident to me. Normative liberalism alone would be unable to account for Natasha's experience at Kyle's party.

The Owner of the Hillside

As it turns out, only someone who benefited from the freedoms afforded by the laws of the Hillside (a favela liberalism) could make sense of Natasha's observations. Narco-traffickers dominated, undemocratically, the territory of many favelas, constituting their own "state" apparatus. They obtained power through symbolic and physical violence, but not only through those. The leading political authority in Rocinha was known as the Owner of the Hillside (O Dono do Morro). The position combined economic power, mainly from the profits of drug trafficking, with political power, resulting in strong authority over the territory. The Owner of the Hillside exercised legislative and judicial functions. He established rules on issues of common interest in the daily life of the favela: the laws of the Hillside. He also conducted trials in cases of conflict between neighbors, domestic violence, and other infringements of favela laws.

The Rio de Janeiro media often described these powerful traffickers as tyrants. As such, the normative liberal chimera of the elites was reinforced; the Owner of the Hillside was presented as the embodiment of an anti-liberal figure, a leader who ruled with brute force, rendering any freedom impossible in the favela. From the perspective of the Hillside, the story was quite different. It was true that the Owner's authority was not democratic; libertarians would probably regard this form of governance as an unacceptable limitation on freedom. Nevertheless, the Owner of the Hillside obtained legitimacy by other means and legislated in favor of alternative, minoritarian, forms of liberties.

"What's going on here?" I asked Amélia one day, after noticing the unusual presence of large, colorful inflatable toys scattered around Rua do Valão. She responded cheerfully, "Oh, that's the bandits! Every Children's Day [October 12], they put those toys there. The little ones have lots of fun!"

Thinking out loud, I said, "Paternalistic provision of services to the poor?" Amélia didn't hear me. For her, it was a chance for kids to enjoy themselves. It was another piece of proof that the drug traffickers were supportive of the community.

Amélia assured me, "These people from the *movement* [traffickers] help, Moisés! Those animals are bad, but they're good. They give money for medication and even burials, you see? There were people in our alleyway who needed them in some emergency situations, and they helped!"

Between 2009 and 2010, when I lived in the favela, the Owner of the Hillside was a slender light-skinned Black man, named Nem. He had joined the trafficking movement—that is, the faction called A.D.A.— when his first daughter was about to die. With no money for her medical treatment, Nem asked the drug dealers for financial support. Intelligent and good at numbers, he quickly discovered that he would make more money doing accounting for drug traffickers than working as a salesman in a shoe store. Once he was in, he was a fast climber in the trafficking hierarchy. Eventually, the sick daughter recovered, because he could afford her treatment, and Nem became one of the richest and most powerful men in Rocinha. That's the official story, as told in the newspapers all over Brazil.[17]

Nem wasn't as attentive to the locals as other previous drug dealers had been. Still, he was respected. He had an infamous violent streak, but the trials he conducted were considered fair. "If you get beaten up by traffickers, it is because you deserved it!" one of my neighbors remarked, after seeing a young man being severely bashed by drug dealers. Nem's popularity was especially evident among my LGBTQ friends. Some laws of the Hillside directly benefited our group, by provisioning certain freedoms to the queer population of the slum. "He likes us!" my friend Auro assured me. "You can't mess with faggots around here!" Auro stated, and further explained: "He inherited this law from a former drug dealer called BTV, and it was clever of him to keep it in place!" Laws that guaranteed minoritarian freedoms like this had a profound impact on the legitimacy and the authority of the Owner of the Hillside. This fact was implicit to Natasha's observations when she compared the liberties that she had in Rocinha to the liberties she couldn't have at Kyle's party in Flamengo.

In the past, Valão was one of the main stages where the famous trafficker BTV used to shine.[18] The Owner of the Hillside between 2004 and 2005 was a seductive man. Amélia remembered him fondly: "Strong. Like this!" She flexed an arm muscle and continued: "A strong northeastern man. BTV was attractive!" He was charming, and he knew it. He liked to exhibit his body, women, and money.

CHAPTER TWO

"BTV was the most loved drug dealer of this favela. Holy shit, darling! You, lady, should have seen him . . . The faggots around here would go crazy for that man!" Auro told me excitedly. The three-letter nickname came from the beautiful yellowish bird called Bem-Te-Vi in Portuguese (or kiskadee in English). He was known for owning a golden gun, which Auro described nostalgically to me: "It was real gold, you know! The man had a pistol crafted out of gold!" Sometimes these memories from my friends would spill out when we passed by the place in Valão where a sniper from the special police force shot BTV in the head. A dead bird.

BTV had become spectacularly famous—the first drug dealer/celebrity in Rocinha. He was even more of a star when in the company of other celebrities. (Celebrities and wannabes were abundant in Rio de Janeiro, the Brazilian capital of TV shows and soap opera productions.) But a drug dealer who overexposes himself becomes a vulnerable target. On another occasion, when I was talking with Auro about the line of succession of different Owners of the Hillside, he asked, "Do you know the secret formula of his parties?" I didn't know the answer. I hadn't met BTV or danced at any of the memorable parties of that period. "Heavily armed security provided by his traffickers," Auro told me. "Huge rifles! Enormous, faggot. A lot of rifles! Lots, faggot. Power! Celebrities, a lot of celebrities. Football players. It was crazy! Whiskey, lots of cocaine, and the beat of funk. Oh, and us too! Lots of gays, fags, travestis, and prostitutes." He paused briefly, just to catch his breath: "Look, BTV really valued freedom, especially sexual freedom. He knew that without us fags, there could be no fun! There wouldn't be these incredible parties in the favela." Auro knew very well that BTV himself profited a lot from these events in the favela, too. He continued:

It wasn't just the love for the nightlife! He did love it, and he did party hard. Because you know, right? A drug dealer never knows if he'll be alive or free the next day! A drug dealer's destiny is to end up either in jail or in a coffin. They have to enjoy life! Only BTV did all that at the same time as he was packing money. The amount of drugs he was selling, just imagine. Do you think a gun made of solid gold is cheap, sweetheart?

Auro's analysis was very perceptive. The capitalist logic of encouraging drug sales was an important aspect of BTV's liberalism. These same drugs that enslaved high numbers (including some residents) through addiction and labor are what guaranteed the legitimacy of the drug lord. He used his power to attract more power. The laws of the Hillside, combined with the provision of heavily armed non-state security, ensured a different territoriality for sexual freedom and drug use. By contrast, drugs are

LAWS OF THE HILLSIDE

still strictly illegal in the Asphalt, as I write. This political arrangement, which I call *favela liberalism*, made certain types of freedom possible in Rocinha and not so in other neighborhoods, such as Flamengo.[19] Natasha's observations regarding the different modes of liberalism between the favela and the Asphalt make even more sense when considered within this broader territorial assemblage of drug trafficking, queer laws of the Hillside, celebrities, and sexual freedoms in Rio de Janeiro.

Favela Freedom in Practice

BTV's governmentality had widespread purchase on the daily life of Rocinha residents. I witnessed some of these effects one night when I went to get dinner with Auro at a pizza place. He wanted to go to the food court in a supermarket that had just opened in São Conrado. Auro knew many people who worked there. As the nephew of a former drug lord, he knew people everywhere. While the bourgeois architecture of the supermarket reminded me of some nouveau riche place, both workers and customers of the new supermarket were mostly Rocinha residents. ("At least this place is, like, more pleasant . . . And it doesn't stink like Sendas!" Amélia once remarked, comparing the new location with an older supermarket also located in São Conrado.)

On our way down the hill, Auro and I came face-to-face with a group of five teenagers playing cards in a shady alleyway. Two of them stared as we walked closer. Auro noticed their intimidating looks and started to move his hips around, as if on a catwalk. The teenagers pointed their fingers at us and laughed, "Biggest faggot, man! A big wimp and a little wimp!" (*Maior bichona, mané! Um viadão e um viadinho!*) I felt the weight of their words, and Auro did, too. He stopped, turned ninety degrees to the right, and went to have a word with the group. I anticipated a fight, or even worse. Auro started in a low tone, but soon he was yelling, shaking his finger, and demanding respect from them. The boys shut up. Auro walked back toward me and said: "Come on, love. Let's eat our pizza." I looked back once more to make sure no one was following us. I couldn't quite understand what had happened, and I didn't want to ask, either. We went on ahead.

On the way back, after eating our arugula pizza, Auro chose to take the same dark alley. "I'm still angry. I want to look those kids in the face again," he declared. I refused to go back. I couldn't imagine we would have the same luck again. "I know what I'm doing!" he insisted. Auro was a big man with a heavy bone structure. I gave in. Once we were back

CHAPTER TWO

in the alley, we approached the teenage crew again. Auro showed no fear. He shouted with hatred in his eyes: "As far as I know . . . the law of the Hillside is not about making fun of fags! Be very careful, huh?" The boys seemed very nervous; they hadn't expected a second round. When he was done, Auro asked me with pleasure: "Did you see the fear stamped on their faces?" He was proud of himself. In a strange way, I was proud too, even though I was trembling with fear. Auro went on, "Since the time of BTV, it's been forbidden to mess around with faggots in Rocinha. The punishment can be very severe. BTV brought liberty to the slum, fags!" He concluded: "Today, it's Nem who guarantees our liberties!" At that moment, I experienced a notable aspect of what it was like to be a fag living in Rocinha. Certainly, it wasn't always easy. But there were winning days. Maybe Auro didn't realize I was slightly emotional. He kept speaking with pride: "BTV used to say: 'Will you mess with my faggots? No fucking way! Don't mess with my faggots!'" The legacy of BTV was alive and well.

Language Learning: Mavambo

In order to better understand queer life in the favela, one must learn not only the favela slang, but also some sort of dialect called Pajubá. "I love *mavambos*! I think it's an addiction!" Natasha said, laughing. She was sitting with me, Samira, and Segata on the curb in front of a bar in Beco do Foguete. My queer friends in Rocinha used the term *mavambo* to refer to drug traffickers—the bandits. Natasha hadn't wanted to get her skirt dirty with dry mud, so she had removed her keys, a cell phone, and a pocketknife from her small cloth purse, then sat down on the purse on top of the curb. She held all of her other items in her left hand. Segata, a Black travesti with long and frizzy hair, was one of Natasha's friends. "And who doesn't like a bandit, Nat? Affff . . . just to talk about them makes me hot. These mavambos are a waste of time, but they always give me a hard-on!"

Samira, one of my best friends, with deep dimples in her cheeks, smiled and waved her finger in negation. "Hey! What about me? I don't like these guys! Are you crazy? Respect me!"

To which Segata replied: "Oh, stop it! You don't like them because you don't even like men. You dyke! Cut the bullshit, okay?" Everyone laughed. Segata confessed, "Once, a mavambo fucked me in an alleyway, in public! A big Black one [*Negão*] who stays around that area in Roupa Suja!"

Natasha replied, "In the alley? I've done many! But not Black men like that . . . I don't like them Black."

Natasha, who wasn't considered Black, was frowned upon by Segata. "What? You racist! And the anaconda? The nigger's dick, darling? I have got a tight hole, okay! Can you imagine my situation?" Segata laughed out loud.

"You people are terrible. What the fuck! What a conversation," Samira complained.

"What was my experience with mavambo men?" I thought. Even though I agreed with Segata regarding Natasha's racism, I didn't even know the word *mavambo* until living in the slum. I was told to keep my distance from them. That was Dona Teté's advice to me when I moved to Rocinha, not to mingle with drug dealers.

I went through intense language learning in Rocinha, despite being a native Brazilian Portuguese speaker. Auro was surprised by my lack of skills at first. "The faggot dialect of the slum, darling, that's Pajubá! Don't you speak it?" he continued, with contempt, "A lot of Pajubá stuff comes from *macumba*! And are you into macumba, love?" Auro asked, referring to Afro-Brazilian religious practices.[20] When I expressed an interest in learning Pajubá, though, no one wanted to tutor me. My friends liked to speak the queer dialect, but they didn't like to talk about it, much less to teach it. Giulia, one of Rocinha's best-known travestis, also made fun of me: "What a *kosi* faggot!" *Kosi* was a term used to indicate a lack of knowledge, refinement, or education. I was kosi because I didn't know Pajubá. If I were not so unrefined, I would also have known that kosi is a derivation from the Yoruba language (something I learned much later), predominantly spoken in Nigeria and Benin in West Africa; it literally means "there is not." A limited Yoruba lexicon was still used in Afro-Brazilian religions to different extents. It was more present in Candomblé, and less so in Umbanda and Quimbanda. The latter two more commonly used Portuguese language in their rituals. The linguistic heritage from slavery had been reverted into a strategy for queer liberalism outside religious contexts too.

Auro was the only one who was more didactic:

Oh, we talk like that so no one will understand it, *adé*! See? *Adé* means faggot in Pajubá! Fags are *macumbeiras*. They like witchcraft. They keep learning these words in their religion. Then they come here and use them with their friends, and soon everybody is speaking it. Everybody? No! Just the faggots! It's our thing. So no one really understands it, do you understand me? For example, we can talk about other people's bums, and no one understands anything. I laugh so hard!

CHAPTER TWO

From Auro, I also learned that in the Yoruba dictionary, *adé* means crown. Queens wear crowns, and faggots are queens. Could that be the logic? Auro told me that the term *mavambo* had Bantu origins, maybe Kikongo. Together with the Yoruba, the Congo-Angola region in Africa had significantly contributed to the formation of the so-called macumba in Brazil, and also to the constitution of a Pajubá lexicon. "*Mavambo* and *mavula* are similar. Meaning drug dealers," concluded Auro.

Traffickers knew that they were called mavambos; they knew they were ardently desired by the "faggots" in the favela. Many other women were attracted to them, too. Drug dealers cultivated these desires, dominating others, in part, through their erotic and phallic power. In addition to guns and gold, they relied on their muscles and sweat. Heteronormative men were also seduced by them. Even if they did not necessarily want to have sex with the bandits, they wanted to be around them, largely because of their power, wealth, and bravado. Traffickers had different hierarchical occupations within the faction, but most of them were Black and young. They lived intensely and died young; drug dealers over the age of thirty were rare. Kids started to serve as watchmen, packagers, and deliverers, and teenagers were being recruited all the time to fill the ranks. "I like the young ones! I hate old men. Old men only if they have money!" Natasha told us.

The trafficking business was complex. It involved area managers, submanagers, bouncers, soldiers, accountants, and executors. In my area in Rocinha, the manager was Belenzinho, a short and skinny white man with a limp. Belenzinho wasn't handsome. Still, the power he carried drew a lot of attention. Belenzinho was cruel. His semi-automatic machine gun caused fear and desire. He was hated by many and feared by almost all. At dawn, he was constantly seen having sex with teenage girls in the alleyways of the favela. Kayanna, my front neighbor, complained to me: "Another recreational snack? I despise that man! He is always around these alleyways fucking till early morning. Like a dog! And you should see it . . . he chooses only the youngest and cutest teens!" From her window, which was higher than mine, she followed the live shows all night long. Kayanna doubted that all of Belenzinho's relationships were consensual. "How is that possible? That ugly man, just because he's a bandit! Or is he forcing these girls to go out with him? It must be on the basis of money, at least that!"[21]

The aggressive mavambo masculinity was a striking feature of the fear and want that bandits awakened. For my travesti friends, it was sometimes a fatal attraction. I never heard of a famous drug dealer who was openly LGBTQ in Rocinha. Still, there were many stories of sex between my queer friends and drug dealers. These were sweaty stories, full of danger and hard-ons. Not all of them were true, but all of them were lived somehow, even if under the form of desire. When these encounters actually happened, absolute secrecy was required. Nevertheless, gossip circulated, as if on the edge of a sharp blade. What if one of the wives of these traffickers found out?[22]

Auro told me about one of these encounters in detail as we sat drinking coffee and eating baked corn cake in Amélia's living room. "Do you remember that guy I told you about? Who went out with me and was armed?" he began. I nodded. He continued:

So, darling . . . he came looking for me again! He came knocking on my door yesterday. Sister, what a scene. I looked out the window and saw who it was. He knocked, knocked, knocked on my door. I didn't want to open it! But who can resist a hot man, huh? When I opened the door, he ran inside, upset because it took me too long to open it. I guess he just didn't want anyone to see him coming. He started to grab me, sticking his hands up my ass. I stopped him. I pushed him and shouted, "Where's the gun?" He pretended he didn't understand me. "Where's the gun?" I said. He took off his shirt. The gun was stuck by his side, like this, in his waistline. I saw it. Meanwhile, my legs were trembling, right? He started to rub himself against me. I pushed him and I ordered. "Take the gun off!" He held me tight and gave me a kiss. I got dizzy. I didn't know what to do! Then, he got the gun. He ran the tip of it right across my face, like this. He asked if I wanted to suck it! Can you imagine, my dear? Look, it was crazy! But then we fucked so hard and hot, you should have seen it. One of the best fucks of my life!

My relationship with Auro was mostly based on swapping stories like this—storytelling meetings. Natasha also had her torrid sex episodes, but she didn't always tell me about them. The time we spent together was usually going out somewhere. But I never witnessed Natasha's encounters with actual mavambos. Was she really a mavambo's travesti? It didn't matter so much if the stories were real or fantasy. Instead, it was the long trajectory of transformations that she had made since moving from Ceará that were important to her—from boy-fag to mavambo's travesti.

A Liberal Heterotopia

The territoriality of the favela affects different possibilities of existence. "I have a lot more freedom in the favela to be who I am!" Natasha stated after Kyle's party. Before we went to the party, she seemed to be filled with doubt. "Was she free to be herself?" I wondered. At the same time,

CHAPTER TWO

Natasha wasn't looking for a single self with a fixed body. Flexible possibilities of being were more important to her. Her body was malleable; it took many forms. Some days, her body was more feminine. On others, her body was more masculine.[23] This was the reason that Natasha didn't like hormones or plastic surgery. Over her years in Rocinha, the possibilities of being for Natasha, of being Natasha, were open. In many ways, this instability was reflected in the favela itself, which was a territory of accelerated changes—a different temporality compared to the Asphalt. So many people moved in and out every day. Natality and mortality rates were both high. New constructions were being built all the time. Despite the disastrous presence of the state in favelas, despite the paternalism of drug lords, and despite the prejudice of the brothers with whom Natasha was at times obliged to live, the favela kept offering different possibilities to her (queer) gender and sexual practices.

Auro once articulated some of these principles of favela liberalism: "Well . . . whores live here, right? Dykes live here, okay? Bandits live here too, don't they? There are faggots all around, right? There are thieves, drug addicts, workers . . . all living here. The favela has got everything! You have got it all, sweetheart. You have to learn to deal with these differences and live your life." Rocinha constituted a "liberal heterotopia" of sorts.[24] If operations of territorialization to the benefit of the elites were among the main mechanisms of normative freedom, in the favela other freedoms were available due to operations of deterritorialization (even when these were followed by other processes of reterritorialization).

Deterritorialization made the favela territory as heterogeneous as possible, accommodating for the differences of those who would be considered deviants in the Asphalt: criminals, addicts, fags, and many others. In the case of travestis, it was their particular vulnerability in the Asphalt that made their favela rights exceptional. Even if their submission to the masculine power of the Owner of the Hillside operated as a vector of territorialized gender relations, this was not a normative case of exchanging obedience for protection as in the heteronormative marriage example provided by Carole Pateman, for instance.[25] There was a radical accommodation of difference in Rocinha governmentality, in a minoritarian spirit.[26]

"Peace, Justice, and Freedom"

Favela liberalism was not a simple affair. It could be better understood within wider territorial relations, beyond the favela itself. I remember an early morning in late July 2009 when, as I prepared to leave my house, a woman passed by my alleyway talking loudly, chatting to a friend. I had never seen them before. She told her friend that a relative of hers had been arrested. She added something I didn't quite understand. Faced with her colleague's astonishment, she asked: "What would you prefer? To buy your freedom or to rot in there?" I couldn't hear the answer either. They were getting farther away from my house and harder to hear. All I could do was to write in my field notes: "What happens when freedom becomes a commodity?" Many freedoms could be bought. More and more, freedoms are being sold in late capitalism. They even sell motorcycles in the form of freedom. Condoms are sold in the form of freedom. Favors from prison security officers are sold in the form of freedom. Favela liberalism is part of a drug-selling scheme with complex financial flows. It is not disconnected from capital, and it certainly benefits elite people who are involved in trafficking. The types of freedom that favela liberalism produces, however, also benefits the favela population.

I was done getting dressed as I had an early commitment in another favela. This time, I was headed toward Pavão-Pavãozinho-Cantagalo (PPG), a conurbation of three slums in one. There, I met Rose, a Black lesbian and a photographer. Her beautiful curly hair was covering up most of her face. She wanted to know about me. How did I end up in Rocinha? How did I end up in PPG? Due to an exhibition of photography taking place, the territory of that slum complex in Copacabana was open to the Asphalt public that day. "Fuck! If this were another day, would you be able to get here alone? With that playboy face? I doubt it, my brother! I think Rocinha is a lot more liberal in this sense," Rose said.

At the same time that favelas were incredibly diversified internally, and safe for difference, the maintenance of such territories was also based on the existence of well-surveilled boundaries in relation to the Asphalt. In most favelas, the bourgeoisie was only welcome in the capacity of customers. According to Rose, this was less the case in Rocinha. Still, the favela borders were relatively closed to the outside public, and even more so when it came to some representatives of the nation-state. The border mechanisms to prevent police invasions were very elaborate and expensive for the traffickers to maintain. They involved not only bribes to corrupt policemen, but the deployment of a favela "security force"—which involved bodyguards to protect the higher-ranking traffickers, onlookers with radio equipment positioned near the favela borders, and even emergency alarm mechanisms, such as the use of fireworks, to alert the residents of imminent conflict. How could there be freedom under such strong surveillance? Internal deterritorialization processes happened alongside other processes of territorialization of favela borders.

Rose offered me a potent theory of minoritarian liberalism:

PPG is for those that are real *cria*, those who were born and raised in the favela . . . For us, shit is different! Life here gives a type of freedom that doesn't exist elsewhere. Do you know why? It follows a lot of what happens in prison. People grow up here, they become bandits, and a lot of them go to jail. They stay there and everything. People here will visit and all, you know? You can stay locked up for a long time, as long as you have to. But one day, one day you'll come back! So how do people come back? Crazy shit! They come with a prison mentality, man. They come back well connected in jail and with their connections in the Hillside. A lot of them just returned and they're already running the favela. Many laws of the Hillside are derived from the laws of prison. But ex-convicts, what do they like? Freedom, man! That's why you have a special type of freedom in the favela! But for a playboy, you don't have that freedom. This freedom is for us from the Hillside. What is the motto of A.D.A. [the Friends of Friends faction]? What's that? You don't know it? "Live and let live!" What about C.V.s [the Red Command faction]? It's "Peace, Justice, and Freedom." There you are!

Prisons are territories in intimate connection with favelas. The Owners of the Hillside knew the realities of jail. Not all of them knew it through firsthand experience, but the possibilities of imprisonment, like death, were always there, a phantasmagoric presence.[27] At the same time, the networking that took place with those in jail was an important asset; those connections made with fellow drug dealers came in handy to help in the governance of favelas. The territory of the prison clearly influenced the possibilities of freedom in the favelas.

Natasha's liberal possibilities in Rocinha depended on complex arrangements, including BTV parties, the drug trade, and the laws of the Hillside: "Don't mess with my faggots!" A statement that expresses contradictions typical to liberalism: authority and possession along with protection and freedom. Minoritarian liberalisms propose freedoms based on multiple differences within a heterotopia that extends even to jail. "Live and let live!" Rose taught me so much in such a short encounter. Unfortunately, our paths never crossed again. Regardless, that episode assured me that I should keep following multiple paths in my research, wherever they took me. To better understand liberalism in favelas, I ended up exploring territorial relations internal and external to Rocinha. Sometimes, really far away from Rocinha, even if still connected to it.

THREE

Northeastern Hinterlands

If the ability to effect change in the world and in oneself is historically and culturally specific (both in terms of what constitutes "change" and the means by which it is effected), then the meaning and sense of agency cannot be fixed in advance. SABA MAHMOOD, *POLITICS OF PIETY*

According to the sociologist Licia do Prado Valladares, the distinctions and connections between urban centers and the Brazilian hinterlands are constitutive elements in the historical conception of Brazilian favelas.[1] Often, when referring to favelas as a problem to be solved, public officials point to their similarities in relation to the "poorest" and most "backwards" regions of Brazil. This is not just because migrants to favelas tend to come from the hinterlands, but also because events such as the war known as Guerra de Canudos, in the interior of Bahia state, offer an important repertoire for concepts regarding social justice and liberty in Brazil.[2] In this chapter I will revisit some connections between favelas and the hinterlands of the Brazilian Northeast, while I trace how queer experiences of liberalism interact with issues of migration, abuse, and some peasant conceptions of freedom.

For my birthday in January 2010, there was no big celebration. Instead, my gift was a trip from Rio de Janeiro to the interior of Ceará state with Amélia and her daughter, Maria Beatriz. The plan was to explore relations between the initial site of my research in Rocinha and the place from which a lot of my friends had migrated, including Natasha and Amélia. More than twenty years had passed since

CHAPTER THREE

my upstairs neighbor had left her homeland without turning back. "I really need to see my mother . . . she's sick!" Amélia had told me, crying. We were sitting in front of her television in Rocinha, when I decided to grab us some plane tickets during a flash sale. Amélia and her daughter took their inaugural flight in my company. They were excited by the adventure, but nervous as they entered the airport, a space traditionally occupied by people for whom Amélia used to work as a house cleaner.

The destination of our flight from Rio de Janeiro had been Fortaleza, the capital city of the state of Ceará. Once in Fortaleza, we took a taxi from the airport to the largest bus station in the capital, and from there the bus trip would take another eight hours to reach Amélia's hometown in the interior of the state: Guaraciaba do Norte, with around 37,700 inhabitants in 2010.[3] We arrived late at night to Amélia's family home and slept well that day. The long journey from Rocinha had made our bodies tired, and the cherished reunion with Amélia's northeastern family had warmed our hearts.

Unfortunately, Natasha refused to travel with us. She had no interest in Ceará. Still, I asked her to arrange for us to meet her family members living in the Brazilian Northeast at that time, and she promptly agreed to it. At Natasha's request, one of her younger brothers in Ceará, named Vadson, instructed us over the phone that if we really wanted to get to the village where their family lived, we would need to travel farther inland. From Amélia's hometown, we would have to embark in the back of an old truck, a D-20, that served as public transport connecting Guaraciaba do Norte to Martinslândia.[4] Natasha's homeland was not an easy place to reach.

After spending a few days at Amélia's mother's home, we decided it was time to venture out. We looked for the stop where a red D-20 was awaiting people and cargo at the central square of Guaraciaba do Norte. From the takeoff in Rio de Janeiro all the way to Guaraciaba, and then Martinslândia, we would have traveled thousands of miles—only to end up in a vehicle designed more for the transport of cattle than humans. The D-20 was the modern *pau de arara*, the only transportation mode that some northeastern migrants could afford until recently, and the same name given to a technique of torture widely deployed during the last Brazilian dictatorship (1964–85).[5] "Would the elites approve of our D-20 journey? Was the pau de arara deployed as a form of movement containment, or punishment?" I thought, without much clarity, only resentment. At that moment, I remembered Armando, the director of the Friends United School (FUS) in Rocinha, mocking a common saying of the Asphalt elites: "One must not give too much liberty to the poor!" (*Não pode dar liberdade demais para pobre!*)

In the South and Southeast regions of Brazil, even within favelas, the Northeast is often perceived as the place from which "undesirable" migrants come, associated with extreme poverty. Although there were also significant flows of remittances and goods circulating between regions, those didn't get much attention.[6] Interestingly, little has been said about other flows in Brazil either, such as the large numbers of migrants who leave Rio Grande do Sul (in the southern region) to colonize the Amazon, in the northern region of the country. Not all Brazilian migrants are northeasterners; not all northeasterners are migrants. Moreover, not all migrants were the same. Queer bodies could not always circulate under the same conditions as others. For instance, disparate freedoms and liberties available for travestis in different territories profoundly affected their ability to travel between Rocinha and Martinslândia.

The Issue with Kinship

The small village of Martinslândia sat within the legal limits of the Guaraciaba do Norte municipal district. Driving toward Croatá, on a road called CE-192, we would have to turn left at a place called Várzea dos Espinhos (Floodplain of Thorns). Unlike the territorial boundaries between the favela and the Asphalt in Rio de Janeiro, the administrative limits in the interior of Ceará were not conspicuous. Várzea dos Espinhos, however, seemed to be an adequate name to mark the entrance to the place where Natasha had spent most of her life before migrating to Rio de Janeiro. The interior of state of Ceará is known for its dry land and lack of resources.[7] Whenever Natasha started a sentence with "back in my homeland" (*lá na minha terra*), I knew that painful memories would unfold. Clodoaldo had been born in Ceará. Natasha was born in Rocinha.

Natasha had called my cell phone from Rio, just to make sure we would be able to identify Vadson at the central square in Guaraciaba on the day of our trip to Martinslândia. Dona Rosário had sent Natasha's brother to town to pick up cassava flour and then accompany us back to her house. We didn't know him, but he was easy enough to spot. Amélia was the one who pointed him out in the crowds. Maria Beatriz, meanwhile, refused to smile at the unknown man. He was around twenty years old and looked a little like Natasha, despite being even taller than

CHAPTER THREE

his sister. He carried a fifty-pound bag of flour in his arms. Soon after we met up and got to our seats, the driver announced: "We'll depart soon!" Passengers squeezed into the back of the truck, not speaking. It was hard to talk while traveling in that pau de arara. The wind and discomfort blew all our words away.

During the journey to Martinslândia, the D-20 kicked up the thin veil of dust that covered the banks of the unpaved roads. The calendar year and the start of the rainy season often coincided in those hinterlands, but that day there was no sign of rain. It was unusually dry and cold upon our arrival in Ceará. Guaraciaba do Norte stands at almost a thousand meters above sea level—a much higher altitude than the beaches of Rio de Janeiro. It felt especially cold to us, coming from the height of the Marvelous City's summer. (A famous Brazilian song goes: "Rio, 40 C! The Marvelous City of beauty and chaos!")

After about a twenty-five-minute drive, the truck stopped on the roadside to let an older lady get off. I was next to Vadson and risked a few words: "Are we still far away?"

Vadson responded in a deep voice, much like Natasha's: "We should have arrived there already."

I didn't want to let the conversation die: "Do you know Rio?"

Vadson said, "Just on TV."

I persisted, "When are you going to visit your sister Natasha?"

He replied, "Natasha? That plague!" (*Natasha? Aquilo é uma praga!*) I thought of the bubonic plague, then HIV—the conflation between disease and sexuality. I shut up. Would the fate of any pau-de-arara trip involve physical and emotional suffering? My first field notes about Natasha's family in Ceará were about kinship relations and abjection. There are families we are born to, and there are families we choose.[8] As feminists and queer studies scholars have often argued, within the family domain, structures of kinship can be deeply oppressive.[9]

In what world does Natasha's liberal lifestyle become a plague? What sort of plague would this be, and what were the potential damages it could cause? I knew that it was important not to take for granted what I understood about families as universal.[10] It was important for me to spend time in Ceará to better understand specific arrangements of land ownership, morality, labor, religion, and kinship that turned Natasha's freedom into libertinism and favela liberalism into the work of the devil. What were the politics of freedom through which Dona Rosário and her family lived in Martinslândia? What were their liberal desires, if any? It was challenging, as a queer ethnographer, to deal with Vadson's homophobia.[11] It was hard for me to hear his transphobic remarks. But my positionality as a boy-fag didn't prevent me from conducting that research. Instead, it allowed me to mediate between Natasha and her family. Even if it required a delicate commitment on my part, if nothing else, understanding the different modes of liberalism between Martinslândia and Rio de Janeiro could prove to be an important effort toward conflict amelioration.

Dead Father

The rusty D-20 stopped in front of a two-window house, painted a very light beige. The whitish dust from the streets made the color even paler. The roof was laid in the Brazilian colonial style called *cangalha*, A-shaped, with thick, irregular, and seemingly old tiles. A parabolic object decorated almost every roof in the village: satellite TV antennas. Martinslândia was not destitute, as people believed in Rio de Janeiro. The houses were not elaborate, but they were well cared for and relatively spacious. The village landscape was filled with dusty colors; most of the homes had a backyard.

Dona Rosário showed up smiling at the window at our arrival. Vadson quickly jumped off the truck and unloaded his purchase. I got out more clumsily, and some passengers helped Amélia and Beatriz to get down. Dona Rosário opened the door and stepped down two steps to reach ground level. She hugged her son, then turned to hug me tightly: "How long, Moisés!" I introduced Amélia and Beatriz. Amélia said they had seen each other before in Rocinha. Dona Rosário was excited: "So you got here, huh? Martinslândia. Who thought you would make it!"

I thanked her for sending Vadson to meet us. "I would never find it by myself!" I remarked.

She laughed and replied, "Yes, you would . . . You'd just have to go around asking. Everybody knows everybody around here. But Vadinho [his nickname] is really good. This is my best son!" Vadson had already left with the heavy load of flour on top of his head. The D-20 pulled away, leaving more dust behind.

Vadson was the best? Maybe his shyness prevented me from getting to know him better. Or perhaps the truncated dialogue we had during the trip had negatively biased me. He had said Natasha was a plague. Maybe Vadson didn't know I was a boy-fag, and that's why he felt comfortable cursing his travesti sister. Maybe he wanted me to think he was a "decent man"? He could have been trying to morally distance himself from Natasha. Why was he Dona Rosário's favorite? Something about

CHAPTER THREE

that situation made me feel melancholic. Dona Rosário knew I was a boy-fag, but, as she put it once to me when we were in Rocinha, "At least you wear male pants, Moisés! I just wanted Natasha to wear decent pants too."[12] Now I was in her territory. I feared being mistreated for being a fag, even if I was in pants.

Dona Rosário continued with her praise, "Vadson will be a teacher and will look after our little piece of land [*sítio*]. He doesn't even think about going to Rio to waste his time! This one won't abandon me." She invited us inside, and Natasha's youngest brother, Dudu, welcomed us. He was lying down on the sofa in the living room, watching TV. This was the brother that Dona Rosário and I had gone to Ipanema about, the one who needed orthopedic treatment. At that time, we had managed to get an appointment for early October 2009. Then it was rescheduled for December 2009. Finally, they changed the medical consultation to March 2010. Fresh into adolescence, the young boy stayed home most of the time. He occupied the entire sofa, which was covered in a magenta fabric. "Get up from there, Dudu . . . Let the visitors sit down!" his mother ordered. The boy turned sideways first before lifting his upper body, revealing a severe lateral deviation of the spine.

"Don't bother, Dona Rosário!" I reacted almost instinctively after seeing the boy's condition.

"I don't want to sit either," Amélia quickly agreed. Dudu smiled and went back to his original position.

Dona Rosário told me, "If you don't want to stay in the living room, come to the kitchen!"

"The kitchen is the best place in a house!" said Amélia, nodding. The two ladies headed into the other room, while I got distracted looking at an old photo hanging on the wall, just above the couch. A man and a woman were dressed very formally, perhaps in wedding attire. They seemed very serious. The colors of the photograph looked surreal, as if painted with watercolors.

"Come and have a cup of coffee, Moisés! Where is he?" Dona Rosário called me. I came into the kitchen and found everyone sitting around a small table. The room was illuminated only by the bright light that entered through the back door, which led to the backyard. The internal walls of the kitchen were not painted. Dona Rosário must have noticed that I was observing the walls because she quickly explained: "The kitchen is under renovation. This month I think I can buy the remaining material to finish this part. Construction material is expensive! But I'll finish it. It's our home!" She continued, "I'm just waiting to deliver some green beans we grow in our sítio. I sold them to a man who hasn't paid me yet. We have our little piece of land, and the family works there. Once in a while, some money comes in!"

Amélia replied, "Don't worry about the walls . . . Nobody cares about these things in Rocinha!"[13]

Natasha's mother smiled but disagreed: "I do care about these things. Here in Ceará, if you don't plaster and paint the house? Oh my God! Only the very poor wouldn't paint their house!"

After some silence, I asked about the photograph in the living room: "There's a picture in the other room, an old picture. Is that you, Dona Rosário?"

She replied, "What picture, that old portrait of my children's father with me? I was still young then, and we'd just moved in together. I had a pretty face back then, did you notice?" I was interested to hear about Natasha's father. My friend didn't talk about him. I knew that he was no longer alive, but not much else.

Amélia was as curious about the situation as I was. She straightforwardly asked, "Do you have a husband, Dona Rosário?"

"We never really married on paper. But he was the only man in my life," Dona Rosário replied.

Amélia, who had never officially married her partner either, continued, "And where is he now?"

Dona Rosário told us:

He died a long time ago. He smoked a lot. Even I smoked, do you believe it? I only quit smoking after I went to see a spiritual healer [*benzedeira*]. I gave her my 25 reais, thinking it would never work. Look at me! It really worked. He's the one who never stopped, not even when he got sick. He had lung cancer, and all of a sudden, he was gone. He left the boys and me. These younger ones? I raised all of them without a man. All by myself and with the help of God.

Amélia remarked angrily: "See, Beatriz! Do you see why I complain so much about your father? He should quit smoking! He will die, listen to me. He will die!"

Dona Rosário added, "I am always watching my boys in Rio! I've caught a couple of them smoking and almost punched their faces. I don't accept that!" Natasha didn't smoke, not even marijuana. She didn't like alcohol very much, either.

I drank a glass of tasty clay-filtered water, then we went out the back door. Beatriz marveled at the yard: "Look, Mom! So much space!" The land looked dry, without much life. Vadson was busy stacking twisted logs to use in the wood-burning stove.

CHAPTER THREE

Dona Rosário called out to him, "Shall we take them there to see if your grandma is home, Vadson?" He agreed quietly. To us, Dona Rosário said, "Let's go for a walk until lunchtime. The other kids will come back from the sítio for lunch. We'll go now and come back to finish cooking the food." We went out, following a dirt trail through the yard. The dry bushes along the path were covered in fine dust. The sun was heating up. As we walked through the village, I noticed kids playing with an old car tire. We soon reached a shed made out of zinc sheets, covering a large, round cemented area. "Mom! Hey, Mom!" Dona Rosário shouted.

Amélia explained the use of the shed to Beatriz: "This is to roast cassava flour."

Dona Rosário commented: "My mother makes flour here. She hasn't worked for a while, however. This is the flour I like to eat. The one that we make ourselves. The one we purchase in the market is no good!" It was important for Dona Rosário to produce her own food.

A lady with sharp facial features and a warm, reddish-brown skin tone emerged. Her long, bright silver hair reached all the way to her waistline. We finally heard Vadson's voice again: "Your blessings, Grandma?"

Dona Rosário told the old lady, "These are Clodoaldo's friends from Rio, Mom!"

"I'm Natasha's friend!" I corrected her almost instinctively, then immediately regretted it, wondering if Natasha's grandmother would even know her by name.

"Natasha's!" Grandma repeated, using the female name. "How's my Natasha?" she asked affectionately.

I repeated the female pronoun and answered, "She? All right! All right, she is well!"

Natasha's grandmother responded, again by using the feminine pronoun. "I really like her! People like Natasha have a lot of protection!" Protection? I thought of how shrewd Natasha was in the arts of self-defense. She always had an answer to verbal offenses, and she always carried a pocketknife or a steel ball in her purse to help in case of a street fight. Natasha was skilled with the cops, too. Yes, it was true that I felt protected in her company. She was keen to take care of me; it seemed satisfying for someone who was attacked continuously to be able to offer some comfort to others. But Grandma was referring to another level of protection—spiritual protection.

Dona Rosário explained, "Mom is the daughter of indigenous people [*filha de índio*]. She likes to pray to the saints and the ancestors [*encantados*] for protection."

The older lady smiled and said: "I always pray for the protection of my grandchildren in Rocinha!"

Grandma offered us a cup of coffee, even though we'd just had some. Beatriz complained that she was tired and wanted to return to Guaraciaba do Norte. Amélia, in turn, complained about Beatriz. "Give me a break, Bia! We're going soon!" Beatriz hugged her mother by the waist and wouldn't let her move. "What is this, girl? You are too old for that. Eleven years old!" her mother complained. They all laughed at Beatriz. The girl was bored.

"Have you had lunch, Mom?" Dona Rosário asked. "In the countryside, people eat early," explained Natasha's mother.

"Not yet . . . Is it because of hunger that this girl is behaving like this?" Grandma remarked, looking at Beatriz.

Amélia said, "It's nothing! She is just annoying. You know, after we have children, our freedom is over!"

Dona Rosário laughed and said, "And you only have her, huh? Imagine me. I had thirteen kids! And that's not counting the ones who died."[14]

Amélia replied: "I have two children. This girl and an older boy. Children take away our freedom. How did you manage?" Those of us with no children listened quietly.

Dona Rosário returned to the original question, "Will you have lunch with us at home today, Mom?" Grandma pulled the silver hair off her face, thanked her daughter, and regretted she couldn't come to lunch because she had to finish some chores. Dona Rosário replied, "It was good for them to meet you, Mom. But I need to go already! I still need to finish cooking for the children."

Women's Liberty and Family

Kinship ties people up. In most of Brazil, rearing children—feeding, surveilling, and caring for them—are activities meant to be performed by women and to take place in the domestic sphere. In the hinterlands, women's morality seemed to be protected, and even elevated, by a lack of freedom. At times, Amélia and Dona Rosário complained about the situation that followed from maternity and domestic life. "It's all on our backs: mothers! Because a lot of fathers don't even want to know about their children. They don't help at home. When their daughters come home pregnant? It's all our fault!" Amélia said. "I always tell Beatriz off. I tell her to behave herself! A girl can't just play around loose in the alleys

CHAPTER THREE

of Rocinha." Even if Amélia was aware of her own lack of freedom, she believed that what was best for her daughter was to be surveilled, not taking liberties. Part of the challenge of being a dutiful mother was precisely to recognize a woman's place in the family and to *honor* their roles as mothers and good daughters. The normative liberal (universal) obligation to be free did not seem to apply well to situations in which women used their moral agency to subject themselves to certain limitations on their freedom.[15]

In Favela da Rocinha, however, not all women accepted the subjection of motherhood. Many of them "rebelled" against what they called the "slavery of motherhood." My neighbor across the alleyway, Kayanna, who had gotten pregnant as a teenager, was one of them. She was a good-looking woman of short stature. "I'm a mother of three, but I'm not dead. I have a life to live!" she told me. After long journeys working as a cleaner in Barra da Tijuca, Kayanna would not always go home to cook, clean, and look after the children. More often, she would go home, shower, and get dressed to enjoy the nightlife—despite the disapproval of some neighbors.

Teenage pregnancy was a common concern in the favela. At the NGO where I taught English, this was a favorite source of gossip, as well as a frequent topic in sexual education classes. When one of the teenage students would turn out to be pregnant, Armando would announce to the future mother, "Your freedom is over, darling!" Many of the students told me that they were scared of losing their freedom. Not only did they not plan on having babies; they did not want to get married at all. Lilica, one of the most dedicated students at FUS, once told me: "I don't want kids. I don't want a husband. I want to have my own life, to have my own freedom. I'm studying so that I can have a job and be independent." To me, it looked like a move away from the "sexual contract"—in this case, the expectation that sex exchanges must be regulated through marriage.[16] In Rocinha, it was evident that kinship ties were a threat to liberties, even more so for girls and women. Not all women were happy to live their lives for the sake of their children, limiting their own agency to the domestic realm. Due to different circumstances, almost half of households in Brazil are headed by single women.[17]

People like Amélia and Dona Rosário were at the forefront of an intergenerational war with their own daughters, trying to regulate their lives and, most importantly, their sexuality. Both Beatriz and Natasha were closely watched at home, although under different forms and with different expectations—Beatriz was supposed to remain a virgin until marriage, and Natasha was expected to marry a woman and constitute a heteronormative family. Natasha loved Dona Rosário, and she told me that once or twice. At the same time, Natasha felt trapped when she was with her family: "My mother suffocates me! And my brothers picked it up from our mother. That's why I prefer to be out in the streets!" For her, the street was a place of freedom, whereas the house was a place of oppression. On a related observation, Brazilian anthropologist Roberto DaMatta makes the point that public spaces in Brazil tend to be gendered as belonging to men, while the domestic spaces are understood as belonging to women.[18] Natasha challenged some of these associations: she became more of a woman when she was out in the streets. "This one? She likes libertinism [*libertinagem*]!" Dona Rosário used to complain about her daughter. At home, heteronormative gender surveillance was more intense.

Dona Rosário had thirteen living children, with another four or five who had died. She told me that among those who didn't survive, there were some miscarriages. Others died shortly after birth. No mention of induced abortions, if any. Dona Rosário claimed not to remember the exact number of the dead, but perhaps she preferred not to think about it. She used to pray for their souls, though. She also prayed for her living children, and she did her best to control them. In the interior of Ceará, if the good mother was the one who gave up on her liberties, the good son was the one who submitted himself to the family leader—usually, to the father. In this case, Vadson subjected himself to his mother. He was grave, silent, and Catholic. Natasha's brother seemed happy with the idea of looking after the land, to produce his own offspring, honor family values, and reinforce heteronormative gender structures.

Peasants Against Slavery

Dona Rosário was not a tyrant; she was doing her best to lead an ethical life, which to her meant trying to prevent her family from suffering economic and moral humiliation. To accept limitations on freedom (as happens in other forms of liberalism) is not necessarily the same as supporting slavery. In fact, for Dona Rosário, a more restrained life could even save their children from falling prey to the dangers of life in a metropolis. "I didn't give birth for one to be a slave!" (*Não pari ninguém para ser escravo!*)—I once heard Dona Rosário venting.

Other studies set in northeastern communities have found that particular arrangements of land ownership, freedom, kinship structures, family values, and labor have shaped the distinct ways that "peasants" lived their lives. Ethnographies of the Brazilian northeastern state of Paraíba not only help to support some of the observations I derived from Ceará but add complexity to the analysis of how these arrangements inflect different possibilities for freedom. For instance, Klaas Woortmann, who experienced the rural lifestyle in Paraíba, argues:

In peasant cultures, the land is not thought without thinking of family and labor, just as labor is not thought without thinking of land and family. On the other hand, these categories are closely linked to central organizational values and principles, such as honor and hierarchy. This type of society can be opposed to modern, individualized, and market-oriented societies; in other words, a moral order can be opposed to an economic order.[19]

For Dona Rosário and for Vadson, to be "good" was equivalent to establishing appropriate relations in the assemblage involving land, labor, kinship, and liberties. Her best son was the one who was willing to stay in Martinslândia to marry a "decent" woman and take over the responsibilities for the family property (sítio), whenever Dona Rosário decided it was the right time. Vadson was good because he was not looking for easy money in Rio de Janeiro; he worked hard and accepted that life in the northeastern interior could be challenging but ultimately more fulfilling than life in Rio de Janeiro. The other siblings who had migrated to Rocinha, including Natasha, were accused of compromising family ties in their search for adventure and money. Along the way, Dona Rosário claimed they had lost their moral values. They even lost their Catholic habits (if not their faith). Dona Rosário did not hide her sorrow at seeing her children "lost" in the world, untethered from the family and their land in Ceará.

For Natasha and her siblings, however, migrating to Rio de Janeiro was an assertion of liberty. It was a way to disconnect from family ties and to look for opportunities away from the suffering of manual labor and the daily challenges of cultivating land among the thorns of dry bushes. "Clodoaldo" had gone further still. Not only had he migrated away from an "honorable" peasant life; he had abandoned Catholicism and frustrated all the family expectations that one day he would marry and have his own children, establishing and perpetuating the most appropriate moral relations among family, labor, and the land. As some would say, Clodoaldo had literally become another person. For Dona Rosário, this was an unacceptable series of insurgencies.

If she was strict in her relationship with Natasha, Dona Rosário was also always trying to care for her daughter. Sítios in the interior of Ceará were often perceived by their inhabitants, as Woortmann has argued in relation to sítios in Paraíba, "like islands surrounded by an ocean of dangers: a peasant world surrounded by the filthy universe of merchandise, private mercantile property unconnected with work, ambition; a universe that threatens the moral order, but with which we must also know how to deal."[20] Dona Rosário resisted what she saw as the dangers of Rocinha; for her, that place was equivalent to hell. She wanted Clodoaldo back in Martinslândia to protect him. To achieve that feat, the only solution she could think of was to exorcise the devil out of Natasha's body.

Dona Rosário wanted Natasha married to a woman and to wear what she considered to be proper masculine clothing, and she also wanted her child to have a different kind of job. For Dona Rosário, sex work was not only "indecent," but it also implied putting one body's for sale in the public market of the streets, like an object. When working as a cleaning lady, Natasha received more respect from her mother. Still, Dona Rosário couldn't help but to remark that doing domestic work for other people like that was also a form of exploitation. Ideally, for Dona Rosário, Natasha shouldn't submit herself to others in Rio de Janeiro at all. Had Natasha chosen to stay home in Martinslândia, she would have the family land to cultivate and wouldn't have to face the exploitation of working-class life in a metropolis.

Money was considered evil but also necessary to prevent humiliation. Dona Rosário considered a life in the favela to be demeaning and unhealthy. One of the reasons Dona Rosário held Vadson in high esteem was because he accepted the difficulties of life in Ceará without resorting to selling his labor working as a "slave" in Rio de Janeiro. Vadson was the best because he would make a living from their own land. It wasn't much money, but at least he was without the daily humiliation to which others in the favela were subjected. At the same time, Dona Rosário also benefited from the money her children earned in Rio de Janeiro, even if indirectly—through gifts, interstate bus tickets, and other life's necessities when she visited them in Rio.

A Man Is a Man

Once we got back to the house from our visit to Natasha's grandmother, Dona Rosário finished cooking lunch. The lovely smell of freshly boiled beans wafted from the kitchen. Beatriz was still restless. Amélia tried to calm her down: "We'll just have lunch and leave, okay? Life here doesn't have the same agitation of Rocinha! Get used to it."

CHAPTER THREE

I waited in the living room. Natasha's youngest brother was happily telling me about his forthcoming surgery: "After surgery? Oh! Then it is going to be so good. Imagine, I'm going to be able to run around the world!"

I asked, "Do you want to live in Rio?"

He replied, "Sure! So much. I'm going to be operated on in Rio and hope to stay there for good. I just don't know if my mother will let me do it. If she doesn't, as soon as I turn eighteen, I will move there. At eighteen, she won't be able to hold me. It will be my manumission [*alforria*]!"[21] He was just waiting for the right age that marked the official "liberation" (*emancipação*) of children from their parents in Brazil. Voluntary emancipation before that age was possible, but parents rarely agreed to it. The dream of leaving his mother's sofa in the hinterlands and venturing into the world made Dudu smile. "I'm going to work with my older brother, the one who cooks in a restaurant in Ipanema. He said that when I get better, after surgery, he will help me. This [rural] life is not for me. Not even if I wanted it to be. The doctor has already told my mother that I cannot work the land because of my condition!" Dudu explained.

A third son of Dona Rosário's arrived from the sítio for lunch, along with a nephew. Their clothes were dirty from the heavy work. I didn't know either of them, and they remained mute in our presence. They were eating their food in a hurry because there was more work to get done. Dona Rosário had a fourth son still living in the village, the eldest in Ceará. She told me about him before, and I was keen to meet him, but he didn't show up for lunch. The eldest son would spend days roaming around from bar to bar, only going home when he was out of money or when he got into trouble. "Why is everyone in silence? Is the food that good that we can't even talk?" Amélia remarked and laughed, trying to break the ice.

"These ones? They hardly speak . . . I don't know how they find all the girls to date. They are like horny dogs!" Dona Rosário complained, gesturing at her son and nephew. We laughed.

"What can I do?" Natasha's cousin murmured. I noticed that Natasha's deep voice was a family trait. (Even Natasha's closest friends in the favela would sometimes make fun of her voice and quick manner of speaking.)

Over lunch, I witnessed another episode that demonstrated the family's unwillingness (Grandma excluded) to conceive of a queer, nonnormative, more fluid form of life in the hinterlands. I tried to make conversation with the boys. "Are you familiar with Rio de Janeiro?"

"Not yet!" the cousin replied.

Amélia said, "When you go visit Natasha, go to my home so I can cook lunch for all of you!"

Vadson replied, "These ones don't even know who Natasha is. They only saw Clodoaldo once."

Dona Rosário added, "Clodoaldo only came to Martinslândia one time after he started messing around with this thing of becoming a woman. I remember that day very well. He got here wearing a short jacket, with his hair on his shoulders. Like this here, you know?" She gestured around her face. "He had on some small earrings and a pair of Lycra pants. My heart was broken when I saw that he didn't come home as a man. You should have seen it! It was so shameful. Ask the boys what happened?"

Vadson responded with pleasure, "They kicked him out of the village! He was almost stoned here in Martinslândia. Seriously! What a disgrace to the family. If he had been properly stoned, I am sure he would have become a real man again. In Ceará it is like that: a man is a man! Don't let a man come here wearing makeup, okay? We will beat the shit out of him!" The boys laughed loudly. I lost my appetite and stopped eating.[22]

No Longer an Innocent Boy

Clodoaldo was born at the hospital in Guaraciaba do Norte, Ceará, on May 20, 1985. His family brought him back to Martinslândia, where he grew up. Natasha was born in Rocinha. Her birth happened over an extended period, starting in 2000. "I'd much rather live in a favela than return to that hell called Ceará," she snarled. Once, she described in detail an episode of sexual violence she had suffered there in the Northeast. "I've always been a different boy. I was curious about men since I was little. I liked to play with the boys in the middle of a sugarcane plantation near our house. I began to discover my sexuality in those days," she told me. "Guess my favorite game?" she asked. "We played something called 'little house [*casinha*].' Each boy had to get a wife and make babies, but there were not enough girls among us. So, I was always the wife, right? Because I'm not stupid!" She winked at me and laughed.

"However, it was not only the young boys that liked to play with me!" Her smile faded. She got emotional: "It's so hard to talk about this!" She described a scene of sexual violence, which I prefer not to reproduce here. "To this day, I'm so angry at these old men! I'm disgusted by them." That's why, she confessed, "I only look for the young ones [*novinhos*]."

I asked her, "And you didn't tell anyone?"

CHAPTER THREE

"Who could I tell, fag? Are you out of your mind?" she replied. "What I did was try to clean up as quickly as possible so no one could ever find out what had happened. I washed myself right there in the creek. I came home, holding my tears. I don't even know how. Nobody noticed anything, do you believe that? And the pain?" She went on, "Up to this moment, I haven't forgiven that man. I was so happy when I heard he had died."

"Was he ever arrested?" I asked.

She replied angrily:

Arrested? Who? In Ceará? These older men spend their lives looking for children to fuck, and nothing happens to them! Even eight- or ten-year-old girls prostitute themselves, darling! In Guaraciaba, there used to be a whorehouse, owned by an obese woman, called Titi. It was a shack by the road going out of town. That place was full of old men abusing young girls. Some girls would even wear high heels and red lipstick to look older, but everybody knew they were children selling themselves for as cheap as two reais. A lot of them took the money home and handed everything to their mothers.

I was speechless. It took me a while to be able to ask, "But isn't it true that there is prostitution for two reais in Rocinha too?"

She answered: "Sure, but that is because there are people in the favela who are drug addicts, and two reais is the smallest amount of cocaine traffickers will sell, you know? Young girls like that the traffickers wouldn't allow!" she explained. "There is a lot of rape in Rocinha too, but if the traffickers find out, they must kill the rapist. That is for sure." I didn't have anything else to say and was reminded of Belenzinho and his girls—would his case be a contradiction in the favela rules? In the face of certain horrors, words failed me.[23] Natasha concluded, "You know what I wanted to see? If that old bastard would abuse me nowadays. Damn him! I'd kill him with my teeth. I'd stick an iron ball inside his ass and tear him into two! I'm not an innocent boy anymore. I'm a travesti!"

"Nothing in Rio Is Good!"

Before leaving Martinslândia that day, Dona Rosário made a point of introducing us to some neighbors. One of them turned out to be the mother of Nivaldo, Natasha's cousin, whom I had also befriended in the favela. Dona Rosário told me, "That's my *comadre* here![24] She is Nivaldo's mother, your friend in Rocinha!" I was excited about the unexpected encounter, but the woman didn't get up to greet us. Unlike Dona Rosário, she didn't smile at all.

Nivaldo's mother was sitting in front of a large house on a green chair made of braided plastic wires. Her gray hair, pinned on top of her head, formed a perfect bun. She was wearing a brown shirt and a formal skirt, slightly darker than the top. She asked us in a low voice, "Are you coming from Rio?" We nodded yes. She replied grimly, "Nothing in Rio is good. Nivaldo was an Evangelical boy when he lived here. He moved to Rio and look what happened . . . Right?" She vented about her son's sexuality, while Dona Rosário agreed with her. The woman continued: "My other son was wonderful, older than Nivaldo, but he made the mistake of going to live in Rocinha too. He got rich there, and soon after he died. It was a motorcycle accident right here in Martinslândia that took his life. He came home to visit us, full of money, full of pride. He bought a damn motorcycle, and the following week he crashed it and died. I never liked motorcycles!" Nivaldo's mother didn't look well. She had almost no emotion in her voice. Dona Rosário listened to her lamentation with no reaction either, until Nivaldo's mother concluded the conversation: "But the Lord Jesus will help us!" Amélia asked for a glass of water before we left, but Nivaldo's mother didn't move from her chair. She quietly asked Dona Rosário to serve the guests.

As soon as we left the house to walk to the D-20 stop, Dona Rosário hastily told us:

Please, don't mind her, okay? Ever since her son passed away, she hasn't been right in the head. It is like she no longer wants to live. She goes out of the house to go to church and then goes straight back home. That is all she does. Nivaldo's brother was messing around, misbehaving. They say it was some bank fraud business. I don't know exactly. I don't understand it very well. I don't even have a credit card to understand anything of card fraud! I know he got rich back in Rio. When things got dangerous for him down there, he'd run back here to hide for a while, you know? He built that big house for his mother and everything. Unfortunately, he changed a lot after he went to Rio, and the punishment came soon. What a horrible end he had in that motorcycle accident. He got crushed like minced meat.

Amélia shared her own afflictions: "Look, Dona Rosário! If we don't keep a close eye on these boys, nothing good will turn out. I have my son in Rio, the brother of this one here." She gestured toward her daughter. "I keep him on a leash. He complains, complains, and I say no! I don't let him go out. Does he want freedom? No . . . we can't give them all this freedom! It's full of bad people in the favela. You know that, right?"

Dona Rosário angrily replied:

CHAPTER THREE

Yes, but not all mothers think like us! A lot of them pretend they don't see the wrongdoings of their children, most of all if there is money coming home. I know a fellow who was hiding in his mother's house in Martinslândia after killing someone in Rocinha. Imagine. But the traffickers in Rocinha found a way to punish him. Somehow, they got rid of him. And what about those bandits that come here because in Rio they cannot go freely to the streets? They come here to show off their money. As if we didn't know where all this dirty money comes from!

Amélia added: "Oh! Am I going to raise a son for him to become a bandit? Not me. I don't accept that!"

"Even with all the money?" Dona Rosário provoked her and continued, "You'll see just how many new mansions there are in Guaraciaba. All built with this dirty money!" The two ladies shook their heads together, in disapproval, and kept walking side by side along the dirt road. Beatriz complained to me about the long walk. I thought of the notes I'd write later.

Peasant Liberalism

Back in the nearby town, Guaraciaba do Norte, time went by very slowly. We spent most days at home with Amélia's mother, who was suffering from an inflamed heart. The most entertaining moments were the conversations in the living room, as family members sat around in a semicircle around the grandmother. One time Mimoso, Amélia's youngest brother, explained his reasons for never wanting to move to Rio de Janeiro. "Look, whoever goes to Rio only has three destinies: to work like a slave, become a junkie, or become a bandit," he said. "At least here in Guaraciaba, there are no slums!"

Amélia got upset. She responded, "It's not like that, Mimoso! One day I'm going to buy my own house and will not need to work so much. The children are growing, and my partner, Bezerra, is employed now. And I am not involved in any wrong business. You know me."

Mimoso said: "Exactly! It is because you are honest that you end up working like a slave, cleaning madams' houses [*casas de madame*]."

Amélia defended herself, "I like living in Rio!"

Mimoso continued, "At least, it is quiet here. There is room for children to play and all." As we talked, Maria Beatriz was out playing in the street with her younger cousins. They were teaching the Carioca girl how to ride a bike.

Amélia simply responded: "It is too quiet!"

Their mother remained silent, watching television. Then, just at that moment, a favela appeared on the screen. It was a scene from Rio de Janeiro. At the image, the old woman jumped into the conversation: "Rio is beautiful. I wish I'd moved out of here when I was young! When I was a girl, I was very deprived of any liberty. There was nothing I could do. Everybody watched me all the time. I decided it was better to get married than to live in a prison! They handed me up as a wife to an uncle of mine, who had become a widower."

I joined in, too. "Did you marry your own uncle?"

Amélia replied, "Didn't you know that, Moisés? My father is my mother's uncle!"

Amélia's mother continued, "At that time, those things were normal! I should have run away from home. What happened instead? I ended up full of children and even more stuck at home. All these years at home. Now I spend my days sitting on this couch, waiting for the time of my death." The old woman took off her glasses to wipe away her tears. Mimoso rushed to cuddle his mother, worried about her swollen heart.

Amélia, in turn, maintained deep grudges from childhood; she often complained about how her family had exploited her in Ceará. Once in a while, she would open up to me. That day in Guaraciaba, she turned to me and offered more details: "It was a lot of clothes I had to wash, you see, Moisés? For the whole house! I washed everything by hand in the river. I don't even know how I could carry everything on my head until I got there. I was so thin then. So much suffering!" Then, proudly, she added, "One day I got so upset here that I promised I would run away. Soon, I was gone! First to Fortaleza and from there to Rio."

Mimoso, still hugging his mother, kept talking, "Almost everyone here wants to go to Rio. They think they're going to make so much money! These soap operas only show the beautiful side of Rio. Do people think soap operas are real? Every kid here dreams of going to Rio. I never wanted to go there, not even to see it!"

Amélia countered, "I did well to move there! I suffered a lot at first, but I have my own life and my family in Rocinha now. In the old days, things were very tough in Ceará. Now I see it has improved a little bit."

Beautiful images of Rio de Janeiro did not seduce Mimoso. He was the only son who had stayed at home. Amélia's father had died already, and Mimoso took care of his mother and looked after the family's house and property. Like Dona Rosário, he looked down on migrants who went to the big city to sell their labor force. He knew they were underpaid and would end up overworked. According to Mimoso, to become an object for cheap consumption in Rio's labor market was a form of slavery. Instead of valuing normative liberalism, capitalism, and individualism, he defended values that were more aligned with what I call "peasant liberalism." For him, work outside of the family domain was a moral issue; the commodification and exploitation of labor was a problem. Other forms of making easy money in Rio related to drug trafficking, which he considered immoral. Mimoso argued that many migrants lost their dignity, getting addicted to drugs and alcohol (a form of prison too), or lost in life (*se perdendo na vida*). He preferred his life in Ceará, looking after his mother.

Although my time in Ceará was more limited than I would have liked (ethnographic research takes time), there are at least two considerations that can still be made. First, just as the hinterlands have been operating as a counterpoint to favelas in Rio de Janeiro, I conceive of peasant liberalism as a helpful counterpoint to understand minoritarian liberalism in Favela da Rocinha. Second, I would also point out that the wider literature on peasantry (*campesinato*) in Brazil offers support to some of my own observations. There have been several other studies, focused solely on the hinterlands, which have come up with similar conclusions to the ones I have formulated based on my experiences in the interior of Ceará state.

Reflecting upon what Giralda Seyferth calls "peasant ideologies" in Brazil, the value and attachment to the land in "peasant societies," for instance, goes well beyond a mere economic logic. She highlights the value of "freedom" in their work with the land, "unlike the pure wage earners, [the peasant] has freedom of choice, because he has no boss or schedule; although he has a job that requires dedication, hard work, traditional knowledge, love of the land. These are themes common to traditional peasant ideologies."[25] This is a similar ideology to what I observed in Martinslândia, regarding the way Dona Rosário referred to her land, family values, and work. The same could be said of Mimoso and his concerns of falling prey to slavery in Rio de Janeiro.

Having said that, there is another aspect to peasant liberalism that could help us understand the attitude of those who decided to migrate too. Based on observations in the hinterlands of another region in Brazil, the North, the anthropologist Otávio Velho reflects in a book entitled *Capitalismo Autoritário e Campesinato* (Authoritarian capitalism and the peasantry):

The attitude of peasants in the Marabá [Pará state] region toward the future may also have a common element with traditional peasants: they fear the "return to captivity." In fact, together with the attachment to their "freedom," this can help explain a phenomenon that has puzzled scholars for a long time and that has to do with a certain prevailing trend among Brazilians from the lower classes to a constant and apparently inexplicable migration which in the past led to the assumption of an "atavistic migratory instinct" inherited from the Indians. In our terms, in fact, it is as if from an attitude of basic distrust in the system they are always fleeing from the possibility of being caught and put in captivity or in any structure that in their view resembles or might indicate a tendency toward that accomplishment.[26]

I consider Velho's observations on peasant liberalism helpful to better understand both attitudes for and against migration that are prevalent in Martinslândia and Guaraciaba do Norte. We should not expect this minoritarian mode of liberalism to inflect on the lives of different subjects in the same fashion. Migration to escape oppression is common among other peasant populations. Why would Amélia and several of Dona Rosário's children not migrate too, when they feel like they are in "captivity"? In Amélia's case, limitations on her freedom that derived from becoming a mother seemed more acceptable than a situation that felt like domestic slavery when Amélia was still a child. Natasha felt entrapped in Martinslândia, and even her younger brother, Dudu, had his own dreams of mobility and reasons to escape the hinterlands. Others, like Vadson or Mimoso, had a different relationship to the hinterlands and peasant liberalism. They feared the captivity of "modern" life in the metropolis. Rather than eliminating difference, my ethnographic analysis of the favela-hinterlands connection recognizes a multiplicity of liberal possibilities and their heterogeneous effects.

Trans-Politics

Life in Ceará was not always caring. A few days before returning to the Brazilian Southeast, we visited Neuza, one of Amélia's friends. She and her husband lived in Rocinha but were originally from Ceará, like Amélia. Neuza's husband had been employed for a long time as a doorman in Ipanema. With great effort, they had managed to invest in the construction of a small building in the favela. Gradually, they built more shacks to rent. After many years, they were finally in a comfortable financial situation, and they planned on using their savings and the income from the rentals to move back to Ceará when they retired. In preparation, the middle-aged woman and her husband were building a house in a town near Guaraciaba, called Varjota.

Neuza invited us to join her and her sister for a day trip, to swim in

CHAPTER THREE

the lake formed by a dammed river, the Acaraú. Maria Beatriz seemed much happier then. It was sunny and Amélia was glad to meet her good friend Neuza, who had known Amélia for years and was even present at the hospital when Beatriz was born in Rio de Janeiro. She was a redhead, with freckles, and quite tall. "I look like an awkward German woman [*alemoa*], don't I?" she said, laughing at herself. Neuza's sister, who also joined us that day, was very critical of Rio de Janeiro and the choice that her sister had made when she moved there. She was proud of Ceará and wanted to show the best attractions of the state to visitors.

At the lake, we told Neuza about our visit to Martinslândia. We talked about Natasha, and I complained about her brothers' transphobia. "That's the way it is around here. Or even worse!" Neuza's sister replied, while sunbathing on a large rock. She turned on her side to tell us a story:

I have a friend called Márcio, right? But people call him Cinho. So, this boy suffered so much around here . . . He suffered, he suffered. All in front of our eyes. He wanted to be a girl. His life was hell, all that confusion. His was a family of Evangelicals. Imagine? The boy kept saying he was a girl and an army of people were praying around him, forcing him to go to church, locking him up at home. Cinho's father was very rude, like an animal! Until one day, you know what happened? You're not going to believe this . . . His family were away on a trip, and he managed to stay behind at home, alone. He invited a friend over, this other boy who was not just a friend. You know, right? They went to Cinho's room. I know this because Cinho himself told me everything. Cinho wanted to have sex, do you get it? The other boy said no, that he was a male and wasn't going to fuck another male. I think Cinho was in love, because he insisted. His friend then told him that first he'd have to put on female clothing, including a pair of panties. He put all that on, and his friend still didn't like it, right? He said that Cinho was ugly. He insisted that he was not a fag and that he could still see Cinho's dick in the panties, and the day Cinho was born again, without a dick, they would fuck. Márcio was completely heartbroken when he heard that. He got angry and kicked the boy out. Minutes after his friend left the house, Cinho cut his own dick off with a kitchen knife! Do you believe it? He almost died. There was blood everywhere. It was a big scandal. He was almost dead when they saved him. What a mess and what a shame for the family! Cinho ended up in a hospital in Sobral. He really almost died! Even the TV people went to the hospital. TV Record registered everything.[27]

Márcio didn't die at the hospital. Still, I wondered if he was reborn, free from the unwanted penis. Perhaps Márcio was a transsexual, or else he was a transgender person obliged to become a transsexual. He could also be a boy-fag trying to please the man with whom he fell in love. It is impossible to make this judgment from a story recounted quickly.

Nevertheless, the critical point is that, for whatever reason, Márcio felt compelled to cut his own flesh under the pressure of a heteronormative male. With his bare hands, Márcio tried to transform his body into the one that his desired partner demanded it to be.

Natasha had a penis, which I know because she wouldn't always hide it. Depending on the occasion, however, she made more effort to hide (*trucar*) the organ. When she wanted to wear a tight-fitting dress or go on a first date with a new guy (*bofe*), she would take extra care with it. "Darling, you have to pull it back between your legs and hold it in place with a strong tape. I don't like to do that all the time, but there are some days you just need to do it right (*trucar bem trucado*). It's more elegant!"

Other days, even when wearing tight clothes, Natasha made no effort to hide her bulge. Sometimes, her travesti friends would make fun of that fact: "Nat, faggot! You're showing a full package (*mala*) today, huh?" someone would remark, laughing.[28]

Natasha, sometimes jokingly, complained about the excessive sexual demand for her penis: "Oh, faggot! There are hardly any real men in Rio anymore, you know? Everybody wants dick these days! I am desperate to get fucked! I meet a bofe [man], and what does he want? He wants my dick. What an unfortunate situation!" In Rio, Natasha was an empowered woman with a penis, in high demand. In the interior of Ceará, Márcio felt obliged to cut off his penis, trying to please a potential boyfriend through emasculation.

After conducting ethnographic research with travestis in Salvador, the largest Brazilian capital of the Northeast, Don Kulick noted: "This specific combination of female physical attributes and male homosexual subjectivity makes travestis almost unique in the world."[29] Natasha was a travesti, and she liked to be a travesti. Natasha cultivated a feminine body, though she was skeptical of the more permanent bodily transformation techniques that some of her friends relied on, such as plastic surgery. Subjectively, Natasha sometimes identified as a woman: "Yes, I am a woman. I'm just not cracked [*rachada*]!" she said, smiling.[30] She also had a penis, which was a valued organ.[31] This seemingly heterogeneous bodily assemblage certainly contradicted normative expectations of what a woman should be in Ceará.

Migrations

Spending time with Natasha in Rocinha, she seemed satisfied with the queer possibilities at her disposal. Natasha, the person who existed in

Rocinha, could not exist in Martinslândia without great turmoil, though. Natasha knew that power over gender and sexuality was not only about control, but also about possibilities for sex and gender.[32] The LGBTQ cause, as a political struggle, should not solely depend on normative liberal resources. Indeed, it would be against its best interests to do so. The normative liberal notion of individuality, constituted as a person with rights and liberties, is far from universal. Instead, it has European roots and it is heavily dependent on specific discriminatory arrangements. The mobilization of a global liberal apparatus of universal rights presupposes a homogenized field of freedom, uniformly operating across all territories of power. In practice, being a bearer of universal freedom is itself a positionality afforded through a dominant mode of power and not a default setting attached to some sort of natural human essence. Universal freedom is not (even if some think it should be) a condition equally enjoyed by all across the globe. Slum dwellers struggle daily to realize their rights in the Brazilian state. As we know, in the favela, it was the laws of the Hillside that prevailed and guaranteed some queer freedoms.

Favela liberalism affords its own conditions of possibility in terms of gender and sexuality. Queer people exist in Ceará, too, according to Natasha and my own experiences. Nevertheless, they live under different arrangements. Being aware of that fact, why would she travel back to visit Ceará as Natasha? Beyond an anti-normative disposition, I suspect that there was also a desire to test the limits of power. Travestis are known for presenting challenges to social norms. Natasha used to say: "Sou afrontosa mesmo!" (I am keen to affront, indeed!) If I were to guess, I would say that Natasha traveled to Martinslândia as Natasha because she refused to mold herself to the liberties afforded in her homeland; she refused to be the ideal moral subject of peasant liberalism. After the "near-stoning" episode, Natasha made an important life decision: "I will never return to Ceará again! I am only going to go to places where I am welcome!" If Natasha could not easily change the territorialities of power and was not willing to reterritorialize her body, presenting radically different gender embodiment for each place, then she would restrict her existence to Rio de Janeiro. In the Marvelous City, a travesti existence was possible for Natasha.

Natasha did not always enjoy peace or justice. But in Rocinha she enjoyed liberties and freedoms that she couldn't have had either in the "formal" city of Rio de Janeiro or in the interior of Ceará state. The innocent boy-fag from Martinslândia became a *travesti matesca*, with the possibilities afforded by a particular type of favela liberalism.[33] It wasn't the favela that had caused this transformation; it was not the place that turned boy-fags into travestis, as Dona Rosário seemed to believe. Even if it was necessary for Natasha to experiment within the liberalism of the favela in order to constitute the body and subjectivity she had always wanted, this wasn't a sufficient condition. It helped that, in Rocinha, Natasha didn't feel obliged to wear pants, or even to hide her penis, before going out to meet friends. She didn't have to obey her brothers' wishes, no matter how hard they tried to impose them on her. She didn't have to hold sexual abuse in silence either; the laws of the Hillside were rigorous against rapists (although when the rapist was a trafficker, things got more complicated). Natasha worked within the possibilities of being according to these different assemblages. She tested the limits of her existence and was a risk taker. She liked to speak to strangers, to venture out into the night, to seduce armed traffickers. For all those reasons, she was criticized by her own family, judged by her Christian neighbors, and remained a target of violence.

The Asphalt and favelas of Rio de Janeiro were united in contrasting their urbanity against the assumed backwardness of the interior of Ceará, "the bushes" (*o mato*). This is partly due to peasant liberalism's preference for a family-based economy over a free-market-based one. Normative liberalism tends to value individuality, something that appeals to Asphalt queer politics too. Meanwhile, a strong marker of peasant liberalism, as I witnessed it in the Northeast, was a concern with the prevention of modern forms of slavery, coupled with very little regard (and even distrust) toward individual freedoms, including in terms of sexual difference. As such, peasant liberalism could be accused of being complacent with oppressions such as homophobia and transphobia. For that very reason, life in the interior of Ceará felt violent to people like Cinho, Natasha, and me.

But the northeastern hinterlands should not be defined by a lack of freedom any more than the favelas should be; both territories are constituted by different modes of liberal arrangements. The adoption of a normative liberal ethos is not the only possible response to the queer oppression tolerated in peasant liberalism. Favela liberalism can also serve as a minoritarian alternative to peasant liberalism, for example. The very sensitive resistance to any form of slavery that marks peasant liberalism could be exactly what led people like Natasha to take an interest in favela liberalism, and not in the normative liberalism of the Asphalt. The next chapter shows that favela liberalism may be more attuned to capitalism than other minoritarian liberal modes; at the same time, it also creates important alternatives for queer liberalism as a collective endeavor.

FOUR

Queer Kids and the Favela Closet

In Latin and Greek the free man, *(e)leudheros*, is positively defined by his membership of a "breed," of a "stock"; proof of this, in Latin, is the designation of (well-born) children as *liberi*; to be born of good stock is to be free; it comes to the same thing.　ÉMILE BENVENISTE, *INDO-EUROPEAN LANGUAGE AND SOCIETY*

My small home in Rocinha had only one window at the front of the building—the one way to get some fresh air from the narrow alleyway outside. On either side, the neighboring buildings had been erected so close that they blocked my other side windows. It was still possible to open some of these, but I had to use screens at all times; otherwise, rats would scurry in, searching for food. Along with the front window, which I always kept open, I also liked the front door open as much as possible. Neighbors rarely locked their doors, as it was against the laws of the Hillside for residents to steal from one another. The little breeze that channeled through the alleyway, combined with the flow of air generated by an old ceiling fan, provided some relief from the heat and prevented mold and damp from taking over the interior of my *barraco* (shack).

Amélia and her family used a narrow corridor at the front of my house to access the staircase to their place on the second floor. There was a wall that came up around my waist and divided the alleyway from this corridor. One day Amélia, Auro, and I were standing with our elbows resting on the wall, watching a group of kids running, shouting, and laughing on the alleyway outside. Amélia remarked, "What is this? These children running free around the favela? Look at what they are doing!" We realized that the children were playing with the corpse of a huge rat, carrying it by the tail.

Auro laughed out loud. He turned back to us and said, "Oh, I used to do that a lot . . . I used to hold rats by the tail and kill them by smashing their heads on the ground. When I was a child in Rocinha, I had much more freedom than nowadays! I would say, even more freedom than this group of young fags that go around the favela scandalizing people [*tocando terror*]!" Amélia laughed.

I understood well the reference that Auro was making to the crew (*bonde*) of young queer friends—known all over the slum by the name of PAFYC[1] or As Novinhas Flexíveis (The Flexible Young Ladies). In fact, Auro knew that I had been hanging out with this crew in the favela and did not approve of it. Spending time with PAFYC members allowed me to understand some alternative liberties that existed for queer kids in the favela. The experiences that I had with them help me to demonstrate the oppressive potential of normative liberalism in the life of children and to discuss the existence of alternative desires, struggles, and achievements in terms of queer liberation—specifically, in this case, among kids who are often viewed as simply marginal, loitering in the streets, passive victims of poverty and suffering.

Liberi

Childhood is a particularly contested territory for liberalism. On the one hand, children are supposed to be the very embodiment of freedom. It is not by chance that the Latin word for children is the same term used to refer to liberty: *liberi*. However, in the ancient Roman Empire, only those considered "well-born" children would be liberi; the others were simply slaves.[2] Nowadays, privileged Brazilian children still occupy a special place when it comes to freedom. Not having to concern themselves with the responsibilities that constrain adult life, the "good" childhood is meant to be a time of innocence, learning, and free play.[3] For Hannah Arendt, children are the embodiment of newness. They are associated with freedom to the extent that possibilities for freedom are possibilities for actions geared toward a new reality.[4] In this sense, it is not that "well-born" children are the ones who are free, but that "good" children are the ones who bring change to the predictable, ingrained structures that govern our lives.

At the same time, children are also perceived of as incomplete beings, lacking in rationality and full awareness of social rules. Therefore, they can be taken as potentially dangerous subjects; if given too much freedom, they have the propensity to "misbehave," to violate established norms. Given their disruptive potential, it is not surprising that control is also one of the most marked concerns regarding childhood experiences. Freud framed this in terms of a need for the infant's repression,[5] while Foucault observed that, historically, the sexuality of minors has been subjected to the same strict control as the sexual practices of other groups considered "deviant," such as homosexuals.[6]

The historic Greco-Roman understanding of the liberties of childhood still holds well as a framework for reflection upon the contemporary distinction made between the sons and daughters of the Carioca elite versus other children in the city of Rio de Janeiro, such as favela kids (*crianças de favela*) or street children (*crianças de rua*).[7] Elite families tend to believe that children should not be allowed to engage in paid labor; instead, they should enjoy an abundance of free time for play. By contrast, children from the favelas or living on the streets are not supposed to be allowed liberties. For part of the Brazilian elite, the offspring of the marginal classes would be better off engaging in some "occupation" from a young age, even if they receive low wages, just to keep them out of "trouble."[8] While normative liberal ideals state that "we are all born free and equal,"[9] in practice, this only works well for elite children. The actual possibilities for freedom in the life of children in minoritarian positions of power, therefore, rest more on disidentification, or other forms of radical liberalism, such as Arendt's vision of freedom as difference (deterritorialization), rather than sameness (territorialization).[10]

False Imprisonment

Had I not traveled with Amélia and Maria Beatriz to the Brazilian hinterlands, I might not have understood that Amélia's memories from her childhood in the interior of Ceará state were polarized between extremes of oppression and moments of freedom.[11] When we were in Guaraciaba do Norte, I heard Amélia tell stories of forced labor during her childhood; her migration to Rio de Janeiro was justified as an escape from domestic slavery. But at other moments, Amélia would also contrast the oppression of life in a big urban center to the freedom she felt living in the boundlessness of the hinterlands.

One day, Amélia and I visited a large mall in the West Zone of Rio, called Barra Shopping. She wanted to buy some clothes for Beatriz, who came along with us. We looked around many stores, but in the end Amélia could only afford to purchase a single jean skirt. On our way out, as we walked to the bus stop, I noticed a full-size replica of the Statue of Liberty decorating the entrance to the shopping complex. I found it weird, but probably something meant to attract the liberal elite of Rio. It wasn't our case. The three of us took the bus back to Rocinha. Beatriz complained that her mother wouldn't buy her the clothing she wanted. Amélia looked sad and tried to explain to her daughter that shopping malls were not for poor people. I felt sorry for Amélia, and she felt sorry for Beatriz. She told me, "Children in Rocinha have a hard time, Moisés. I pity these children. No money and not even space for them to play! Real freedom we had in Ceará, where we used to run loose playing around. There is space in Guaraciaba, lots of land. That is what I call freedom!"

Different from Amélia's experiences of the hinterlands as a landscape of freedom, the British social historian Patrick Joyce argues, focusing on places quite distant from Guaraciaba—mainly London and Manchester of the nineteenth century—that liberalism is more intimately associated with life in urban centers. The author evokes once again the relationship between modernity, the metropolis, and the normative liberal project:

> . . . a city of wide streets, straight lines, improved visibility, a city where people and things could circulate freely. This city was cleaner and better lit than ever before. In short, a certain freedom was realised. And this freedom was realised around the city and the person as both now themselves sites of free movement, free association, with the person now freely choosing, responsible and therefore self-monitoring. Indeed, the city and its streets were constituted in such a way as to remove all impediments to this person, this liberal subject, being able to exercise freedom (the impediments of danger, darkness, traffic, the very mundane impediments of unpaved roads, mud and horse droppings). . . . This freedom is where I take "liberalism" to reside. And the action of these pipes, sewer, roads, and lights comprised what I have called the "agency" of material things.[12]

In many aspects, however, life in Rocinha offered the opposite conditions to those described above. The favela constituted a territory of danger, where people could easily get lost, step on dog droppings, and cross paths with bandits. For families that hoped to achieve a certain moral respectability in the favela—and above all the Evangelical ones—the solution was to keep their children at home and to distance themselves from the risks of the streets. For children, and also those with disabilities, the option of home confinement was tolerated. Amélia and other neighbors were aware of some concrete cases, but I never witnessed formal accusations on the grounds of false imprisonment. The lack of open public spaces like those available in the Asphalt was a constant source of complaint in Rocinha. There were not many public squares, and even soccer fields were limited in number; I only knew of two in the whole slum. The areas that once existed for public recreation had been occupied by housing. Some limitations on freedom were self-imposed, however, and based on specific moral considerations. There were still masses of children who spent almost all of their time playing around the narrow and bent alleyways of the favela.

The (Ir)Rational Slum

If we were to delve into the study of some other city in the world, such as Chicago, we would be reminded that classic urban studies of the Chicago School held in-depth discussions regarding the interrelations between moral judgments and urban form. For example, Robert Park and Ernest Burgess have argued that "the city is rooted in the habits and customs of the people who inhabit it. The consequence is that the city possesses a moral as well as a physical organization, and these two mutually interact in characteristic ways to mold and modify one another."[13]

Considering that normative liberalism also relies on a Kantian assumption of universal rationality and autonomy,[14] certain normative freedoms were not expected to thrive in the chaos of the slum; because the "modern" urban infrastructure developed in the Asphalt was not really operational in favelas. State powers were perfectly aware of this situation. The slum continued to be a dense territory of twisted alleyways, without effective police monitoring and not much open space. From this scenario, Asphalt dwellers concluded that there was a lack of liberty in favelas, which prevented slum children from achieving a desirable experience of an idealized childhood. If favela children were not entitled to liberty, according to this elite reasoning, it was not because normative liberalism excludes those outside of dominant groups. Rather, the blame was transferred to the urban poor, who were expected to "pay the price" for their illegal and irrational occupation of urban land. In short, the favela way of life—which was said to violate property laws and went against elite norms of order, morality, and sanitation—was considered to be *the* problem.

Most nation-state projects geared toward the solution of the "favela problem" in Rio de Janeiro aimed at introducing infrastructural elements to the slums that would "rationalize" them, fostering their incorporation into the "formal" city.[15] The Favela Bairro upgrading program, for example, was launched by the Municipal Government of Rio de Janeiro in 1994, with a focus on the provision of public services (such as sewage, roads, staircases, and ramps) to improve accessibility to (and within) favelas, and with the final goal of integrating favelas as neighborhoods of the Marvelous City.[16] In particular, the Favela Bairro program was supposed to increase opportunities for free movement by provisioning and upgrading public spaces in favelas.

The impacts of this municipal project were barely visible in Rocinha when I lived there, despite its intentions. State projects were branded as providing the favela population with an opportunity for liberation—a normative mechanism of governance in the name of liberty, or territorialization as liberation. This discourse would be mostly incorporated within the slum by people who aspired to have social mobility and elite values—such as my Evangelical neighbors. Amélia, however, when upset or feeling caught up in the slum, would vent her desire for some freedom by mobilizing positive memories of a peasant liberalism. She did not necessarily look toward the Asphalt as an alternative to her problems, as did most Evangelicals.

Double Abjection

There were other reactions to the particular urban conditions of favelas. At night, the crew of queer teenagers and preteens known as PAFYC would gather and hang out in Rocinha, chatting away until very late. They liked to meet at a spot near Natasha's house, and she enjoyed talking with them. However, the significant age gap between Natasha and most of these kids somehow disconnected her from the group.[17] Most of the time, Natasha had different priorities in her life, too. As an anthropologist, I had more time to be with the crew, despite my radical age difference to them. I never claimed any membership in PAFYC. It would have been ludicrous to do so. I was certainly queer, but too prudish, too old, and too foreign to the favela. I had managed to connect with these kids through other queer relations. They hung out with me

CHAPTER FOUR

because Samira was considered the godmother (*madrinha*) of the crew, and she had become a close friend of mine. She was a little older than most in the group, an out and proud lesbian.

We were all sitting on the pavement in front of an arcade (a sort of internet café) located in the infamous Firecracker Alleyway (Beco do Foguete), about ten meters down from the group of heavily armed drug dealers who spent the night shift in the area. Most of the PAFYC members lived around the Valão area of the slum, my area, but one or two had moved to different favelas and kept coming back to meet the group in Rocinha regularly. A few lived in the higher parts of the hill and would make an effort to walk down to meet us almost every day.

The PAFYC kids insisted on talking about their sexual adventures. A very young travesti called Pituca (the letter P in the PAFYC acronym) said she wanted to buy a big bottle of Coca-Cola to split with the gang. We were a group of more than ten people, so a few coins from each were enough to finance the bottle. Once she was back from the bar, and people started passing the Coca-Cola around, the phallic shape of the bottle caused some commotion. One of the guys grabbed the bottle, put it on the ground, and started dancing low, with his ass touching the bright red top of the container. Up and down, up and down. His name was Yan, and he was also one of the founders of the group (the letter Y in PAFYC). He was very thin and not even a meter and a half tall, with dark skin and a short, bleached Afro. He wore very tight jeans, sneakers, an orange tank top, and big hoop earrings. Someone else grabbed the bottle to take it from him, and Yan screamed: "Oh, babe! Give me that cock!" Some of the passersby turned to look at him, shocked. He kept shaking his ass violently.

To my left, Samira talked to a guy with a mohawk. In a low voice, he told us that he had spent the previous night at a very wild party. He recounted that more than fifty straight men had gathered for a sexual encounter in a house at the top part of the favela. Some of them were drug traffickers, and he loved sex with traffickers. "Delicious!" he screamed. The party had lots of men, with whiskey and Red Bull for everyone: "It was paradise, darling!" he told us.

"And what were you doing there?" Samira asked him.

He told us that he was one of the few lucky fags to have been invited to join them that night. "But now my asshole is on fire, all fucked up, darling! Too many men for just a few fags. Oh, delicioussssss!" Samira shook her head, saying that they were crazy to attend such events. I kept imagining the scene—young guys being gangbanged by muscular drug traffickers—and felt a moralizing type of anger.

A few seconds later, I turned to Samira and asked, "That story has got to be a lie, right?"

She replied, "It could always be a lie . . . But these boys do things that not even the devil would do!" I was clearly disturbed. Samira noticed my expression and added: "I also worry about them, but what can I do? All they think about is a nice cum, and they cum all the time!" She went quiet and looked thoughtful before offering her final words on the matter: "But maybe they exaggerate in what they tell us? I don't know! It is all about fun for them!"[18]

Pituca noticed my discomfort and joined our conversation. "These people are too liberated!" she said, disapproving of the gangbang story. "Too much. Oh my!" Once Auro told me that Pituca was the only one who commanded some respect among the older generations of fags in Rocinha; the latter despised most of the other PAFYC members. Pituca herself had an ambiguous relationship with her cohort. She spent a lot of time with them but often did not approve of their attitude. She cultivated a "well-behaved" image. That night, Samira remarked on how much more feminine Pituca looked. I took the liberty of asking Pituca if she considered becoming a woman permanently, maybe going through surgery and all. Samira interrupted me and said, "I find those fags who are women inside and men on the outside to be better-looking!"

Pituca replied, "I have not decided yet."

Samira was often abrupt in her manners and was not afraid of letting her strong opinions be known. She said:

This is what I think: people have to choose one or the other, either you are a fag, or you are a travesti! I don't care . . . What I don't like is this business of people that don't know what they are . . . some go halfway only. They keep walking around wearing male pants, trainers, and put on female tops that only cover their tits! Just like this top that Pituca is wearing. Look at that! Long hair, short top, and pants . . . Is Pituca a travesti or not? Pituca is a mess! Fucked up.

I looked at the young Pituca and felt sorry about the harsh words coming from Samira's mouth. Pituca didn't look angry, but she went quiet and seemed hurt. After some silence, she told us, "I am too young to make a definite decision to become a woman like that. I think I'm a travesti. As you said, there is surgery for dick removal now, isn't it? I am fourteen. Not sure what I really want yet!"

Samira then laughed and told her: "Shut up! You look like a perfect girl already. The most beautiful travesti in PAFYC!" This last comment brought a slight smile back to Pituca's face.

CHAPTER FOUR

Whereas some of my favela friends preferred to keep their children at home, and certainly tried to avoid that particular alleyway (Beco do Foguete), I soon realized that I was spending more and more of my time around the area. Given the criticisms I was receiving from my neighbors for hanging out at the same place as traffickers, drunkards, and travestis, I started to realize that the Firecracker Alleyway was a unique "moral region" internal to the favela.[19] If those in the Asphalt tended to treat all favelas as morally degraded territories, favela dwellers also treated certain areas within the slums in that way. In other words, Beco do Foguete was a zone of double abjection.

I started to consider that the normative liberal narrative of a rational city with clean streets and straight lines was not the only possibility for liberty. Dirty, shady, and bent alleyways could also foster a different mode of liberalism. Long ago, in reference to street children in Rio de Janeiro, the medical doctor Carlos Moncorvo Filho wrote: "It is in this toxic environment for the body and the soul that a good part of our childhood lives on the loose, in unconditional freedom, abandoned, imbuing themselves with all disrespect, indulging in all vices, getting trained for all crimes."[20] Here, it becomes evident that some forms of freedom are considered undesirable, above all if these minoritarian liberties are intimately connected to urban territories at odds with the "modern" European cities.

Incubated Faggot

Going down Beco do Foguete, in mid-September 2009, I ran into a friend named Peterson. He was talking to an Evangelical woman who frequented the area as a missionary, trying to convert souls for her church. I knew him through the PAFYC group. However, Peterson refused to identify himself as a member of the crew. This was not only due to his age (twenty-two), but mainly because he had been raised Evangelical and still claimed affiliation with the church—something that most of the PAFYC members found to be in contradiction with their radical queer ideals.[21]

I decided to wait for Peterson to finish his conversation and walked into a nearby store to buy some sweets in the meantime. Peterson must have seen me loitering because he was waiting for me with a broad smile and a friendly hug when I walked out of the store. Adilson (a cheerful boy-fag and the letter A in the PAFYC acronym) was also passing by Beco do Foguete at that moment, with some other guys from the crew. He greeted me in the PAFYC style: "E aííí?" (What's uuup?) he said loudly, then lifted his right hand to high-five me. Adilson noted my brown bag of sweets and asked if he could have some. Other young queer guys from the crew soon followed, asking me for sweets too.

Adilson tried to greet Peterson the same way that he had just greeted me: "What's up, faggot?" Peterson ignored him. "What is your problem, fairy?" Adilson said.

Peterson answered, "Look at you, Adilson! What do you take me for? Behave like a man, will you?" A general booing followed from the other PAFYC guys.

A chubby travesti, around the age of fifteen, with blond curly hair and green eyes, yelled at Peterson: "What's the problem with you, darling?" To break the tension, Peterson laughed, as if he had been joking all along.

Adilson did not miss the chance to tell him off, loudly: "Peterson, stop being such an incubated fag [*bicha encubada*]![22] When will you be liberated? Here, look at us. We are all liberated already, my love! Why are you like that?"

At times, Natasha seemed to have some contempt for the liberties of these younger queer kids, who didn't have to endure the same harsh conditions as she did growing up in the hinterlands. "These people are practically born fags in this favela. Look at these PAFYC boys, right?" she told me one day. "I think there is one now who is six years old and hangs out with them. You know they go around the slum provoking everyone. They dance, they walk around rolling their hips, they don't hide they are fags! Me? I had to hide it for a long time, my friend!" Natasha had told me that after moving to Rocinha, away from her hometown, she started to feel that she could finally "become herself." As she put it, "Ah, darling! In Rocinha, I am at liberty to do these things!" She continued: "In the favela everything is possible. All things happen [*acontece de tudo*]! Look around you. There are all sorts of fags. What about the Young Ladies [As Novinhas]? If they can be travestis at that age, why not me at my age? I stopped being an incubated boy-fag! Here I am, Natasha Kellem!" she said, laughing.

Captains of the Alleyways

At first, I thought that Natasha's coming out as a travesti could be explained as a case of normative liberal ideals (such as individuality and autonomy) territorializing favela life. Natasha had moved out from a

CHAPTER FOUR

peasant community in the interior of Ceará, so I assumed that processes of migration, modernization, and urbanization accounted, altogether, for her sexual liberation in Rio de Janeiro.[23] In a historical reflection on early processes of urbanization in the United States and Europe, John D'Emilio explains more about this kind of assemblage, which I had taken as a template:

The interlocking processes of urbanization and industrialization created a social context in which an autonomous personal life could develop. Affection, intimate relationships, and sexuality moved increasingly into the realm of individual choice, seemingly disconnected to how one organized the production of goods necessary for survival. In this setting, men and women who felt a strong erotic attraction to their own sex could begin to fashion from feeling a personal identity and a way of life.[24]

According to D'Emilio, the possibility of queer identification, as we often conceive of it, follows from modernization processes. Both of these elements above—"an autonomous personal life" and "the realm of individual choice"—are core principles of normative liberalism. As I came to learn more about Natasha and the lives of other queer folks in the favela, however, I realized that an understanding of travesti experiences of liberdade would be partial without taking into account that the very conditions of possibility for freedom and liberty could be different in favela territories.

Beyond the wider context of favela autonomy in relation to the Asphalt, which included the existence of distinct laws of the Hillside to mediate relationships in the slum, there were other aspects of queer liberalism in the favela that were not based on universalist notions of rights, the rationality of urban forms, or the moral approval of the Brazilian elites. The sense of freedom in the PAFYC type of liberalism was more radical than normative liberalism could tolerate because it wasn't grounded on class privilege. On the contrary, the group was born against and in spite of liberal ideals of governmentality. PAFYC children were not liberi in the Greco-Roman sense. Instead, they were the children of highly stigmatized favela dwellers—often accused of being criminals—who, faced with the most solidified class structures, insisted on "affronting" norms to assert their freedom.

The fact that we can only easily imagine queer liberalism of the normative type is "always already" an effect of dominant power. But not all senses of queer liberation derive from the same source; not all of them are grounded on European and North American political ideals. In the case of the favela, the "interlocking processes of urbanization and industrialization" described by D'Emilio created alternative possibilities for queer liberation.[25] The PAFYC sense of queerness was not simply based on their identification with categories of classification fostered by the Brazilian state to promote sexual diversity as a "liberal" policy.[26] Rather, their queerness seemed to derive much more from a sense of "disidentification" with normative liberalism[27]—theirs was a collective effort of cultivating a lifestyle that challenged the limits of normally accepted freedoms.

Such ideals of liberation resonate with the experiences of other kids from the poor classes who end up living periods of their lives away from the "domestication" of adults and families. One of the great ethnographies on this question is Jacques Meunier's research among street kids in Bogotá, Colombia. Although Meunier does not make claims related to queer gender and sexuality, he does observe assemblages related to what could be called minoritarian modes of liberalism. The children he observed in Bogotá also looked for ways to make an alternative living. When walking in groups, they felt stronger. They tended to take over certain "undesirable" territories in the city and were called rebellious, dreamy, bold, and adventurous. At the same time, they could also be rude, obscene, and very aggressive. One of the strongest claims in Meunier's ethnography, however, is that these street kids value, above all, their freedom. Theirs was an attempt to free themselves from an adult world marked by severity, brutality, injustice. Although they could not take this attempt to live freely very far, these children constantly fought for it, which, for the anthropologist, constituted the main reason for people to feel scandalized by them.[28]

In *Capitães da Areia* (Captains of the sands), Jorge Amado, the great Brazilian novelist, describes the life of "street children" in Salvador da Bahia. In fact, he calls them "children of the sands," who live as much on the beaches of Salvador as in the streets. Amado moves away from clichés of poverty and suffering to focus, instead, on the collective libertarian consciousness of these kids. One of his central characters, Pedro Bala, who at first is described as a "gang leader," becomes, in adulthood, a militant worker. Still a libertarian, he is said to organize strikes and to fight against capitalist exploitation.[29] In the case of PAFYC, I noticed a collective spirit of minoritarian liberalism that resonates with the one narrated by Amado. Theirs was an effort to create and sustain a collectivity that existed in the alleyways of Rocinha and would be able to challenge the forms of oppression that most impinged on them: PAFYC kids were minoritarian to bourgeois children, to adults, to those who lived a domestic life, and, importantly, to heteronormative folks.

A Favela Coming Out

Natasha never once told me that she was in search of a stable identity. If anything, she would affirm that what she enjoyed the most about being a travesti was the potential for disorientation that she created through her being. "What I like is to be the center of attention, and to confuse people. I adore it!" she said, smiling. "I like this thing that people cannot say for sure whether I am a woman when they look at me. And always *giving an it* [*E sempre dando um it*]!"[30] she added. Natasha didn't deny the desire to keep cultivating the female gender expression that pleased her most. Nevertheless, when Natasha talked about the process of "becoming herself" in the favela, she wasn't referring to a stable, rational, and self-interested (her)self. It was almost a requirement for the PAFYC and other queer groups in Rocinha that members be liberated fags as a collectivity. "We are all liberated already, my darling!" Adilson proudly told Peterson, echoing a phrase I'd heard Natasha use on several occasions, as well. In this particular sense, Natasha joined the PAFYC group and, as members of a wider non-normative collectivity in the favela, shared similar aspirations.

Encubada, like other words in queer favela-talk, is a concept with Pajubá origins. Though it might more easily be translated as "being in the closet," that would be an oversimplification; the extent to which this is a concept equivalent to "being in the closet," in the "Euro-American" sense, depends on the difference between normative processes of queer liberation and minoritarian processes of queer liberation.[31] Making a similar point, based on his ethnographic research with Filipino immigrants in New York, Martin Manalansan argues that the LGBTQ liberal ideal of coming out of the closet is a political-identity issue that makes more sense in the context of white middle-class North America than in the impoverished Filipino migrant communities he knew. Gay Filipino migrants dispute the supposed universality of the "closet" and suggest that not everyone had the need to declare their sexual identity or make public their private sexual practices. In other words, not everyone would be keen to assert a queer public identity. The normative liberal conception of universal freedom of expression is also constitutive of the formation of "the closet."[32]

Unlike Filipino migrants in New York, young queers in Rocinha tried to draw attention to their gender and sexual practices, instead of being inconspicuous. Given that the Owner of the Hillside explicitly prohibited the public humiliation of "his fags," favela liberalism protected and encouraged a specific type of LGBTQ expression. Indeed, one of the explicit political objectives of PAFYC members was to aggressively state their queerness in public, taking advantage of, as well as testing, the limits of favela liberalism. However, the PAFYC members did not necessarily identify with normative "coming out" narratives either. Manalansan states: "Coming out, a liberation from the closet, is founded on a kind of individuation that is separate from familial and kin bonds and obligations. This kind of individuation is also predicated on the use of verbal language as the medium in which selfhood can be expressed."[33]

Most of my queer friends in Rocinha did not base their liberation politics on individuation and, I would say, individuality. Quite to the contrary, they actively constituted friendship (and even new kinship) ties as a strategy to promote their liberation. Such groups were the result of a special form of favela relationality that enabled "coming out" as a collectivity. PAFYC members fostered a sense of privileged connections within the group, referring to each other as "sisters," and to trusted older members, such as Samira, as "godmothers." Contrary to normative kinship, which commonly demands that people give up on their sexual freedoms for the sake of the family,[34] queer kinship in the favela enabled particular liberties that are not to be found either in normative liberalism or in peasant liberalism.

The young age of PAFYC members meant that most of them were not independent from their blood relations at the time of their "coming out." Even if the relations with their blood families were often jeopardized in their sexual liberation process, most members kept both forms of relationality operating at once. Above all, however, it was upon membership to queer groups, such as PAFYC, and queer bodily practices that minoritarian liberation was made possible in Rocinha for this group of very young, and otherwise disempowered, fags.

Explaining the complex etymological possibilities implicit in the word "free," the linguist Émile Benveniste explains something that can help us elaborate on the PAFYC situation:

In Germanic [languages], the connection which is still felt, for instance, between German *frei* "free" and *Freund* allows us to reconstitute a primitive notion of liberty as the belonging to a closed group of those who call one another "friends." To his membership of this group—of breed or of friends—the individual owes not only his free status but also "his own self."[35]

What seems to be more remarkable, as an ethnographic observation, is that such potential for freedom—which is derived from strong bonds of friendship, sometimes turned into kinship—is not a privilege of the elites, as the etymology of the word *liberi* seems to suggest. The children of the oppressed, who have been historically deauthorized by normative liberalism from bearing the liberi designation, come together to introduce a novelty in an otherwise determined world. They transform the possibilities for liberalism, affording the term a minoritarian existence.

PAFYC members caught a lot of attention in Rocinha. However, there were other queer groups working on kinship relations and liberal politics too. According to Auro, there was an important one made up of older travestis, which had existed for much longer than PAFYC. As the mathematician explained, he thought that the past generations were much more "serious" in their political objectives—whereas PAFYC members were known for their excessive banter, pranks, and immaturity. For the older generation of travestis, the incorporation of new members to their group was an elaborate process. Auro recalled, "Only through baptism! To become part of their group, you had to be adopted by an older member. You needed a godmother [*Precisava ter uma madrinha*]! Then, there was the actual baptism, a ritual of which there were different versions. In old times, baptisms took place in Valão. All the travestis would hold the novice fag by the feet and dip the initiate's head down into the sewer. From that moment on, you were part of the group!" Auro laughed, hinting at connections through abjection: sewage, deviance, immorality. Still, it was a form of relationality, but disidentified from the moral standards of normative liberalism and, equally, from the heteronormative standards of peasant liberalism.

Body and Metamorphosis

Expressions of queer liberalism in the favela could be seen in dress, sexual feats, and performances of body flexibility. There were different combinations of these strategies; some put more emphasis on their clothing, makeup, and sexual prowess, as was the case with Natasha, while others played more with public displays of their bodies. It was important for Natasha to affirm her *liberation* through her clothing, hair, and makeup. Meanwhile, the youngest PAFYC members were often seen doing splits (*espacate*) in public, among the crowds. The "real" fags were the ones who expressed themselves in bodily form. People like me, who kept wearing male clothing while only verbally claiming an inner queerness, remained very much "incubated" fags, boy-fags. It was not enough to "come out" verbally—it was necessary to hold a different posture in order to be considered a proper liberated fag.

In the favela, coming out was not necessarily a process marked by a singular moment that coincided with the beginning of an independent adult life. It was not a matter of verbal identification, either, of clearly *voicing* one's sexual orientation, desires, or subjectivity. Instead, queer liberation among my friends in Rocinha was deeply connected to the capacity of a bodily type of metamorphosis, either in the sexual use of the body (and here boy-fags would be more acknowledged), in the cultivation of bodily elasticity, or through the deployment of clothing and other artifacts as means of transforming the body. In that sense, clothing is not a simple matter of identification through consumption, either. Following a perspective elaborated by Eduardo Viveiros de Castro and other ethnologists within a different minoritarian (Amerindian) context,[36] I would suggest that "clothing" should be understood not as a superfluous item in queer life in Rocinha, but as privileged equipment for the expression of their liberation. More than an external layer to the body, the care and time Natasha and some PAFYC members dedicated to their outfits indicated that clothing and makeup were also part of their bodies—these bodily performances were inscribed with efficacious meanings as acts of minoritarian liberation.

Adilson was the most flexible member of PAFYC. (I say this at the risk of being hated by all the other PAFYC folks, who competed daily for the public recognition of their bodily abilities.) When the group gathered in Beco do Foguete, one of their main activities, aside from sharing queer stories and adventures, was to practice all sorts of stretching and dance moves in public. Cacau, the letter C in the PAFYC group, was a Black boy-fag in his early teens. He used to challenge the others to see who could go further in the leg splits, and, for that reason, he was known as *afrontosa* (insulting). His sudden moves always startled me. He would be standing talking to someone and, all of a sudden, would let his slender body drop to the ground into the splits. His legs would stretch open and, with his crotch against the ground, he would start to bounce up and down, dancing, simulating an orgasm. The scene used to provoke generalized commotion in the group, and soon there would be five or more of the PAFYC members doing the splits in the alleyway. Some were more skillful than others, and the youngest learned from the established experts. The crew was known all over Rocinha for such collective performances of flexibility that at once shocked and amazed the general public.

Natasha had not grown up in Rocinha and rarely risked the splits—another reason for the PAFYC group not to consider her a full member of the crew. Natasha's bodily performances were more related to her sexual prowess—such as having more than one man penetrating her at once—and her concern with bodily artifacts. "Have you ever thought about getting silicone implants, darling? Like huge silicone boobs?" I asked her one day as we walked to the beach.

She shook her head emphatically, moving her chemically straightened hair from side to side. "Not me! Are you crazy?" she promptly replied in her usual deep voice. Natasha commented on her friend Paulette's use of industrial liquid silicone injections, which were available in the favela to make bodies curvier and more feminine: "To be pumped with silicone? I don't want to! Paulette herself is pumping, you know? She even offered her services to me! I said no. I'm not crazy!"[37] Had I offended her? Silicone implants were such a frequent topic of conversation in a country obsessed with plastic surgery. I didn't mean that she *should* pump cheap, dangerous, liquid silicone into her body. I was simply curious if Natasha had the desire to stop using foam inserts inside her bra to produce bigger breasts. Natasha kept talking: "Not me! What if someday I decide to go out like this, *boyzinha* [as a little effeminate boy]? What am I going to do with the silicone then? Let me be as I am. Whenever I want bigger tits, I use my foam, and men go crazy for them. On other days, I will go out with no tits at all. That is how I like it!" She smiled. I smiled. Even if not in the exact fashion as the PAFYC group, she obviously held a profound interest in queer bodily performances.

No Address, More Freedom

The fact that most people in Rocinha don't have individual home addresses, another particularity of the "irrational" urbanity of favelas, also contributed to my friends' collective liberties. On November 1, 2009, Natasha came around to my house in the early evening and asked if I'd like to go for walk. This usually was a cue that she wanted to cruise for sex at the beach.[38] She didn't mind cruising alone, but some days she preferred to have company. I got used to the idea that I could be sent back home at any time if Natasha found something more exciting to do than talking to me. Going toward the ocean, we walked by the tall buildings in the neighborhood of São Conrado, through a tree-lined avenue called Aquarela do Brasil. There was about a mile separating my house in Rocinha and the beach. About halfway there, a black Mercedes-Benz almost hit us on its way out from the garage of a luxurious building on Aquarela do Brasil. The opulent middle-aged woman, who was driving the big vehicle, still felt entitled to blow the horn at us. Instead of getting out of the way, Natasha moved closer to the car and stopped in front of it, putting her face right up to the windshield. My friend shouted as loud as she could: "Son of a bitch! [*Filha da puta!*] Knock me down with that car, and I'll have to beat the shit out of you!" I got scared. The driver got even more scared and drove away as quickly as possible. I later relaxed and laughed.

"Natasha, one day, someone will sue you or something!" I warned her.

She laughed at me. "Sue me? Are you serious, fairy? Who is going to find me in Rocinha? I am free [*Eu sou livre*]! I don't even have an address, darling! You are so naive sometimes . . ."

In addition to the laws of the Hillside, queer kinship groups, and bodily performances, a vital element in the assemblage of minoritarian queer freedoms in the favela was the territorial dynamic between the Asphalt and the Hillside. In contrast to normative liberalism, which depends on the possibility of surveillance to maximize governmentality, the lack of formal addresses and grid-like roads and pathways in the favela generated the conditions for a different form of liberty: the inability to be located, monitored, or tracked down. In arguing that she could not be sued, Natasha positioned herself as an outsider to the system of governmentality effected by the nation-state and the rule of law. If one cannot be located, one cannot be officially notified by the judiciary system.

In the Asphalt, travestis like Natasha were often treated as criminals. Even if some did commit (mostly petty) crimes, they were frequently unfairly stigmatized and subjected to all forms of exploitation and police brutality.[39] But in the favelas, travestis could count on being part of a more extensive "safety network" that helped criminals, marginals, and other "deviants" against the nation-state. For drug traffickers and others considered "on the loose," there was hardly a better place to hide than the favelas. This is partly how drug trafficking was networked with many other activities considered "illegal," such as bank frauds, robberies, and internet scams. As long as the Owner of the Hillside agreed to host a fugitive, it would be almost impossible for the police or the judiciary system to locate that person unless they were to venture into the favela territory—which would be considered an "invasion," as people in favelas would put it. This protection was afforded by urban form, favela boundaries, and the laws of the Hillside—in what I have called a "liberal heterotopia."[40]

CHAPTER FOUR

Gay Pride in the Asphalt

These different forms of minoritarian liberalism in the life of slum dwellers often collided with other, more normative, modes of queer liberation. I realized this when I attended the Rio Gay Pride Parade in 2009, which took place at Copacabana Beach in early November. Amélia was straight but had heard about it on TV and was curious to see the event live, so we arranged to go together. When we arrived, there was loud electronic music, colorful flags, and half-naked bodies all over.

During the parade, I met Raimundo, one of my students from FUS, the Rocinha NGO where I taught a Basic English class. I was surprised to see him because I always assumed he was straight. He was shirtless, displaying his well-defined abdominal muscles. Maybe he was queer-friendly, I thought. Raimundo asked me if we could hang out, as he had come alone and didn't belong to any of the queer crews. I was expecting to meet up with other friends, including Mazinho, a bicha-boy studying in the same class as Raimundo and infamous for his insatiable sexual appetite. Natasha and most of the PAFYC members were a confirmed presence in the event too. They were in the mood to "go down to the Asphalt" (*descer pro asfalto*) that day and meet up with some "gays." As I've noted, for my queer friends in Rocinha, the word *gay* was a marker of an identity connected more to the Asphalt than to the Hillside (although self-identifying gays were emerging in the favela too).

My FUS student briefly told me about his life. His mother was an Evangelical woman who had migrated from Ceará to Rio de Janeiro. "And she is one of those fanatics! She is a member of the Universal Church of the Kingdom of God [UCKG]," Raimundo said, in reference to one of the largest Neo-Pentecostal groups in Brazil. Since we were talking about this topic and it was Gay Pride, I felt at ease to ask him for more details. "When I arrived in Rocinha, there were only women and men, and some travestis. There was no such thing as gay people. Do you understand? Gay people like you and me," he said. Raimundo continued, "I never thought of myself as a travesti. For this reason, I had many girlfriends, and I even have a son. But I am less confused now. I have realized that I am gay. I call myself gay, do you understand?" I did. It sounded to me a bit more like one of those verbal "coming out" stories that I was used to. I asked him about the time when he lived in the Brazilian Northeast. "In Ceará, there is a lot of prejudice, even today. But my family in Rio accept me better. I have an independent life. Even my mother, who belongs to the UCKG, accepts me!" he replied. The unanticipated encounter with Raimundo highlighted that there is a place for more normative forms of liberalism in the favelas too.

Loud parade floats passed by as we chatted, blaring messages of liberation. One of them read: "É direito nosso amar e viver livremente!" (It is our right to love and live in liberty!) Another truck carried a banner: "Devemos lutar pela vida, amor e liberdade!" (We should fight for life, love, and liberty!) Yet another car carried the message: "Duque de Caxias deve respeitar a liberdade de expressão!" (Duque de Caxias [a city in Rio de Janeiro state] must respect freedom of expression!) There was also a big moving structure dedicated to religious freedom (*liberdade religiosa*), which was carrying representatives of different religions (Catholicism, Protestants, Afro-Brazilian religions, Spiritism), some wearing ritual clothing. This last truck was called "Carro da tolerância religiosa: Brasil é país laico" (The truck of religious tolerance: Brazil is a secular country), in reference to the fact that all religions should have a place within the nation-state and the state itself should be free from religion. The sequence of liberalisms being promoted were based on normative concepts of universal rights and respect for difference within a framework of liberal multiculturalism. It made more sense for the realities of Asphalt dwellers than most favela queers. The celebration went on until very late at night, ending up with many of my friends having lots of sex at the beach. Sex, it turned out, is what attracted most of them to the Gay Pride Parade in the first place.

The Need for Limits

Auro was a puzzling case. He told me that when he was young, he had been a favela travesti. After growing up, however, he decided to quit the travesti life and dedicate himself to the study of mathematics. More recently, Auro seemed to have started to conceive of himself as a gay person. "I am still friends with all the travestis. I know them all, especially older ones, from my generation," he told me proudly. At the same time, he was very judgmental of the new generation of fags growing up in Rocinha. From the perspective of a gay favela dweller, he used his seniority and moral standards to pass judgment on favela liberties. One day he told me about his cousin, a member of PAFYC, who had gotten involved in some petty crime. "My cousin, that little faggot I showed you the other day, know? He is working with Dona Elza, dear. I think he is like that because my aunt gave too much liberty to her children!" "*Dar a Elza*" or "*trabalhar com a Dona Elza*" was the Pajubá way of referring to the action of stealing. Auro was so agitated telling me this news that his mouth went dry. He had to pause to drink some water.

I witnessed more judgment of PAFYC one night when Mazinho stopped by my house. He shouted my name through the window until I came to open the door. "Let's go for a walk on the beach!" he said. Mazinho was considered a boy-fag. He was not shy at praising the size of his manhood and was very successful when he went cruising for sex at the beach in São Conrado. When we reached the area near the famous Hotel Nacional—designed by Oscar Niemeyer, right across the road from the ocean—the air became damp and warm, smelling of salt. At that point, some friends were passing by on their way back from the beach and stopped to greet us. Marcos, who belonged to the PAFYC group, was one of them. After greeting me, he turned to Mazinho and demanded, "Faggot, give me fifty cents!"

Mazinho looked him up and down and replied, "No! Not me!" I reached for some coins in my pocket and handed to them, and we got going. A few minutes after the episode, Mazinho remarked, "Oh my. Did I give him the liberty to talk to me like that? I didn't! To call me faggot as if we were at the same level and then have the guts to ask me for money? How do you tolerate these people?" I laughed at the situation, but Mazinho was truly upset.

Similar complaints regarding a perceived excess of freedom on the part of PAFYC members reached me from all sides. It was as if people thought I should bear some responsibility for their acts and somehow help to "tame" their freedoms. My friend Paizinha, a teacher at FUS, explicitly told me once: "I was thinking of you the other day in church, Moisés! You know I teach children in Sunday school? So, we were discussing the limits of freedom. Isn't that what you are researching? For us, because of Adam and Eve's mistake, which was an outcome of their free will, Christian freedom had to be limited. We learned from our mistakes, and we know our limits! We are different from other people. We know the limits of our sexual freedom. For example, freedom for your friends from this group . . . what is it called again? PAF . . . , or something like that? Yes, their freedom seems to be unlimited. For us, this is really not good! They need limits."

Liberation and Respectability

On a rainy afternoon, Amélia noticed that I was talking to Auro downstairs. She offered to make us some coffee. We went upstairs, and the whole house smelled as if she had just been roasting coffee beans. Auro told us a story about a friend of his named Walda, who was a travesti with some clout among the fags in the favela but not respected by other residents. "One day, Walda was walking down in Rocinha and a woman called her a screwed faggot (*bicha escrota*), for no good reason. Walda got mad, as if she had incorporated the spirit of a female devil, and crashed a glass bottle against the woman's head!"

I was surprised and asked, "Oh! Just like that? And then what? What did they do to Walda?"

Auro replied, "Guess! She earned a lot more respect that day. Nobody in the favela messed with Walda, ever again."

Amélia laughed, but Auro remained serious and added: "It is exactly because of the struggles and victories of these past generations of fags in Rocinha that nowadays these young fags have such liberty!" I reached for my notebook and started to write. Auro looked at me and said, "You want to take notes? This is important now: the struggles of the previous generations helped to change the favela attitude against us. Because of them we got respect, even from the traffickers." I listened attentively. Auro had lived those earlier times of queer life in the favela. He continued his reflection: "But now the older generations of fags are really worried about the way that these young fags are behaving. Look at these PAFYC people. With all this excess of liberty, all the gays and travestis from Rocinha, all of us could end up losing respect again!" Auro paused for a moment. He put his cup down and added one last thought: "That is why I keep telling Peterson, that incubated fag, to stop being crazy. To stop hanging out with these little fags of Beco do Foguete. And he replies that he is not crazy, he is the 'reality.' What does that even mean? Life is crazy, and he is a crazy bitch!" At that point, Auro finally relaxed and laughed at the situation. I knew that Auro liked Peterson and found him entertaining.

Favela morals and ideals only look homogeneous for those who never experienced the complexities of life in one of these territories. Not all slums existed under the same political and social arrangements either. The conditions of possibility for liberdade in the life of my queer friends in Rocinha did not emerge homogeneously. Some queer folks were reaffirming normative principles, seeking to regulate the conduct of others based on dominant standards of ethics, power, and morality. Yes, there were favela dwellers who believed that queer liberation could only come through nation-state mechanisms, constitutional rights, and upward social mobility. The PAFYC group was part of a wider queer scene in the favela and, at the same time, stigmatized within it—starting with the older generations of travestis.

CHAPTER FOUR

This disdain for PAFYC group members was often manifested as a critique of their liberties. These hypersexualized queer kids from the favela challenged so many rules and expectations that I myself felt uncomfortable hanging out with them. Not only were my moral standards put into question, but people kept approaching me in the hope that I would act as an agent of normalization of their excessive freedom. Some of these complaints were more religious in form, others related to the control of interpersonal attitudes, and some were related to the preservation of the heritage of queer liberties in Rocinha. I certainly had my own concerns regarding PAFYC liberalism, which I expressed directly to them when I had a chance. I worried about their physical integrity and their sexual health. I tried to talk to them about their expectations for the future, schooling, employment. More often than not, though, I was ignored, and their banter would proceed, avoiding *assunto de velho* (a conversation topic for the elderly). For my part, my contact with the PAFYC crew was carefully balanced. Too close, my presence as an adult could become oppressive. Too far, I could risk losing contact with them. While tracing other assemblages of liberation in the favela, however, I would end up meeting several PAFYC members again, sometimes, in very unexpected territories, as we will see next.

FIVE

Encountering Demons and Deities

"If you continue in My word, you are truly My disciples. Then you will know the truth, and the truth will set you free." "We are Abraham's descendants," they answered. "We have never been slaves to anyone. How can You say we will be set free?" Jesus replied, "Truly, truly, I tell you, everyone who sins is a slave to sin."
2 JOHN 1:4-6, BEREAN LITERAL BIBLE

Religion is not liberalism's nemesis, despite what some secular views might suggest. What we usually conceive as the "religious domain" can be an important territory for liberal politics. Demons, spirits, and deities can both support and challenge different modes of liberalism, for example. I started learning all this with Fafá, my student in the English as a Second Language (ESL) program at FUS. She had joined the group late, a few weeks after the start of classes. Armando warned me that I had a special mission with Fafá. She was a talented singer who had performed throughout Europe, mostly singing gospel songs; however, her career had been severely jeopardized because she couldn't sing a word in English. Fafá even managed to speak some German, but English was her Achilles' heel. "I know you can teach people to speak English. Now, can you teach Fafá to *sing* in English?" Armando asked me, laughing, knowing I was a terrible singer.

Fafá was born and raised in Rocinha, from a Black family, and she had come back to the slum for a few months to be with her relatives and her Evangelical community. When we met, I noticed that her teeth were slightly wider

CHAPTER FIVE

than her mouth could accommodate. She was vivacious. "I've been to places I never imagined that a Black woman from the favelas could ever reach!" she told me. Once in a while, she would come up to me at the end of classes with lyrics in English that she hoped to learn. "I need help with pronunciation! I don't understand why I find English so difficult!"

In late May 2009, I stayed with Fafá after our regular class to help her prepare for a musical performance. That is when she told me more about her religion. She was an Evangelical Christian from a traditional church near Rua do Valão. Curious to learn more, I asked her: "Have you ever been to one of those other churches, such as the Universal Church of the Kingdom of God [UCKG]?" The latter had an international presence; their "universal" mission was even part of their name. Fafá affirmed that she used to attend their services once in a while. "Which services?" I asked her, hoping to find out more about the liberation services (*cultos de libertação*) offered by the UCKG. These events had a regular presence in the weekly schedule of several Evangelical denominations in the favela and were tailored for people hoping to free themselves from demoniac forces disturbing their lives.

"Whenever my friends go to the Universal Church, I go too!" she replied.

"And have you ever heard of their liberation services? Have you ever been to one of those?" I asked.

"Sure! Many times!" she answered.

"Really? And how do you like them?"

She commented:

They hold powerful mysteries. Sometimes, I can't cope. I get so scared when they turn off all the church lights. Lord, have mercy! It's midnight, pitch-dark, and they start calling out all those demons. Shit! The devil starts to manifest, and all you hear is people howling and grunting. It's so scary! I'm glad there is an army of pastors and helpers, the Army of Jesus, to deal with them. They liberate everyone. They chase all the demons away.

"Have you seen possessed people?" I asked.

"Many, many times!" she replied. And she kept talking: "Do you know As Novinhas, the crew of young fags that hang out in Beco do Foguete?" I nodded yes. "So," she told me, "they are always going for liberation at the Universal Church. They are always getting possessed!" I never imagined that anyone in the PAFYC crew would attend services at an Evangelical church, since they were openly critical of Evangelicals.

My friend Samira used to say: "I hate Evangelicals! I want distance from these people!" I got really puzzled after that conversation with Fafá.

I always found Natasha to be intriguing in terms of her religious practice, too. She used to say: "I hate the believers [*crentes*]!" This is how she liked to refer to Evangelicals. Natasha seemed removed from any particular faith. Except that she once told me that some people looked for her help when they needed "witchcraft," especially the type that could bring lovers back together. "What do they think I am? A love witch?" She laughed. "And you know what? When I do stuff like that for other people, the magic works in less than seven days!" She kept laughing. Natasha would never be seen in the Evangelical church; why would some of the PAFYC members attend liberation services?

Overcoming Secularism

Being raised in a "secular" family,[1] I started to realize the actual significance of Evangelical liberation services only after moving to Rocinha. From my very first weeks living there, I had observed that the overall number of Evangelical churches in the favela was well beyond what I was used to seeing in other parts of Brazil. I found out about the very existence of "liberation services" when I noticed an old banner hanging on top of a very small church on Estrada da Gávea, in Rocinha. It read: "Congregação Evangélica da Libertação" (Evangelical Congregation of Liberation). The sign informed people that liberation services were held on Wednesdays and Fridays at 7:30 p.m. Curious, I took notice of the discovery: "Culto de Libertação? [Liberation Service?]" I wrote in my little notebook. The following day, I mentioned the church to Carcará, an Evangelical neighbor of mine, but hearing about the small and unknown congregation didn't seem to impress him. After some consideration, he agreed to accompany me to the Evangelical Congregation of Liberation. Also, along with other neighbors, he helped me attend several other liberation services in a variety of congregations while I lived in Rocinha.

As mentioned, Latin America has a long history of power struggles between oppressors—colonizers turned into contemporary elites—and the oppressed—Black, indigenous, queer, and disempowered mestizo populations. "Religion" figures as a prominent force mobilized in the mediation of these (post)colonial relations. This has been the case at least since the first Christian mission was sent from Europe to educate and evangelize native populations in Brazil, landing in the state of Bahia in 1549. As

CHAPTER FIVE

such, it shouldn't come as a surprise that religion would also figure as an important element when it comes to discussions of liberalism. Nevertheless, in its modern liberal, state-based version, normative liberalism promotes such a strong separation between "political" and "economic" issues from issues of "religion" that, prior to my fieldwork, I had not seriously considered the oppressive and liberatory potentials of religion in the life of favela dwellers.

The anthropologist Talal Asad, whose important work has been dedicated to the analysis of religion and power, argues:

Religion is not an archaic mode of scientific thinking, nor of any other secular endeavor we value today; it is, on the contrary, a distinctive space of human practice and belief which cannot be reduced to any other. . . . Yet the insistence that religion has an autonomous essence—not to be confused with the essence of science, or of politics, or of common sense—invites us to define religion (like any essence) as a transhistorical and transcultural phenomenon. It may be a happy accident that this effort of defining religion converges with the liberal demand in our time that it be kept quite separate from politics, law, and science—spaces in which varieties of power and reason articulate our distinctively modern life. This definition is at once part of a strategy (for secular liberals) of the confinement, and (for liberal Christians) of the defense of religion.[2]

Therefore, rather than reaffirming a "secular" understanding regarding the place that "religion" should occupy in contemporary power assemblages and in the life of favela dwellers (be they my Evangelical neighbors, Natasha, or the PAFYC crew), ethnographic research forced me not to take the operations of the category "religion" for granted. Quotidian experiences with historically oppressed populations in a colonized nation, such as Brazil, were also an opportunity to unbracket religion, and to open up the concept to its actual operations of power as part of liberalisms that were not so familiar to me. Through a fieldwork method of tracing and mapping the assemblages through which liberalisms are mobilized, I (literally) ended up on my knees in the Evangelical liberation services of the favela.

Demons and Deities

Living in Favela da Rocinha, I was confronted with situations with similar complexities to the Colombian colonial context described by Michael Taussig: "Colonization and enslavement inadvertently delivered a special mystical power to the underdog of colonial society—the power of mystic evil as embodied in the Christians' fear of the devil."[3] In Brazil, the Society of Jesus, a religious order of the Catholic Church, was a vital part of the colonial enterprise. A salient historical concern of the Jesuits has been the education and conversion of non-Europeans to Christianity.[4] In the Bible, there is only one true God, the Christian God. Any other gods posed a challenge to this universal truth. Despite their ethnocentric violence, these European colonizers inadvertently recognized the power of other gods, even if in a negative sense. Despite all the trauma of colonialism, some of the most vulnerable in colonial society—Amerindians, Africans, and people of African descent—managed to keep their own gods alive. Gods that were feared by Europeans (even if as manifestations of the devil). The struggle between demons and deities reverberates to contemporary times in Brazil.

In the favela, one of the most evident manifestation of this phenomenon currently takes place in the intense struggles of Neo-Pentecostal Christians against the practitioners of Afro-Brazilian religions. This concern that Christianity—especially in its Evangelical variations—have historically demonstrated in relation to the powers of entities of African origins has been noted in other Latin American colonial contexts. Again, from Taussig:

Two generalizations are necessary to any discussion of black slave religion in Latin America. First, the whites were apprehensive of the supernatural powers of their subjects, and vice versa. Second, religion was inseparable from magic, and both permeated everyday life—agriculture, mining, economy, healing, marital affairs, and social relations in general.[5]

I soon realized that to research Neo-Pentecostal liberation services in Rocinha, I would have to trace the relationships between Christian and Afro-Brazilian practices. Remarkably, it would be much easier for me, as a gay man, to participate in Umbanda rituals than to attend Evangelical churches. Afro-Brazilian religions were in a minoritarian position in relation to Christianity in the same way that queer identities were in a minoritarian position in relation to heteronormative ones. It was not a coincidence that Auro was an expert in macumba and that Natasha hated Evangelicals.[6] In fact, most of my LGBTQ friends in Rocinha had good knowledge of Umbanda but not necessarily of Christianity.

Presenting themselves as an explicit counter to Afro-Brazilian religion, however, are the Evangelical churches. And although several denominations offered liberation services in Rocinha, the belligerence of the Universal Church of the Kingdom of God is unique amongst them.

CHAPTER FIVE

As Ronaldo de Almeida argues: "Above all, the symbolic battle is more acute against Afro-Brazilian religions. . . . [I]n this confrontation process, the UCKG constituted itself in relation to the symbolic universe of its opponents, becoming alike to the religions they fight against."[7] Though my disposition is to move beyond a symbolic analysis, I am interested in the strong attachment from the part of the UCKG to Afro-Brazilian religions.

The UCKG was one of these Evangelical churches with a great focus on spiritual liberation. They occupied privileged sites in the slum, one at a main corner of Estrada da Gávea, facing the upper-middle-class neighborhood of São Conrado. Estrada da Gávea was the only wide road that crossed the whole favela, going all the way uphill from São Conrado and then downhill toward Gávea. The UCKG was a Neo-Pentecostal congregation that operated in many other locations all over Brazil and even abroad. Their Solomon's Temple in São Paulo was one of the largest religious buildings in the country. In Rocinha, their flagship church was located at the main entrance to the favela, but there were smaller ones with which I was not so familiar. Compared to the infrastructure of other churches in Rocinha, the UCKG's main building was quite monumental, holding around eight hundred people during the busiest services.[8] The church was painted beige and white, with the highest point of the façade decorated with a big red heart containing a white dove, representing the Holy Spirit. Below the UCKG emblem, one could read in capital letters: JESUS CHRIST IS THE LORD. Most of their six thousand (or more) churches around the country—and even abroad—carried this same message.

Afro-Brazilian entities such as Exu were a constant presence in territories both minoritarian and normative. For most Evangelicals, Exu was the representation of the devil par excellence. For most of my queer friends in Rocinha, however, Exu and its female counterpart—Pomba-gira—were entities known for their power to do both harm and good. They could trick and deceive, but, at the same time, they could help, assist, and counsel people. Although Exu and Pomba-gira were also recognized as the devil in some Quimbanda and Umbanda rituals I attended in the favela, that did not necessarily make them enemies of the minorities who attended these religions.[9] To cite Taussig once again, as he remarked regarding Christianity in Latin America:

In their devil worship, the slaves appropriated their enemy's enemy. Ironically, through its very attempts at suppression, the Church indirectly validated devil worship and invested it with power. By acknowledging the fear of the slaves' spiritual powers, the credulous Spanish inadvertently delivered a powerful instrument to their bondsmen. . . . Finding their spirits defined as devils or one in particular defined as *the* devil, the blacks did not readily attribute evil to the "devil," at least not at first.[10]

In the context of my research, the ethnographic material from Rocinha allows for the following analytical move as it concerns liberal politics: if religion affords power to the "underdogs" of colonial society, I suggest that this power has been significantly mobilized toward the actualization of minoritarian modes of liberalism. At the same time, dominant powers mobilize their own religious apparatus in an effort to normalize these minoritarian freedoms. As such, religion is integrated into the liberal apparatus, but in arrangements that sometimes seem to counter state power and other times seem to complement it.

My First Time

The first time that Paizinha, an Evangelical colleague from FUS, heard that I was interested in liberation services, she offered to take me to her church and show me what they did to help people find freedom. I met her in front of my house, in the same alleyway as she lived, just before 7 p.m. She was wearing a patterned dress down to her ankles, and her hair was wet. She had showered so that she could go to church clean (*limpa*) for Jesus. Her two daughters came along with her, dressed up in formal clothes. We walked down the alleyways toward the church, which was located in Raiz, the same area where I had encountered Natasha when she got ill. The name Raiz (Root) relates to the fact that this was one of the few locations in the lower parts of the slum that kept a standing tree, with long roots that were entwined with brick, water pipes, and cement.

On the way to church, we came across another of one my neighbors, Cristina. She was wearing a white T-shirt that read "Grupo de Libertação" (Liberation Group) and had a picture of a dove nesting in pieces of a broken chain. Cristina was returning from a liberation service in her own church. As we walked on, Paizinha told me: "We also have a special task force within our church that is specifically in charge of liberation. I used to be the leader of that group for a while, but it was such hard work. With my domestic life being so busy, I had to quit my position. It was a lot of responsibility!" We got to the church, and Paizinha greeted some people standing near the entrance. She introduced me as a friend. They looked excited to see a new guest. She then said I had come for the liberation service, and a woman wearing a long mauve dress informed

CHAPTER FIVE

her that the liberation service would only happen the following day, on Friday. Paizinha turned to me and said: "And what day is it today, Thursday? Oh, no . . . See how the devil is dirty? Tricking us, trying to turn you away from your path toward liberation!"

Paizinha wouldn't give up. A few weeks after our first frustrated attempt, Paizinha and her sister Laiza decided to take me to what they guaranteed to be a powerful liberation service. We took a van from Estrada da Gávea and got off at a place in Rocinha known as "99," which faces Gávea and Lagoa Rodrigo de Freitas, on the opposite side of the favela from that where we lived. The van stopped at a very sharp bend, and we alighted. Laiza vaguely remembered where the church was located. Her sister stopped an old lady to ask for information: "Excuse me! Do you know of a church around here called Tanque de Betesda [Pool of Bethesda]?" The benevolent woman told us the way.

We soon started to follow the loud music coming from the main room of the church, which was underground. In the basement of this old building, there were many chairs and some benches scattered around in front of musical instruments and a microphone. A few people were praying on their knees. Most of the women were wearing long plain dresses, with long sleeves and high collars, and they wore their hair long. The men were wearing long-sleeved shirts and dark formal pants, with some clad in full suits. A few people started singing while others trickled in. The newcomers would kneel and join the group in prayers. Paizinha told me that I didn't have to kneel, but it felt more appropriate to get down onto the ground with her.

A pastor got on the microphone and said, "God, bring us liberation! Liberate us from the desire for mundane things! Liberate women from prostitution! Liberate the Kardecists, Buddhists, and all adepts of witchcraft![11] Liberate my daughter Sheila, God."

Laiza told me that she was always happy to visit other Evangelical churches. "I am addicted to God's pleasures!" she said while looking at the preacher with admiration.

During the service, the pastor told us that nobody should be sad that night: "The enemy wants to see you sad, my brother! But God? He wants to see you happy!" They started to sing a song that reminded me of a military march, proclaiming: "I am Pentecostal! When I sing, the devil gets nauseous!" And as they kept singing and singing through the night, the Holy Spirit started to touch some people. Some women began to spin and spin as they danced. Their bodies moved faster and faster, while their long dresses started to inflate like blossoming flowers. Even if uncomfortable at the service, at different moments I felt profoundly absorbed by the experience.

After what she deemed a successful first time, Paizinha continued to invite me to more Evangelical events. I agreed to go with her and her two sisters to another liberation service, which she told me would take place near the Residents' Association (AMABB)—in a more "formalized" part of Rocinha called Bairro Barcelos.[12] In order to get to the small church located on the rooftop of a three-floor building, we had to climb a steep staircase. As we sat down inside, I noticed a slightly unpleasant smell. The pastor was a handsome young man. Despite the heat, he was wearing a suit that made him sweaty. His prayers were loud and passionate. He prayed for the youths: "Liberate this young generation!" I thought of the liberties of my young friends in the PAFYC group. He then prayed for couples: "Liberate troubled couples!" After this prayer, we sang from a hymnal called the *Evangelical Harp*, which most people carried around together with their Bibles. The lyrics of the song went: "Liberate the sinners from sin! Real freedom? Only with Jesus!" After singing that last song, the pastor invited another young man to take over the microphone for a few minutes. He was a teenager, who prayed with his eyes closed: "Jesus told me that in this liberation service He will free us from all disease! The prison of sin? We need to get out of this prison, brothers!" People clapped vigorously.

Toward the end of the service, Paizinha was invited to stand up and give her life testimonial. She said: "At first, I used to go to church just to be liberated from the demons that attacked me. Later on, I dived into it, and I tell you that God exists. He is real, and he has done wonders in my life!" The good-looking pastor closed the evening telling us that we should always be faithful to God. He warned us what could happen if we frustrated God: "Earthquakes! The world falling on top of our heads!" He used the then-recent earthquakes in Haiti as an example of God's punishment to voodoo practitioners: "God kills to punish! What if he decides to let this whole rock upon which Rocinha rests slide down on top of our houses, our families, and our heads? Let's be responsible with our faith!"

I went to bed late that night, after taking notes on the liberation of sinners, the mercy of God, and earthquakes in Rocinha. I thought about how Paizinha had made a distinction between a life dedicated to the church and people who go to the church only to get rid of their demons. If my PAFYC friends had been attending Evangelical liberation services, was it to get rid of demons? I wondered what sort of liberation they were looking for at the Universal Church of the Kingdom of God.

CHAPTER FIVE

Young Women Weeping

In late July 2009, I attended a liberation service at the UCKG main temple in Rocinha, all by myself. An acquaintance of mine, however, noticed me coming into the church and walked toward me. She sat on my left side. Mariana was a very white girl, not older than twenty, with long curly brown hair. She was Peterson's friend, the "unofficial" member of PAFYC who had been raised in the Evangelical church. "I didn't know you came here," she said, surprised to see me.

"I am interested in liberation. Do you come here often?" I replied.

"I need liberation. See how I am trembling already? I worry I will get possessed again!" She showed me her right hand, which was shaking.

"Does possession happen to you?" I asked.

"Some people doubt it. They say that I am faking it! I wish my possessions were fake . . . Unfortunately, they are not," she replied, with sad eyes.

Suddenly, it got very loud around us. The high moment of the service was starting. The voice of the pastor was rising in volume. He kept moving back and forth on the large stage at the front of the church. A spotlight followed him, making the pastor glow. Using a wireless microphone, the leader yelled: "Our God is not tied to the Cross! He has been liberated. He is in heaven. You can also liberate yourself this evening, my brother, my sister! All demons must get out of here today. I order you all to get out, demons!" He called for liberation from "witchcraft," specifically mentioning Afro-Brazilian spirits such as Pomba-gira and Tranca-Rua. "All witchcraft made for you, people of God, will be burned today! Pomba-gira, be burned! Tranca-Rua, be burned! All witchcraft be burned!" he declared. The pastor also called out what he saw as other sinful behaviors, like doing drugs or listening to sexually explicit music, such as *funk*, a style of music that originated in the favelas of Rio de Janeiro and was infamous for its sexual content.[13] "God, liberate your people from drug addiction!" he exclaimed. "Liberate them from these funk music fests [*baile funk*]!"

Mariana's body started to shake vigorously. She began to produce deep squealing noises. I was frightened and concerned. Soon, one of the many assistants to the pastor came up and grabbed her by the arm. Along with numerous others, Mariana was taken to the front of the church, near the stage. Dressed in uniforms of white tops and dark blue formal pants or skirts, the assistants started praying over the possessed.

Another woman nearby me started to scream, while jumping up and down: "Liberate me, oh Lord! Liberate me from infidelity!" she begged.

Some thirty minutes later, Mariana returned to her original place, by my side. Her pale skin was all red, and her eyes were filled with tears. The only sounds coming out of her mouth were sobs. She turned to me and said: "I am a lost cause!" She kept crying. The pastor and his team of assistants kept praying for others. Mariana's tears stopped after she told me: "At least I have been liberated from my drug addiction! That is something. Let's get out of here?" We slowly left the church before the end of the service. I didn't even know that Mariana had been an addict. The church had changed that condition. However, there was something deeper going on that made Mariana return to the UCKG. The fact that she kept getting possessed was an indication that her demons were alive. She cried, disappointed, wishing that she had been freed from all evil by then.

The concern with witchcraft was not exclusive to the UCKG. A couple of weeks earlier, Laiza had taken me to a church called Reviver (Revival). While reading Isaiah 61, the pastor referred to people "with chains on their feet" and said: "We don't want to be these people. We can't be slaves anymore! We need to break these chains, to free ourselves from these ties." The Evangelical sense of unfreedom was explicitly connected to slavery. It referenced not just the enslavement of Africans, but also all the other histories of enslavement presented in the Bible. "Not anymore!" the pastor prayed. The fear that slavery has never actually ended was clear in his preaching, the greatest of all slave owners being the devil. The pastor summoned all members of the church to pray against the devil: "Leave these lives, demon! Enough with depression and domestic fights. Let's go! Everybody, let's pray!" In addressing common problems in the lives of those who seek liberation (depression, domestic violence, and addictions), he touched their emotions and a few people started to cry. At that point, a woman grasped the microphone and demanded: "Freedom, Lord! Why live encaged? Repeat with me, everybody. Free me, Lord!" An anthem started to play: "When I am oppressed, He frees me!" Most people started to dance and felt what Laiza later described to me as "the presence of the Holy Spirit." Some started to faint at that moment, including Laiza. When that happened, the pastor covered their bodies with white pieces of cloth while the music kept playing.[14]

At a certain point, the lead pastor took the microphone back, proclaiming that she had just received a revelation from Jesus: "I see flowers for Iemanjá! God is showing me flowers in the sea. I can smell flowers of death! Someone is doing macumba, witchcraft to destroy the life of one of our sisters in this church." The pastor went quiet and closed her eyes. A tense silence pervaded the church. I kept thinking of the Afro-Brazilian divinity Iemanjá. In Brazil, the goddess of the seas. Flowers in the sea are gifts for Iemanjá. But what would "flowers of death" mean? A Trojan horse? Soon, she shouted: "But God just said that the witchcraft was undone. Burn Iemanjá! Lord, free your daughter from all evil. Take away her marital problems. Take away the macumba and offerings that were made to destroy her life!" The whole church cheered. A young woman stood from the crowd and slowly walked toward the pastor, crying. The pastor hugged her. "Jesus' message was for you today? Smile! He will change your life, okay?" she whispered into the microphone. The girl couldn't say anything; she just wept.

Afro-Brazilian Deities

It took me some time to understand the significance of having Neo-Pentecostal churches incorporate Pomba-gira, Exu, and Iemanjá within their liberation services. These are all agents from Afro-Brazilian religions, whose histories are intimately connected with the history of transatlantic slavery.[15] For Nigerians, Èṣù (Yoruba spelling of Exu) is a trickster divinity in charge of crossroads, related to movement, confusion, and, consequently, order.[16] Iemanjá, or Yemọja in Yoruba, is a water deity. Her name would more literally translate (from Yoruba) as "the mother whose children are fish."[17]

Auro was the main interlocutor who helped me to learn about these Afro-Brazilian divinities. He had been involved in Quimbanda and Umbanda practices since childhood, and later in his life with Candomblé—the three most common Afro-Brazilian religious traditions. In fact, Auro almost got fully initiated in Candomblé, but the *terreiro* (the sacred space) he had been attending was located almost two hours away from Rocinha by bus, so it was difficult to keep up regular attendance. On top of that, he also had disagreements with members of the terreiro regarding the strict sense of hierarchy in the religion. He left Candomblé when he realized that the expectations of the community were impossible for him to fulfill. "I am a child of Orixá Ogum and Orixá Iansã, dear! And a child of Ogum with Iansã likes freedom! Candomblé was not for me."[18] Auro then returned to his family tradition of Umbanda, although he also praised Brazilian Spiritism, which was more entangled with the scientific tradition of spiritual studies developed by Allan Kardec.[19] Auro remarked that, for favela dwellers, Umbanda was more accessible than

Candomblé, not to mention cheaper. He often complained of the costs involved in Candomblé rituals, given the complexity of their material practices; also, he lamented the lack of a "natural" environment in the favela, which is required in Candomblé:

There are not many Candomblé spaces in the favela. Some people say they are practicing Candomblé here, but I don't see it. For Candomblé, it is necessary to have plants, trees, pure water, and animals. In the past, there were good Candomblés in Rocinha. Now, it is almost all Umbanda and Quimbanda. It is much easier to keep an Umbanda temple, because animal sacrifice is not absolutely necessary, for example.

Once, I was invited to go down to São Conrado Beach to attend an Umbanda ceremony led by a *babalorixá* (spiritual leader) named Pai Nelson. I invited Natasha. She was not so keen on it, but it was my turn to ask for her company to walk to the beach. Once we arrived, we found a big circle of people, mostly clad in white. They were barefoot on the soft sand. In the middle of the circle, there was incense burning and drummers playing. Pai Nelson was singing: "Oh, gira! Deixa a gira girar!" (Oh, circle, let the circle turn!) People followed the song and started to move around the circle in counterclockwise direction. I was amazed to see most of the PAFYC members at the event, including my friend Samira. "Why are they all here?" I asked her.

Samira replied: "You know that fags are *macumbeiras* [practitioners of macumba], fond of these things! It's a tradition already."

Peterson overheard the conversation and offered his opinion: "I think this is because Umbanda gives people this freedom! There is this freedom of having faggots in the religion!"

Auro joined the debate and added his view: "In macumba they deal with you as you are, do you understand? They don't try to convert you into something else."

Soon after that conversation, a Brazilian indigenous spirit, Caboclo Pena Branca, possessed one of my friends.[20] After dancing for a while, the entity had a message for me: "Today, you will see that this is all real, my son. Stay here, and you will see the truth!" I got slightly frightened, and Auro laughed at my reaction. I stayed until the end of the event, well after midnight. At some point, most of the PAFYC members got possessed. Their Pomba-giras danced and drank and consulted people on the beach. Although not everything that happened will be described in detail (following their request), it was a mesmerizing ritual. Unfortunately, Caboclo Pena Branca never returned to talk to me again. Nevertheless, he was right. I returned from the beach that night feeling much more comfortable in the presence of Afro-Brazilian entities. Instead of the evil figures that some Evangelicals considered them to be, most of the spirits that were present that night seemed dedicated to charity, helping humans in their quotidian problems, even if as part of their job they also enjoyed themselves dancing and drinking alcohol.

The exchanges between Umbanda and the UCKG were messier than I realized, though. Samira came to my place a few months later and asked me to hang out with her in Beco do Foguete. I immediately said yes. There, we found Peterson seated on the pavement with a big group of people, some of whom I knew from the PAFYC crew. Peterson was agitated, wondering if anyone knew of an Umbanda ritual that they could attend that Sunday night. I was surprised to hear that he was looking for macumba, given he had told me he was an Evangelical Christian. He noticed the surprise in my face and told me: "Dude, every time that I go to the Universal Church, it is always the same thing. I get possessed there, and the spirits beat me up. A thousand things happen! So, I think I would be better off just going to some good Umbanda place to deal with my Pomba-gira once and for all."[21]

It was not only that PAFYC members were attending the UCKG liberation services; some Evangelicals who got possessed in Neo-Pentecostal churches in Rocinha were also frequenting Afro-Brazilian terreiros. Samira told me: "Most of these assistants at the Universal Church came from Umbanda in the past. They say that even Edir Macedo, the owner and main leader of the Church, attends a Candomblé terreiro here in Rio! Of course, he refutes it, but I don't doubt it." Peterson also tended to publicly deny the fact that he traveled between the two "assemblages." He was aware that the borders between the two were not meant to be crossed by humans without serious consequences. Usually, the assumption was that people gave up on one territory before moving to the other. The Evangelical concepts of conversion and baptism—and the Afro-Brazilian concept of initiation—speak to such ideals of commitment to one or the other side. Other-than-human entities, however, traveled much more freely between the two territories than humans. People like Peterson, along with spirits and Orixás, challenged the understanding of these different religions as closed systems.

If a great transit of entities were allowed between Neo-Pentecostal and Afro-Brazilian religions, this is not to say that their relationship was harmonious. Iemanjá manifested herself both in Umbanda terreiros and Evangelical churches, but her existence changed as she traveled between these spaces. In Afro-Brazilian religions, she was a deity related to water and reproduction, who helped people to create families and have children. At Reviver, however, Iemanjá was considered an Afro-Brazilian entity who destroyed families, who used flowers to seed evil, like a Trojan horse. In the Afro-Brazilian pantheon, she was one of the most cherished goddesses. At Neo-Pentecostal churches, Iemanjá was among the demons that most often presented themselves during liberation services.

The fact that Evangelical churches in Rocinha sometimes dedicated two or even three days of the week to liberation services was significant. These services were partly meant to free people from Afro-Brazilian heritage, which could be used as evidence that Christianity, as a European colonial heritage, still serves racist purposes. The "anti-slavery" preaching seemed important and potentially revolutionary. Nevertheless, most churches combined that rhetoric of liberation with the demonization of Afro-Brazilian religious power. In terms of racial makeup, even if Christianity isn't a white religion in Brazil anymore—or precisely because it isn't—it struggles to keep its "whiteness" in another sense, as a dominant locus of power. Of course, the Evangelical faithful (*crente*) were not only liberated (*libertos*) from the power of Iemanjá. Spirits such as Caboclo, Pombagira, Tranca-Rua, and other Exus could all be exorcised. These agents were accused of influencing people, making them engage in activities that were considered sinful, such as prostitution, taking or dealing drugs, or experiencing queer sexual desires. All of these "evils" could be liberated from people's lives during the religious services. Paizinha once theorized:

It is in the Bible, Moisés. You should read it. In Matthew (8:28–34), when Jesus meets a man possessed by demons, Jesus asks for his name. The man refuses to answer and keeps making sounds similar to a dying pig. Jesus asks him again, demanding an answer: "Who are you? What is your name?" And a guttural voice suddenly came out from inside him, saying: "My name is Legion, for we are many." The devil is not one; he is a legion! There are many of them, more than you imagine. That is why it is so difficult for us, humans, to recognize them all. Jesus can do it. We can't because we are sinners. The devil is dirty! He torments us under so many different forms. As people of God, all we can do is to remain vigilant. We must remain vigilant! Always.

For my Evangelical friends and their fellow church members, the devil manifested in many different forms. Above all, it manifested itself under the form of Afro-Brazilian deities.

Individual Liberation

I was at a liberation service at UCKG when a pastor summoned a man to the stage. The faithful was possessed by a spirit called Exu Cachaceiro

(Exu of Alcoholism). The pastor prayed while he waited for the possessed man to be taken to the front. His words: "Liberate your child, Lord! Liberate each individual. Each one of them! Liberate from addictions, from debts, from adultery, from AIDS, from prostitution!" While he prayed, his assistants circulated in the space, many of them moving very quickly to help people who were getting possessed. One of the assistants, a young guy wearing a white formal shirt, came near me and ordered: "Pray for your own liberation!" I could hear another helper praying over a woman by my right side. In the middle of a wave of possessions, a mother with many children fainted. Some assistants took the children to the side of the church while others said prayers over the mother. The pastor was still dealing with the first possessed man, struggling to liberate him from the Exu of Alcoholism. The pastor told him: "You will fall, demon! If you don't fall, this is because are not real. Is this brother faking it?" No true evil spirit would resist the power of God. People clapped and cheered when the demon in the man's body finally fell to his knees. One by one, people were getting their individual liberation. Toward the end of that service, the pastor announced: "For next Friday, bring a piece of hair from someone that you want to see liberated, so that we can place it near the Cross. This person's hair contains the DNA of that person, meaning the person's physical and spiritual address, okay?" We left after a final round of clapping, as the deafeningly loud sound of a happy hymn rang through the church. The level of individualization of these liberation projects reached one's DNA.

The scope of liberation also included drug dealers. Although I never witnessed armed traffickers at the UCKG, Paizinha told me that more and more of them converted to Christianity, especially if they spent time in jail. Laiza once stopped at the gate of my house to tell me about a service that she had attended in PPG, a conurbation of favelas located between Copacabana and Ipanema. "I got so scared trying to find my way to this church! I am not familiar with other favelas," she confessed. Laiza had heard about the great works (*obras*) of this congregation and always wanted to attend one of their services. She told me that traffickers ended up approaching her to ask her if she was lost. "Those traffickers belonged to the Red Command, a rival faction to the one that rules in Rocinha. Can you imagine, Moisés? Oh, Lord! I was horrified, thinking that the traffickers would ask me where I was coming from. It was a blessing that they didn't! Nothing bad happened. God looks after me as I walk after him," she told me proudly. I asked her if the service had been good. She replied: "It was great, with a lot of emphasis on liberation work. I closed my eyes and prayed, asking Jesus to liberate the bandits!

Liberate the traffickers! Liberate all drug addicts! It was very intense." As she repeated these prayers for me, she punched her left hand with the right one over and over again.

Paizinha arranged for me to meet a former drug dealer whom God had freed from his previous sinful life. I met the Black muscular man at his fiancée's house, where he lived. His family supported him while he was preparing to become a pastor. Paizinha expected me to record his testimony, and so I did. Murilo told me from behind his thick eyebrows that God had totally changed his life: "Even my tattoos changed their meaning after my liberation. Now they represent the word of God in my life. I was cruel in the past! I have stolen from people. I have killed people! This liberation is a miracle," he told me, and showed me his hands, with some letters tattooed on them. They didn't form recognizable words to me, although they obviously made sense to him. Then he said, "There are recordings of my liberation process and everything. Do you want to watch them?" He turned on the DVD player in the living room. The videos showed Murilo at many different services, at a church that I could not identify. These were short clips of pastors praying over him, asking for his liberation. During several moments, Murilo was possessed and then exorcised.

After that conversation, he invited us to his church. Paizinha agreed to come, too. The place was small, but there were a good number of people attending the service. Green plastic plants decorated the walls. Murilo himself prayed over an older lady who had difficulty walking. He raised the tone of his voice over the microphone, put his right hand on top of her head, and said: "Exu João Caveira, get out of this body.[22] She has been clamoring for liberation, Lord! May all evil be reprehended. Disease, pain: all out! All witchcraft, out now!" The woman fell on the floor. Her demons had been defeated. Murilo smiled, dried the sweat on his forehead, and asked the congregation: "A round of applause, brothers. She is liberated! Where the Holy Spirit is present, there is freedom."

Pomba-gira Dona Rosa

Exu João Caveira and others were also a frequent presence at the Umbanda ceremonies I attended.[23] I took extensive notes from one that happened at the very top of the hill in Rocinha. The location was so high up that the terreiro was still immersed in vegetation, sparse trees dying under the pressure of urbanization. The terreiro looked like a gated yard, fenced on all sides by white walls. At the center of the compound, there was a structure built with red bricks. It looked like a large shed with very low ceilings. Lots of wine and *cachaça* (a Brazilian sugarcane-based spirit) were distributed at the ritual. The abundance impressed me. Samira told me that she was eager to talk to Dona Rosa, a Pomba-gira who liked to wear a red rose in her hair, from whom she needed some advice. However, nobody knew for sure if Dona Rosa would come that night to possess one of the participants.

Much later in the night, that one Pomba-gira did arrive. Cacau's body trembled violently while getting possessed by her. Dona Rosa came almost at the same time that the first golden rays of sunshine began to penetrate through the smoky air in the room. Exus like to smoke cigars, whereas Pomba-giras seem to prefer cigarettes. At that moment, Samira started to tremble a bit, too. Was it an unexpected possession? I wondered. Samira smiled and told me that she was just very anxious to consult with Dona Rosa. The Pomba-gira ignored us for a long time, making Samira even more apprehensive. I advised her to go after Dona Rosa, but, out of respect, she said she preferred to wait for her turn to talk to the spirit. When Dona Rosa finally approached us, she took Samira by the hand and led her out of the house. I got a bit tense, wondering where my friend had been taken. After a while, Samira returned to my company, with a list of materials that she needed to assemble for an offering (*despacho*) to Exu. "I'll prepare it and put it at one of the crossroads in between the favela and São Conrado," she told me earnestly. Dona Rosa had given her exact instructions of what to do to please Exu and, in exchange, get whatever it was that Samira had asked for.

Devilish Powers

Granted that there are several contextual differences, I started to wonder: for certain minorities, such as queer people adept with Afro-Brazilian religions in the favela, would the UCKG have a similar effect as the Catholic Church during the colonization of Latin America? At the same time that the UCKG proposes to remove the devil's presence (in his multiple manifestations) from the lives of favela dwellers, it also invests Afro-Brazilian entities with power. Liberation services operated both as an affirmation of the dominant power of Christianity (at every victory of Jesus over his enemies) and, concurrently, as a form of recognition that the minoritarian power of these Afro-Brazilian spirits and deities should be acknowledged and feared (due to their capacity to affect normative life).[24]

Natasha claimed privileged relations with the devil. I was present during a heated argument she once had with her mother. "Remember that soap opera in which a woman deceived the devil? I'm worse than the devil myself!"[25] Natasha stated, well aware of the fact that her mother, Dona Rosário, blamed the devil for Natasha's "deviant" sexual liberties. She rarely attended Afro-Brazilian spaces, although she did practice what she called *magia* (magic) or, at times, *feitiçaria* (witchcraft). Auro once explained to me that these magic practices in the favela presented a combination of indigenous religious elements and Afro-Brazilian ones, but didn't constitute a "religion" per se. In any case, if the devil is strong, as Christianity recognizes it to be, Natasha used to say that she was stronger than the devil. If her liberties were not accepted by her mother and Christian morality, Natasha was proud to occupy a minoritarian liberal position: *libertinism*.

It was not only Natasha's mother who attributed the violation of gender and sexual normativity to demonic agencies. When I visited Nivaldo's mother in Martinslândia, she had also expressed her desire for the liberation of her queer son. In a dry tone, she told me, "I worry about Nivaldo. This spirit of homosexuality needs to be liberated from him! I do not accept this."

Dona Rosário had tried to cut the conversation short, in case I got offended. Instead, I was curious. "How can he be liberated? Do you mean he should go attend a liberation service?" I asked.

She answered, "It is not so much the service. If you accept Jesus as the truth, you start to get liberated already. If the person wants it, Jesus liberates them!"

Amélia was present during the conversation and later expressed her views: "What an ugly thing not to accept people as they are! I didn't like Nivaldo's mother. No, I didn't."

The Catholic Church and the UCKG

In late January 2010, I went to mass with Amélia during our unforgettable trip to Ceará. Old church bells kept ringing. She also had grown up attending the Catholic Church on the main square in her town. Everyone there was well dressed. Some ladies were wearing high heels. At the entrance, a young woman walked by us in a white T-shirt with the phrase: "I am at liberty to love God" (*Sou livre para amar a Deus*). Mass was due to start at 6:30 p.m., and the church was at full capacity. The smell of frankincense filled the pews. Amélia no longer knew the parish priest, who was a short man with dark and sleek hair. The young priest began the homily by saying: "Freed and captives are both parts of the same church. One body in Christ." Discreetly, I took notes in my little notebook. I remembered the slavery past of the sugarcane plantations in the Northeast and wondered if the homily would be geared toward the pervasive racism that I encountered in the interior of Ceará. The priest continued: "God sent Jesus to free the slaves. Liberate them from all evil! Lord, deliver us from evil."

I realized that Catholics and Neo-Pentecostal Evangelicals held different understandings of the meaning of slavery that appeared in the Bible.[26] For the former, according to my Catholic friend Pedro, who worked in a stationery store in Rocinha, the biblical category of slaves could also be understood as the current class of the oppressed, in a more Abrahamic fashion. The liberation of slaves, in that sense, was a collective affair. This was the more standard interpretation of liberation theology, which was common in Latin America in the 1980s.[27] In those years, the Catholic Church often worked for the well-being of the favela community as a whole, struggling to improve the lives of favela dwellers through the collective work groups called *mutirões*. These groups would focus on collective problems such as water supply, trash collection, sewage management, and even the construction of houses for the homeless. The Catholic Church in Rocinha was also concerned with the broader problem regarding the devil and made an effort to enforce a Christian morality—emphasizing heteronormative relations and "the family" as sacred values. However, they were much less focused on "homosexuality" as an individual issue.

The UCKG, by contrast, focused much more on a variety of individual sins as a form of slavery, providing a more immediate type of liberation—under the form of personal autonomy from evil and without connecting sins to more structural issues.[28] At the UCKG, the liberation of LGBTQ individuals was much more explicit and aggressive. I witnessed a variety of instances in which the female spirits of Pomba-gira were blamed for transgressions of gender and sexual norms. When I met Raimundo, one of my FUS students, at Gay Pride in Copacabana, he told me that his mother was a member the UCKG. My immediate reaction was to ask him: "And doesn't she want to liberate you from evil? Chase your Pomba-gira spirit out?"

He replied, "She tried, she really tried hard, but she couldn't do it! Now she's even stopped trying to liberate the Pomba-gira spirit out of other people. First, she would have to be able to solve the case of my own Pomba-gira, right?" Raimundo laughed and then added, "She says this is not her gift. I think she should just leave us alone."

Despite its shortcomings, the Evangelical mode of liberation has been a growing force in Brazilian favelas. At the same time, regardless of the merits of liberation theology, with the end of the cold war and the global emergence of neoliberalism in the 1990s, the Catholic liberation efforts lost momentum both in Rome and in Latin America. Dona Rosário, for her part, refused to go to the Evangelical church. She praised the liberation efforts of the Catholic Church from the past and longed for the old days. However, as a collective effort against class oppression, Catholic liberation didn't seem very helpful in solving the main problem Dona Rosário had with her daughter. Despite this fact, Natasha's mother used to say that she was a more traditional woman and dismissed the Evangelical church as a "new creation." Meanwhile, the combination of prosperity theology[29] and a more individualistic mode of religious liberation adopted by Evangelical churches are much more aligned with neoliberal aspirations. It is not a coincidence that the power of Evangelicals and the forces of neoliberalism grow side by side in poor urban neighbors in Latin America: they are deeply connected through normative liberalism.

Peterson's Ambivalence

A conversation I had in Rocinha in mid-2009 now comes to mind. Auro and I ran into Peterson waiting for some people on Rua do Valão. His friends were coming back from an Umbanda ceremony. The three of us talked for a while, but Auro soon lost his patience with Peterson's rumblings. He used to call Peterson a "crazy faggot" (*viado colori*). "Keep talking the two of you. I am going home!" Auro said, and abruptly left us.

I stayed and asked Peterson if he had seen Natasha around. "I almost never see her! She is more into sex than religion!" he said, and laughed.

"What about the PAFYC crew? They seem to like both?" I said.

Peterson laughed even louder. He shook his head disapprovingly and told me:

What they really like is dick, but they also like macumba. Sometimes both at the same time! And they go to the Universal Church once in a while. It was me who took them to the Universal Church for the first time, did you know that? I told them about the liberation services there. Many of them attend it now! They get possessed there and everything. Although I think there is a lot of faking going on too! Lately, they have not gone to church so often because their babalorixá, Pai Jair, forbids them. Jair said that they have to choose if they want to get possessed in Umbanda or in the Evangelical church. It has to be one or the other! But some insist on both.

CHAPTER FIVE

He noticed I was interested in the topic and kept talking:

I never faked being possessed like these guys do, you know? Ever since I was a child, I could see spirits, even when I belonged to the Evangelical church and I was firm in my faith as a Christian. Later on, I went off track a bit, but I still go to my own church and also to the Universal Church to be liberated from these evil entities that tempt me. But I've also gone to some macumba rituals lately.

I asked him directly, "And why do you keep going to macumba and the church at the same time?"

He gave me an elaborate answer, recalling one of the biggest Brazilian celebrities of the 1980s, a blond TV presenter called Xuxa. Peterson guaranteed that Xuxa got everything in life from going to macumba rituals. "Fame, money, everything!" he affirmed. Having said that, Peterson also tried to emphasize an important difference between himself and most of the PAFYC kids: "I may go to macumba; I am there to get power. I am not there to be a slave of these spiritual entities." He said this in reference to the fact that the others bowed to the spirits, cooked for them, and bought them gifts. "But I know some of these entities deceive us!" he complained, and recounted: "One day at the beach, I asked a spirit for help, and she pretended she was cleansing my body from evil. Guess what? I got sick right after that cleansing! After that day, it was only when I went back to the Universal Church again that I got better. It was the Universal Church that liberated whatever bad spell that wicked Pomba-gira put into me!"

Peterson and I hung out a bit more. I kept thinking about his Evangelical upbringing and his conceptions of macumba. Peterson trusted the Afro-Brazilian deities to give him power but didn't trust their goodness. As a Christian, he acknowledged the risk of submitting himself to spirits and other deities. His objective was to master Afro-Brazilian entities for his benefit, not to subject himself to them. He noticed that I was quiet, reflecting more than speaking. I guess he got bored. He soon announced that he would have to leave me to meet his other friends.

Self-Possessed Subjects

Spirit possession is usually talked about as some sort of alterity device, producing a sense of "otherness" in relation to post-Enlightenment conceptions of the rational individual—the universal subject in the modern project of normative liberalism. From colonial times to today, experiences of "spirit possession" help to reinforce the binary between modern liberal subjects—those with a marked rationality (who are self-possessed)—and other minoritarian subjects who were liable to be possessed by spirits and other entities, due to their presupposed deficient capacity for self-government.[30] If normative liberalism imposes a particular form of freedom, which is meant to be used for rational self-government,[31] the constantly possessed bodies of my queer friends in Rocinha were doomed to unfreedom. From a minoritarian liberal perspective, however, this binary did not make much sense—queer liberalism in Rocinha was not limited to the conditions of possibility prescribed by normative liberalism.[32] Furthermore, as the social scientists Marco Aurélio Luz and Georges Lapassade remind us, Exu and Pomba-gira can also be interpreted as "symbols of a libertarian proposition."[33]

Can "spirit possession" be understood as empowering a minoritarian mode of liberalism among my LGBTQ friends in Rocinha? Combining the "libertarian proposal" inherent in macumba with Taussig's suggestion that the Christian demonization of minoritarian deities inadvertently served to empower them,[34] the ways that my LGBTQ friends move between relations with Afro-Brazilian deities and Christian demonization point toward a deeper process of recursive possessions and liberations. There are two main points to highlight: first, their refusal to inhabit a normative liberal body (i.e., one ontologically sealed from exterior forces, overdetermined by rationality, and individualized) was itself a deterritorialization of liberalism; second, their constant testing of the limits between what it is usually conceived as distinct and (internally) homogeneous religious practices challenges the normative place that "religion" must occupy in liberal (multicultural) societies.

Still, these experiences seem to pose a central question: Did the UCKG have the power to liberate queer people, helping to turn them into more normative subjects? Every time a PAFYC member attended a liberation service at the UCKG, they were also affirming their existence as queer subjects. Every time one of them was liberated from Pomba-gira and returned the following week to be liberated again and again, they created a recursive loop. The effect was that, despite some defeats along the way, in the long term, it was the Pomba-gira who won. It was the Pomba-gira that they counted upon to promote a minoritarian liberation from Christian morality. As Peterson articulated, the common response that the UCKG offered to explain the victory of the "devil" in some cases was to argue that PAFYC members were faking their possessions.

As for Peterson, his reasons for attending both the UCKG and Umbanda at the same time were based on a different principle. In relation to his experiences in Africa, the anthropologist Peter Geschiere argues that witchcraft can work as a leveling force, empowering the most vulnerable. This is how it seemed to work for Natasha. However, Geschiere also highlights that, with the rise of neoliberalism, witchcraft has been used more and more to create wealth and power, creating "new inequalities and relations of domination."[35] This is how it seemed to be for Peterson. He explained his calculations in terms of power, while making sure to highlight the authenticity of his possessions. Being raised Neo-Pentecostal, he was certain that the devil was evil, and he refused to serve the devil. However, he also strived to obtain empowerment from his relations with demons. He hoped to use the devil's agency to liberate himself from his *individual* subaltern position—obtaining money and power by becoming a celebrity. But if he were to be free exclusively in the sense afforded by his Neo-Pentecostal church, Peterson could not live his life as a queer subject.

Importantly, Peterson's view did not reflect the minoritarian form of empowerment that my other queer friends sought in Afro-Brazilian traditions. In transiting between the two territories, though, he was indeed exploring multiple possibilities for his queerness. While PAFYC members tried to use the powers of Afro-Brazilian spirits and gods to satisfy their minoritarian desires—more men, more sex, more queerness—Peterson looked to the devil to obtain the normalization of his queerness under the form of an affluent liberal lifestyle—more typical of a white, gay, middle-class form of pride.

A Police Case

For one of my last visits to the UCKG, I invited my neighbor Carcará to come along to church with me. He used to be a member of the UCKG in the past and gladly accepted the invitation. That day, the pastor spent almost an hour discussing a federal investigation against the UCKG regarding illegal fundraising and tax evasion. The potential scandal was massive. The main Brazilian TV channel, Globo, was actively reporting the case during the whole month of August in 2009. The pastor started the service that day by warning people that the church was once again under the attack of the devil. "TV Globo is trying to challenge your faith in the Universal Church. Watch out!" he said. A few minutes later, he warned that we all needed to be attentive, because reporters were coming to church services just to collect information and then spread lies to the public. Aggressively, he stated: "If you look and see anyone with a camera or a voice recorder near you, you can grab it and break it! I give you permission to do that, okay?" The atmosphere was tense that day, and the liberation service was unusual because the church was empty compared to previous weeks. Carcará complained to me that he didn't feel much liberation. He preferred his own church in Copacabana.

The following Friday, I returned to the UCKG. This time, I was with a friend of mine from college in Brasília, who came to visit me in the favela while spending a few days in Rio de Janeiro. Although he was a devout Catholic, my friend kindly agreed to attend an Evangelical liberation service with me. Later, we would go out for dinner. The church that day had a lot more people. Notably, there were more church staff present: more assistants, pastors, and even private security, who guarded the entrances to the main hall. Not even halfway into the service, the liberation prayers started. My friend looked uncomfortable. We both started to follow the gestures of the crowds, taking part in the service as much as we possibly could. "Oh Lord, liberate all evil from this room!" the pastor prayed. People brought both hands to their heads and then pushed them away, driving out the evil. The prayers continued. I briefly took a notebook from my pocket, jotted down a few words, and continued to follow the service. People started to become possessed. Then the pastor gestured to one of his assistants onstage and pointed toward me. I figured that someone must be getting possessed near me, so I looked around. I noticed two bouncers talking. I looked at the pastor again. He nodded to the bouncers. I started to realize the problem was with me.

The two bouncers moved closer to us, approaching us from the left-hand side. The men wearing black suits and white shirts pointed at us. But I wasn't possessed, I thought. They insisted we come with them, making my friend and I squeeze through the crowds of worshippers. When we got closer, they said that we had to leave the church. We didn't follow their orders. The two men grabbed us by the arms and forced us through a side door to the outside. In a dark corridor, they pushed us against the wall and inquired: "Do you have any cameras or recorders in your possession?"

I promptly replied: "No!"

They insisted, "Give us your recorder!"

"I don't have one!" I said. I was telling the truth; I did not carry a voice recorder around with me during fieldwork.

"I saw you writing!" one said.

"So what? What is the problem with writing?" I argued.

CHAPTER FIVE

"Either you give us the material, or else we are going to take it from you by force!" the tallest one shouted. We were in danger. Still, I refused to comply with what seemed to be a preposterous request.

My friend tried to leave the church. The bouncers lost their patience with us and aggressively took us to the back of the building, using brute force. At that moment, I realized that anything could happen. The stakes were very high. Because they were under federal investigation, the UCKG assumed that anyone in the church could be a threat to their interests. At the back, two pastors were standing waiting for us. "Take everything from them," the older pastor ordered. The taller bouncer held my arms while the smaller one inspected me, pocket by pocket. I resisted, but he forced his hands inside my clothes. Everything they found went to the pastors for examination. At that moment, I lost the faith I was trying to build in order to understand the church from the perspective of my Evangelical friends. "Why are you stealing from me?" They took my phone, keys, wallet, and notebook, carefully examining everything. The younger pastor returned all our belongings, except for my valuable notebook, which was filled with notes on Neo-Pentecostal liberalism. The bouncers forced us out of the limits of the church, kicking us out through the main gate, onto the street.

I was shocked and felt violated. Standing on the pavement, I wanted my notebook back and justice to be done. I thought about going back inside the church. The friend from Brasília looked horrified. We talked briefly about what to do. He suggested calling the police. I suggested calling the media. Both options could put us in danger, however. It was the law of the Hillside not to attract the police (or the media) to the favela. A horrible thought occurred to me. The UCKG pastors could have connections to the drug traffickers in Rocinha, as they were actively engaged in the conversion of traffickers to Christianity. What if they had told the traffickers about the incident already? What if the traffickers thought we were federal agents conducting a criminal investigation in the area? Or journalists trying to infiltrate the favela?[36] I had not asked for permission from the Owner of the Hillside to live in Rocinha in the first place.[37] I reached for my phone and quickly looked for numbers to call for help. I tried Amélia's first, but I was unable to connect to her. Cell phone signal was precarious at many locations in the favela—calling a landline would be my best bet. I couldn't find Carcará's number in my phone. Finally, I remembered that there were evening classes at FUS on Fridays, and I decided to call the school's landline. The NGO's director, Armando, picked up the phone and listened to me telling a disjointed version of the story. He instructed us to stay still in front of the UCKG until someone from the favela reached me. I tried calling a few more numbers without success. I started to fear that such a traumatic event would also mean the end of my research in Rocinha.

"Moisés! What happened!" Paizinha yelled from a distance. A large group of people from the alleyway where I lived kept coming toward us. Armando was breathless. He had stopped at different houses along the way to gather people to help me. "To the police station now! Let's go!" he ordered.

"The police? Are you sure?" I asked.

"Of course! These Evangelical people have to learn that they cannot do whatever they want in the favela," Armando replied.

"What about the traffickers?" I asked.

"What? Do you want to report them to the traffickers too?" he questioned.

I explained, "No, I mean, will I not get in trouble with the traffickers if we go to the police?"

He reassured me, "We are going to take a taxi to the police station in Gávea! It is not the same as calling the police to Rocinha. Let's go!"

At the police station, I pressed charges against the UCKG. After talking to the police officer, describing in detail what had happened, I was given a copy of an official document formalizing the case against the UCKG. The accusation was based on a particular article of the Brazilian Criminal Code, which referred to the protection of my individual freedom (*liberdade individual*).[38] When I read the document, still nervous, I smiled for a second and thought: "Ethnographic research can be very serendipitous, indeed. This charge is a clear instance of normative liberalism working in my favor. Would Natasha ever resort to the police for justice if in this same situation? Never!" I was living in the favela for fieldwork, a period that would end sooner or later. Whatever happened, even if the traffickers decided to kill me, my position carried privileges, such as access to the judicial system. In any case, that episode had revealed an important distinction between a normative mode of liberalism based on nation-state power and one based on God's power: Neo-Pentecostal liberalism. I was terrified to return home that night because I was still unsure about how the traffickers would treat me. My friend from college told me he would never return to the UCKG again. He went straight from the police station to his hotel room in Ipanema.

Amélia invited me to have breakfast with her the day after the whole episode. She knew I was traumatized. While we ate our food, TV Globo broadcasted a campaign: "Liberdade de expressão é na Globo!" (Freedom of expression has a place on Globo!) After a few more days locked away at home, I decided that I would no longer hide myself. Whatever happened, I would face it. Natasha was the first person I wanted to see. She was totally unaware of the situation; she didn't hang out with my neighbors. I met her in the company of her friend Bira and told them the story, still ashamed of everything: "Guess what? I was kicked out of the Universal Church by some stupid bouncers there! Let me tell you . . ."

Natasha hugged me, and Bira scolded me: "But why on earth would you go to a place like this, fag? The Universal Church? That horrible place!" I explained that I had been going there to learn more about their liberation services. He promptly replied, "Liberation? Oh my God! Right . . . this liberation thing is a lie, butterfly! Are you that stupid, fag? These devilish PAFYC kids (*diabinhos*) only go there because they think it's funny!" If there were people like Peterson who doubted the truthfulness of possessions happening at church, there were also those, like Bira, who questioned the reality of UCKG liberations. He added: "I don't believe in ex-fag, darling! If you are a fag, you are a fag. No church can change that."

Natasha added her own two cents: "I know a travesti who said she was liberated at the Universal Church. She even wears male clothing now! But I don't trust that bitch."

After the incident, even Paizinha told me that she had strong reservations against the UCKG: "They don't follow the Bible as they should. This is a big problem. My father likes to attend their services. You know that. But I already warned him. And he was very sad to hear what they did to you there." Most neighbors were in solidarity with me, even those who were faithful members of the UCKG. "One last thing," Paizinha added, looking sadly into my eyes. "Don't give up on your liberation. The devil might be trying to send you off track, but Jesus is good to you. Isn't he? How many times did Jesus expose your sins during a liberation service? How many times did he reveal in public that you are a homosexual? None. Not a single time, Moisés. The Lord is good! He has a plan for your life."

The Folds and Fractures of Liberalism

Talal Asad argues that there is a modern liberal demand that religion be kept separate from politics, law, and science. This separation would, at once, guarantee the confinement of religion (for secular liberals) and the possibility of religion (for liberal Christians) as part of modernity.[39] In a sense, there is a version of normative liberalism that satisfies the conditions of existence of both state and religion at once. Like any form of normative liberalism, however, the norm that makes it possible for nation-state and religion to coexist freely—that is, secularism—seems to assume a position of dominance and universality vis-à-vis other possibilities of freedom, such as Neo-Pentecostal liberalism. Nevertheless, I would argue that the episode in which I ended up confronting the UCKG, mobilizing the Brazilian judiciary, does not reveal a fracture between church and state in Brazil. It is more like a fold between the two, an encounter between modes of normativity. As the philosopher and artist Simon O'Sullivan poetically explains, "The fold announces that the inside is nothing more than a fold of the outside."[40] Be it through the book of Brazilian laws, the Constitution, or through the book of Christian laws, the Bible, we are still talking about a universal will to govern through a politics of freedom based on capital accumulation (or prosperity theology), normative family values, and individual autonomy. The nation-state and the Neo-Pentecostal church operate together within the same assemblage geared toward the normalization of minoritarian groups, but they do so from different sides.

Folds are relevant not because they demonstrate that different forms of normative liberalism exist in practice, but because they demonstrate that the normative liberal project operates on more fronts than one, not as a unified project, but as different projects that conceive of themselves as universalizing. Despite the idealized separation between church and state, the articulation between these two domains, as a project of power, has become more and more evident in Brazil in the decade since I completed my fieldwork. The current far-right-wing Brazilian president, Jair Bolsonaro, managed to be elected in 2018 as part of a deal with Evangelical churches, and particularly through an alliance with the UCKG.

According to Jean and John Comaroff, anthropologists whose work explores the expansion of Evangelical denominations in Africa, religious expansion, occult practices, and a weakening of the political sphere are all part of the spread of what they call the "culture of neoliberalism."[41] Normative liberalism in the Marvelous City is also based on Evangelical religious expansion and a state that fails favela dwellers while protecting the elites. Both the nation-state and religious authorities are part of a multifold normative liberal assemblage that strives to colonize minoritarian liberalisms, for the political and economic benefit of the Brazilian elites.

Queer favela dwellers are aware of these forms of domination and produce their own "disidentified" reactions, in part by mobilizing the devil and using "witchcraft" as a form of minoritarian empowerment, as Natasha did. Others, however, do so by offering up their bodies to other-than-human agencies, deterritorializing the very normative ideal of self-possessed individuals.[42] Instead of supporting normative liberalism from different angles, another strategy for queer liberation would be to focus on the actual fractures in the normative project. The movement of queer subjects between Afro-Brazilian religions and the UCKG exposes gaps in liberal understandings of self, bodies, and personhood. It took me extended and detailed ethnographic tracing to map these folds and fractures. But there is a value in slowing down our assumptions regarding contemporary liberal politics.

SIX

Roman Slavery

> It is not the product of his or her labor that the worker has a right to, but to the satisfaction of his or her needs, whatever may be their nature. JOSEPH DÉJAQUE, "L'ECHANGE"

One evening Auro's best friend Marcus and I took the bus from Rocinha and got off near Praça do Ó, very close to the beach in Barra da Tijuca. It didn't take us long to find KB7, a sex worker, whom we had planned to interview that night. She walked toward us, wearing a black dress. KB7 was tall with long and sleek caramel hair; she was wearing a wig. Marcus introduced me. He told her that I was living in Rocinha, researching liberalism. KB7 stared at us, puzzled, and remarked: "Liberalism? Well, I can't help. I still need to be *liberated from my sins*, you know? I've never been to the Universal Church, my dear!" She laughed.

As KB7 reminded us, the UCKG was a (normative) liberal force operating in these sex assemblages.[1] Neo-Pentecostal churches delivered liberation to sex workers through spiritual means. According to my friend Paizinha, the Laws of God were explicit in abominating the practice. Both male and female sex workers were considered slaves to sin in the eyes of God.[2] In Quimbanda and Umbanda, Afro-Brazilian religions, spirits under the category of Pomba-gira were celebrated, and even consulted, precisely because of their expertise as sex workers. Those known as Pomba-gira do Cabaré (Pomba-gira of the Cabaret), for example, were referred to as spirits of dead sex workers who offered their sexual knowledge to help the Afro-Brazilian faithful in their

143

romantic affairs. It wasn't by chance, though, that in several Evangelical services that I attended in Rocinha, an everyday clamor was related to the liberation of sinners from the spirits of Pomba-gira. These spirits were among the main targets of exorcisms geared toward the liberation from the "deviance" of sex work, extramarital affairs, and other sexual behaviors considered sinful.

After her sarcastic comment regarding the UCKG, KB7 turned around and took us by the hand to the spot where she usually waited for clients, by the side of the road, where the flux of cars was most intense. She introduced us to the other travestis who were working with her: "These are my friends from Rocinha!" None of the others were from the same favela. Marcus and KB7 talked about old friends they had in common. He asked her for news regarding someone I had never heard about. "Paloma? She is still in Italy, darling! They say she was caught by the *alibã* [policemen] there. I don't know. But I think she is free again," KB7 told him.

"Free and glamourous? And in Milano! I love Milano," Marcus, who worked for an airline, remarked.

A car stopped, and KB7 pulled up her dress up to better show her beautiful legs while she talked to the driver. No success. The middle-aged man drove away. We spoke until Marcus informed me that we were disrupting the influx of clients. Expensive cars were slowly driving by, but they were not stopping near us. We told KB7 we were headed back to Rocinha. Before leaving, Marcus and KB7 made promises to see each other more often. "Sure! I miss you, darling!" She waved goodbye.

Battling Again

Formal interviews, like the one I had tried to host with KB7, didn't seem to work very well in my research context, even if the encounters that they enabled were always valuable. At other times, however, I didn't even need to encounter my friends in person to learn important information from conversations I initially assumed would be uneventful:

"What are you up to? I'm on my way to Lapa [a neighborhood in Rio de Janeiro]!" Natasha told me over the phone.

"Going out by yourself? Hmmm . . ." I remarked.

"Going to work [*batalhar*, literally, to battle], darling! Do you want to come?" she asked me.

"Oh . . . what do you mean, work in Lapa? Sex work [*fazer pista*]? Seriously?" I was surprised to hear it.

"What?" she said impatiently.

"I thought you had quit?" I replied.

"Yes, I did. But . . . you know! You want to come or not?" she asked me.

"No, it's fine!" I lied. I wanted to go.

"You could have fun with a boy-fag [bicha-boy] while I make my money," Natasha proposed.

"No, it's okay . . ." I said, turning her down.

"Since I lost that restaurant job, I have been going back to Lapa. You know, my brothers pay the rent. And I won't starve. But I need other things in life, right? Like, shoes! And who can live without high heels? There are two things I love, high heels and men! They are the perfect combination. I get horny!" Natasha laughed out loud.

"Ha-ha-ha! Okay, Nat. But look after yourself, please?" I begged her.

"Who is going to mess with a travesti like me?" She laughed again.

"I mean, make sure you wear condoms!" I clarified.

"They do offer me more money to fuck without condoms! Did you know it? But do you think I'm crazy, Moisés?" Natasha asked me.

"Be safe!" I said.

"Wish for cute men [*gatinhos*]! That is more important!"

I could hear her smile. "Okay, see you tomorrow!" I hung up, worried.

I had been to Lapa with Natasha on other occasions. I knew this bohemian area of Rio. What I didn't realize was that Natasha had been engaging in sex work again. It didn't seem like a big deal for her in the same way that it was for me. The next time I met her in person, I made a point of talking to her about it. She told me:

I prefer not to do it because my family doesn't like it. I also think that a travesti can do other work, you know? I don't mind cooking and cleaning for money. A lot of my friends work in hair salons. But I am not good with hair! Sex work [*fazer pista*] is good, but I am not a professional. I don't do it all the time, and I don't make much money out of it. My friend, Shelly, remember? She is a manager and makes good money! She even wanted me to join her team . . . But I would have to put in silicone implants and everything. I don't even like to take hormones every day! I don't think I will ever be a professional.

During those days when she was doing sex work, Natasha would leave home in the early evening—all dressed up, carrying only a clutch purse. Some other travestis preferred to be less conspicuous, taking their gear in a bigger bag and getting ready for work (*montar-se*) on the spot or nearby. Natasha would take public transport to get to Lapa, a neighborhood

CHAPTER SIX

known for its iconic white arches, the Arcos da Lapa, which were built in colonial times, Roman style. More than a tourist attraction, it was a bridge for the tram line, and the arches once served as an aqueduct in the Marvelous City. Nowadays, they marked the entrance to a relegated area of town, which the municipality had been trying to gentrify, without much success. As such, Lapa seemed to attract a diverse public, ranging from a heteronormative elite crowd—who frequented some of the most expensive and touristy bars—to queer favela dwellers, who mainly occupied the streets and some specific LGBTQ venues in the area, such as the nightclub Buraco da Lacraia (Centipede's Hole), known as a venue for the working-class public.

Sex Work Venues

During a conversation on the topic, Auro offered up an overview of what could be called a "geography of prostitution" in the city of Rio de Janeiro.[3] "It's not anyone that can work (*batalhar*) anywhere, you know? There is a place for everything. There is a place for women, a place for men, and a place for travestis. And not just that. If you are ugly, you can only work in some areas." He laughed with derision, spreading his lips widely. "Your friend, Natasha, for example! I doubt that they would let her work in Barra da Tijuca. Oh, certainly not in Copacabana![4] No, no . . . only the most beautiful ones work in Copacabana. And Natasha is an ugly matesca! Look at her. Maybe she could work in that other place . . . What is it called again? Quinta da Boa Vista.[5] Maybe there! Or maybe in Lapa?" he continued, with his usual sarcastic personality. Auro knew that I disliked the way he talked about Natasha, but he insisted on harping on her. I wondered if he was jealous of my friendship with her or if he disliked Natasha for the mere fact that she was a migrant. When they met in person, Auro and Natasha would treat each other nicely. When they were apart, both parties expressed their negative opinions of the other.

"Do you know my friend Giulia?" Auro asked me—and then kept speaking. "Giulia is a travesti, but she is a perfect woman! I mean, recently she has become even more beautiful. Astonishing [*um tombo*]! So, Giulia works in Quinta da Boa Vista. But she could do much better than that. Even the beautiful ones find it hard to get a place in Copacabana now. You need to pay rent to the *mocotona* [the most powerful travesti in charge of the area] for a spot. Maybe Giulia doesn't want to move." Auro kept talking, in a conversation that felt more like a monologue. "Natasha? Not even if she wanted to . . . Because she is too thin, no curves!"

He returned to his evaluation of Natasha's prospects in sex work. "Oh, another thing. There is a place for women and a place for travesti in Copacabana. Did you know that, fag? They don't like to mix. In Barra da Tijuca, Praça do Ó is basically all travestis. In Vila Mimosa, it's mostly women.[6] Then, for men [*gigolo*] . . . Real men? Well, they think they are real men, but I think they are all *mariconas* [fags]![7] Anyways . . . for men, there is Via Ápia. But it is not this Via Ápia here in Rocinha. No, I am talking about the Via Ápia there in the city center. In the area near that hospital, Santa Casa, okay? Natasha is more like a Madureira type, a cheap snack for the suburban poor.[8] In fact, the travestis that look more like a wreck don't even get out of Rocinha."

There were several prostitution spots in the favela. Some of them were around the many bars near Rua do Boiadeiro. During my first weeks living in Rocinha, I came across a blue sign while standing on the sidewalk in Boiadeiro, the commercial area of the favela located near the Asphalt. Address plaques put up by the municipality, like that one, were so unusual in Rocinha that I decided to move closer to read it: "Travessa Liberdade [Liberty Street]." I looked down a slope and noticed that Travessa Liberdade connected Rua do Boiadeiro to one of the busiest commercial streets in the favela, majestically called Via Ápia, in colonial fashion.[9] I reflected on the juxtaposition, took some notes, and walked down Travessa Liberdade. The first bar at the very corner of Travessa Liberdade and Rua do Boiadeiro was called Bar da Liberdade (Freedom Bar). My friend Carmélia, a powerful Black woman who owned a day-care center in Rocinha, lived very close to that location. She was the one who explained the importance of those bars, quoting the 1985 song "Mesa de Bar" by Alcione and Gonzaguinha: "É que mesa de bar é onde se toma um porre de liberdade! Companheiros em pleno exercício de democracia!" (It is just that a bar's table is where one gets drunk with freedom! Comrades in full exercise of democracy!)

Almost a year after that initial exploration, in early 2010, I explicitly asked one of my students from FUS about the place in Boiadeiro: "Is that where you live? Near Travessa Liberdade? Why does that street have this name? Do you know it?"

She replied, "Huh! I don't know!" Then she gave it some more thought and added, "Travessa Liberdade is where everything happens. Drug trade, prostitution, all these things. Everything is allowed!" She hit upon an explanation that resonated well with the concept of *favela liberalism* as I had come to understand it, as discussed in previous chapters. I had reason to believe that sex work was also part of a liberal heterotopia that existed in Rocinha and fostered minoritarian modes of liberalism.

CHAPTER SIX

Giulia

The beach areas in Rio were also venues for sex work. As someone born and raised in a landlocked part of Brazil, I saw it as a privilege to be so close to the sea when living in Rocinha. I used any opportunity I had to go to the beach. Swimming by my side, in between the waves, my neighbor Ricky (the one who loved motorcycles) remarked once, "I feel free like a bird when I am in the water!" Liberty is often experienced as a feeling. It was at São Conrado Beach that Natasha, Mazinho, and many PAFYC members had sex almost on a daily basis, often in the evenings. Most of the times, unpaid sex, which seemed to disrupt the scene for more professional activity at that particular spot near Rocinha.

It was also on São Conrado Beach that I had a long conversation with Giulia. She was sunbathing, wearing the smallest imaginable bikini, and her red hair lit up under the sun like fire. As I approached, I got a waft of tanning oil scent. Giulia showed me her breasts. "I am working on my tan lines! These are valuable!" But I confess that she left me wondering more about her penis: how did she manage to tuck it in (*trucar*) so perfectly? I joined her group of friends and listened as they talked about men. Giulia described some of her experiences as a sex worker in the area around Quinta da Boa Vista, a park in the North Zone of Rio, with a hilly topography, old and sparse buildings, some lakes, and tall trees:

Fag! Every time I took that bus to work [*para batalhar*], you should have seen me . . . It was like I had never gone to the Asphalt to do sex work [*fazer programa*]. I was like a virgin! I would go through this tunnel here in Rocinha [Túnel Dois Irmãos], just thinking about what would happen that night. Seriously! I still get a rush of blood every time I go to Quinta da Boa Vista to prostitute [*prostituir*].

Giulia kept talking while her gestures reproduced the scene of her holding on to the bus handle and shaking all the way to Quinta da Boa Vista. "It is a mixture of pleasure and fear. Oh my God! That feeling of not knowing what will happen throughout the night? I loved that part! Other things were terrible. But sometimes tough is good, right? I mean, I like a tough dick inside me!" She laughed and fanned her face, as if trying to cool herself down.

Based on Natasha's experience, I asked Giulia about her family's reaction: "Don't they worry about you?"

She replied, "My mother knows everything that I do! I don't keep secrets. And I am free, my darling!" Giulia also worked as a hairdresser at a salon in Rocinha, just in case the money as a sex worker in Quinta da Boa Vista wouldn't be enough to pay the bills. "You know, I have my needs! I like my *baseado* [marijuana cigarette]. And do you think this body is cheap? Sometimes, the Asphalt is better for money. Some other times, it is the salon that keeps me. But I miss the men when I stay in the salon! Some of the men have been delicious. Straightening female hair all day long gets boring, fag!" I nodded, imaging Giulia standing in a stuffy beauty salon in Rocinha all day long. She continued:

Quinta is very happening . . . I am telling you! Good and bad ones, of course. One day, I met this guy who wanted me to have sex with him for free. He was hot, muscular. I asked him if he wanted to fuck me or get fucked. He whispered in my ear that he wanted to see my dick. I laughed and told him that I would not fuck any faggot for free. No way! This man lost control and tried to hit me. Maybe he was on drugs? I ran toward the train station. When I was crossing the pedestrian bridge to the station, you know? He pulled me from behind. That psychopath! He tried to push me off from the top of the flyover. If I didn't fight him, I would be dead by now, flat on the track down below. Can you imagine the scene, darling?

It took courage to face the dangers of the nightlife. I felt really bad that Giulia had to go through such violence as part of her work experiences as a travesti, but she didn't look sad at all. In fact, she seemed proud of her resilience, excited by the unknown, and kept working toward a perfect tan to attract even more men.

A Professional Pleasure Provider

There were many other sex work areas in the Marvelous City. However, even when these areas were located in the supposed formality of the Asphalt, they were still subjected to flows that connect them to the Hillside. The geographers Rogério Matos and Miguel Ribeiro remind us of the heterogeneity of elements that help to compose urban areas of prostitution in general and highlight some of the particular territorial dynamics in the city of Rio de Janeiro, given the complexities of powers in operation around the sex work industry:

Those "territories" follow the dynamics of the city in which they find themselves inserted, and once established, they are able to develop over some time, tending to increase proportionally to the increase of demands for pleasure. In addition, they may fragment as a result of invasions of other groups to the area, or even the intervention of public powers such as the police, politicians, or county administration. Even the marginal "power" represented by drug-dealing activities may lead in many cases to the complete extinction of the activity in a certain area and its appearing in another one.[10]

I became increasingly aware of the fact that favela dwellers operated within an extensive sex work circuit. Slowly, certain flows emerged that connected people from Rocinha not only to other parts of Rio de Janeiro, but to other Brazilian states and even different continents. Sex work territories are constituted through clients, modes of transport, forms of control, body shapes, sexual practices, and other elements. I was in a position to trace those connections precisely because I was living in such a large favela. From that node, I realized the importance of the slum as some sort of sex work hub. This is not only because a lot of sex work actually takes place within favelas, but because sex workers established a dense network involving Rocinha—some were born in the slum or had families in the area, others owned houses in the favela, others had links to drug traffickers, and some were sex workers under the "management" of folks living in the favela.

These connections were highlighted through fortuitous ethnographic encounters. There was an evening that Auro and I stopped near the store called No Limite. We talked to a woman Auro knew well, Diana. We had run into her in one of those serendipitous moments that often takes place during ethnographic fieldwork. In her sixties, the woman had long curly hair, dyed bluish-black and tied in a ponytail. She was wearing big golden earrings and bright red lipstick. Auro asked her if she was going out to work at that moment or returning home from a meeting. Diana told him that she was going out to Barra da Tijuca. "Going to work, right, dear?" Auro asked.

"We gotta work, Auro!" she replied.

They waved goodbye, and soon Auro turned to me, whispering, "Did you see that old lady? She is a granny already, right?" He tried not to laugh and kept talking, "Do you have any idea of how she makes money to support her family? Diana is a professional pleasure provider [*profissional do prazer*]! She makes a living out of turning people's sexual fantasies into reality. And I know that she joins the fun, too, if they require an old lady for their sex adventures! But her main business is to make everything happen. Whatever the clients ask her in terms of sex, do you understand?" No, I didn't understand much of the topic, but I was learning a lot. Auro seemed to derive great pleasure from situations he assumed would shock me somehow. There were flocks of people passing by us while we chatted about sex in that busy part of the favela. It didn't seem to bother him. He continued his explanation: "For example, there could be a client horny for sex with a well-hung travesti, hung like a horse, or someone who will act violently and carry a whip, okay? This granny knows people in the favela that can offer all that, and she provides the right travesti for the client. Do you get it? Diana is a hard-core lady! She makes any sexual fantasy come true . . . Of course, she makes a lot of money out of that too, babe!"[11]

The circulation of desires, sex workers, fantasies, money, and drugs between favela territories and prostitution territories in the Asphalt seemed to constitute broad "moral zones"[12] that were interconnected through the trading of pleasure. This was part of a wider assemblage in which libertinism was not oppressed but valued and enjoyed. If normative liberalism fostered free trade, commodification, rule of law, and individualism, would there be other modes of exchange and transactions promoted by the values of libertinism, as a form of minoritarian liberalism? Libido, pleasures, excitement, enjoyment, and orgasms seemed to be important "tradables" in this regard, even if sometimes accompanied by the risk of violence.

The Laws of Sex Work

Debates on the implications of modernity for the historical practice of sex work abound. Within the European context, Sophie Day demonstrates that political considerations regarding prostitution have not followed a linear logic of historical progress toward liberalization. To the contrary, Day argues that the case in favor of the professionalization and commodification of sex work grew weaker, especially over the immediate decades following the 1980s.[13] This was the time when feminist arguments most vigorously emerged to the effect that all sex work should be considered inherently exploitative and, therefore, the practice should be abolished instead of legalized.[14] Carole Pateman, an interlocutor in this debate, justifies her concern regarding the (im)morality of sex work based on the absence of pleasure and desire for the workers: "There is no desire or satisfaction on the part of the prostitute. Prostitution is not mutual, pleasurable exchange of the use of bodies, but the unilateral use of a woman's body by a man in exchange for money."[15]

Instead of straightforward prohibition, however, some liberals had (and have) been campaigning to afford sex workers freedom, as long as they submit themselves to nation-state regulations—which, in some countries, such as the Netherlands, imply tax payments. This is not to say that all nations agree on this latter resolution, legislations vary a great deal. In Brazil, the Penal Code, instituted in 1940 and still operational as I write, doesn't criminalize prostitution per se. Since at least 1987, feminist activist and prostitute (she preferred this term) Gabriela Leite had been promoting debates around the issue of sex work in the country. Since 2002, prostitution has been recognized as an official profession by the Brazilian Ministry of Labor. In 2012 Leite helped to create an NGO called Davida, which brought national attention to the cause.[16] The current legislation says that the Brazilian state and its representatives are supposed to give sex workers the same treatment as other workers. It should be illegal to arrest them for the exercise of their profession.

According to what ideals of freedom can we decide if prostitution should be conceived of as a form of pleasure, legitimate work, or slavery? Who, after all, is the contemporary slave? Orlando Patterson, a prominent sociologist, points out that slavery "is best understood as a form of personal, corporeal domination, by the slaveholder or his agent, based on the exercise or threat of physical and psychological violence."[17] Patterson also notes that a second key characteristic of slavery is the uprooting and sociocultural isolation that it brings about to the enslaved. The author refers to the latter as "natal alienation" and clarifies that, nowadays, "the closest approximation to traditional natal alienation are persons who find themselves illegally transported to foreign countries where they are fearful of seeking the protection of law enforcement and other state authorities and are isolated from familial and social ties."[18]

If we were to look for a legal definition of slavery, according to the Brazilian Rule of Law, Article 149 of the Brazilian Penal Code states:

To reduce someone to a condition analogous to that of a slave, namely: subjecting a person to forced labor or to arduous working days, or subjecting such a person to degrading working conditions or restricting, in any manner whatsoever, their mobility by reason of a debt contracted in respect of the employer or a representative of that employer.[19]

To further complicate the situation, based on field research regarding human trafficking between Brazil and Spain, Adriana Piscitelli argues that people in a situation of human trafficking interpret and incorporate notions of law that do not necessarily coincide with legal definitions of the crime of trafficking in persons. She adds, "At the same time, I observed that cases typified as human trafficking do not always refer to human rights violations."[20] At times, normative liberals incorporate sex work as another form of free labor, individuality, freedom of choice—in defense of a free market. At other moments, prostitution appears as indefensible—it emerges as that which liberalism must purge, as the binary opposite of freedom: slavery. And yet, as Piscitelli remind us, sex workers, even those participating in human-trafficking schemes, might have a different understanding of their situation altogether.

The exact nature of the transaction in sex work is one of the most complicated points in the liberal debate. Some feminists would struggle to distinguish between forced and unforced sex work. What exactly is for sale in sex work? If the transaction implies that bodies are made available for purchase in the market, should sex work not to be considered a contemporary form of slavery, a trade in human flesh? Or should sex work be better understood as a form of service transaction? Pateman, discussed in the introduction for her seminal reflections in *The Sexual Contract*, argues that in (normative) liberalism, sex exchanges are regulated through variations of what could be considered a form of "social contract." The derivative version of this contract would be an evident dimension of male access to female bodies through the contract of marriage. In the case of sex work, however, the author explains her discomfort:

Contract theorists argue that a prostitute contracts out a specific form of labor power for a given period in exchange for money. There is a free exchange between prostitute and customer, and the prostitution contract is exactly like—or is one example of—the employment contract. From the standpoint of contract, the prostitute is an owner of a property in her person who contracts out part of that property in her market.[21]

From the perspective of minoritarian groups, however, the situation didn't look the same. For queer favela dwellers engaged in sex work (*batalhando*), for example, the law of the Asphalt and other nation-state institutions didn't adequately protect their rights as Brazilian citizens. The police regularly abused travestis during their sex-trade activities in the Asphalt.[22] Most of my travesti friends from Rocinha either feared or despised the police, having to pay them a share of their profits to be able to work free from harassment. When payments were not made directly, the money was channeled through local (mostly travesti) pimps (*cafetinas*) to the hands of the *alibã* (police)—as payments for their provision of "security."

According to "the social contract" ideal, the protection of citizens should come as a standard state obligation. Therefore, these extra payments implied that, first, sex workers were not fully recognized as citizens of the Brazilian state; second, they did not operate in a fair free market; and, finally, the law of the Asphalt was often manipulated by the police

CHAPTER SIX

to incriminate travestis, a common practice with other Brazilian minorities, particularly street children, Black people, and other favela dwellers in general. While travestis could not be criminalized for their "sex work" per se, if they so desired the police could make up other charges to officially incriminate them. Within the normative liberal scheme, however, pimps were the ones violating the laws for promoting "obscene acts in public."[23] Contradictorily, these same pimps were the ones who received the most protection. They had the necessary money, connections, and political influence to bribe the police force, exchanging money for state protection.

Global Queer Hierarchies

Natasha told me that her family was against sex work. Beyond the moral considerations attached to her non-normative sexuality, from the (minoritarian) perspective of peasant liberalism, Natasha's mother affirmed that a person should not need to sell their body, not even their services, as a tradable merchandise in the market.[24] This was Dona Rosário's understanding of the situation. It was a different take than normative liberalism. Indeed, peasant liberalism seemed to operate in opposition to both state and market forces. Such argument should not just be dismissed in the face of other liberal understandings. Moral considerations of this type bear important implications for the life choices of some favela dwellers.

What has been discussed as a queer liberalism in the favela is also particularly relevant to considerations regarding the trade of sex for money. Given its focus on bodily experiences, prostitution seemed to offer an opportunity for radical and unexpected encounters (as Giulia affirmed). And, as I had learned during my conversations regarding Travessa Liberdade, the existence of a liberal heterotopia in Rocinha allowed for an alternative mode of freedom for sex work.[25] All of these assemblages of normative and minoritarian liberalisms intersected, with different intensities, in the experiences of my travesti friends from Rocinha.

It was late October 2009. It was just getting dark. While doing some grocery shopping at the supermarket, I talked to Auro about a new PAFYC member. Once again, the mathematician seemed to be upset with the crew. He told me: "I prefer not to talk about this issue. I have no respect for these people. They are the lowest of the low. Do you know what I call them? Bread-and-egg faggots [*bichas pão-com-ovo*]! They are not even at the level of Coca-Cola faggots . . ."[26] Hierarchies clearly existed among some of my queer friends in Rocinha. After leaving the supermarket, near the alleyway to my house, Auro and I stopped at a corner before parting ways. He took out a bottle of perfume from his backpack and sprayed it all over himself. "I want to smell nice on my way home! What if I a hottie crosses my path?" He laughed.

"Nice smell," I remarked.

"It's European," he informed me. "I have many friends living in Europe," he added.

"Really?" I interjected.

"Yes! You see, those are travestis that I respect! The ones that work hard in Europe, okay? I know they suffer too. There is no paradise. Europeans are racist! But at least my friends are doing something with their lives. What do these PAFYC people do?"

I asked whether Auro was referring to sex work. He replied, "Yes, most of them are prostitutes in Italy now . . . Some went to Spain, France, Switzerland. It depends on how things go for them."

I asked, "And do they make good money?"

He remarked, "Yes! They have to make money, faggot. If they don't make money, they are in trouble! They struggle to pay their debts. They want their passports back, darling . . . They want their liberty back!" We were blocking the alleyway—somebody complained. Auro got a phone call and had to go home. He walked away, leaving unanswered questions and a trail of imported perfume behind. I went home too, haunted, and determined to find out more about the case of travestis from Rocinha working in Europe.

When Auro realized that I was invested in the issue, perhaps too invested in it, he started to withhold information. At some point, I even began to suspect that Auro could be involved in what looked like a human-trafficking scheme. He wasn't. Over time, I managed to piece together the story: pimps would approach the most "promising" travestis in the favela and offer them money to improve their appearance, through plastic surgery, silicone implants, dental work, and whatever else the agents deemed necessary for a successful career. When their bodies were "ready," the pimps would then finance their trips to Europe. If nothing went wrong, and the travestis managed to reach their final destination, a different manager (another pimp) would be waiting for them at the airport in Milan or Rome.

One of the first things these managers did was to confiscate the travestis' passports and other identification documents. The only way to get their "papers" back was by working on the street, trading sex for money, until they could pay off all their debts, plus interest and the added costs of airline tickets, rent, food, and clothing that they incurred traveling to and while in Europe. By the time the travestis managed to pay all the money back (if they managed to do so at all), their total debt would be many times higher than the initial amount borrowed in Brazil. If they couldn't pay their debt, they would be at the mercy of the pimps, who were the ones with connections both in Brazil and in Italy (possibly with the local Mafia) to make it feasible for these undocumented migrants to work without much hassle while in Europe. Nonetheless, their corruption scheme was not perfect, and even the most obedient of the travestis lived in fear (and real threat) of deportation.

Shelly

Natasha had told me that her friend Shelly had offered her a loan for plastic surgery, which Natasha didn't take. Maybe there was more to that story than I had initially realized? I decided to follow up. On a night out, I took a bus with Natasha from Rocinha to a working-class suburban neighborhood in Rio called Madureira. It was past midnight, and most of my neighbors had warned me not to go out to that part of town so late at night, but I felt safe with Natasha. Vavá, Bira, and Nivaldo had joined us for a night out too. They promised to introduce me to the nightclub Papa G. On the bus, I found a way to ask more about Shelly and the sex work business that she managed. Natasha got a bit defensive: "What are you talking about? Shelly is my friend! She's helped me a lot in the past. You know how these fags are in Rocinha, calling us matescas and all? Shelly is not like that. She likes me. And we gotta respect her. Shelly is one of the oldest travestis alive in Rocinha!" Natasha told me that Shelly worked in Beco 11, a shady alleyway, lined with bars, that connected the large trash dumpster located at the end of Rua do Valão to Largo do Boiadeiro. Shelly owned a house there and rented rooms out for sex work. "She charges by the hour," Natasha explained. "Imagine the money, fag!" Then she reiterated, "Shelly is well connected because she is a good person. Everybody likes her." And Natasha continued to tell me that she had worked with Shelly in the past and knew her husband, too. "They just adopted a baby a few months ago! That's Shelly."

"What about this money that she offered you to become a professional prostitute?" I asked Natasha.

"What about it? She has money, I told you. And I would pay her back. Shelly likes me and thinks that I've got potential. She offered to help me!" Natasha replied.

"Would she be your pimp?" I asked, insistent.

"I would have to take this thing of working in the Asphalt (*fazer pista*) more seriously. She would find me clients and talk to some friends to find a better spot for me to work. I told you, Shelly knows a lot of people." Natasha didn't really answer the question.

"And you said no?" I tried to confirm.

"First, I said, yes. Then I changed my mind. Then Shelly told me that with big boobs I could even go to Europe! Wow, can you imagine? Am I that beautiful? Imagine my big boobs!" Natasha laughed out loud and put her hands against her breasts, simulating melon-sized boobs.

"Europe! Shelly wanted to send you to Europe?" We were finally getting to the question I was after.

"Not Shelly herself. She would put me in touch with people. But I said no. Again, I told you that before! Why are you so weird about it?" Natasha asked suspiciously.

"It's for my research. Remember? I am writing about these things. Work, sex, freedom . . ." I replied.

"Freedom? Oh, yes! Imagine me in Europe? Traveling on a big airplane. Shining in Italy!" She got excited at the thought and started screaming, "Ciao, bello? Totalmente liberada!" [Hello, beautiful? Totally liberated!] I laughed. I hadn't meant freedom in that sense but soon realized that flying to Europe for sex work had implications for which my own ideas of liberalism couldn't account yet. The attraction toward Europe in these travestis' life projects was not necessarily in search of a Eurocentric lifestyle based on "rights." Instead, presented with heteronormative discrimination and a limited job market for travestis in Brazil, working in Europe was used as a strategy to achieve the mode of liberation that mattered the most to my queer friends in the favela: the freedom to have their desired bodies, to experience the adventures they wanted, the men they wanted, and, as we will see, as a form of fostering connections that matter to them, particularly kinship relations.

A Preference for the Street

Natasha and her crowd, including me, got off the bus in Madureira and walked to Papa G. There were huge crowds in front of the nightclub. People were selling drinks on carts, smoking, and talking loudly. Lots of cars were parked with their doors opened, pumping out funk music. Travestis strutted by, making the street their catwalk. Others were

CHAPTER SIX

dancing—their bums moving around to the beat of the music. I got a bit dizzy with all the action and looked up to the dark sky for a second. Instead of resting, my eyes landed on a colorful billboard at the entrance of the nightclub. In big letters, it said: "Papa G: Para quem curte liberdade, sensualidade e tudo mais!" (Papa G: For those who enjoy liberty, sensuality, and everything else!) The message referred to the liberty of sensuality, sex, and all pleasures that escape words. The advertisement on the billboard reminded me that there was also a market for *libertinism*. People were profiting from "liberty, sensuality, and everything else!" There were always economic elites exploiting the commerce of alcohol, drugs, sex, and entertainment to produce a profit. What did this commodification of libertinism mean for my favela friends?

"Should we go inside now?" I asked the group from Rocinha. The billboard had made me curious to observe the nightclub from within.

"Inside where? We are here already!" Nivaldo answered.

"Inside Papa G!" I replied.

"You want to go into the building? We prefer to stay on the street. It's a lot more fun! Trust me." Nivaldo surprised me.

Natasha added, "No way I am going inside! It's boring and expensive. And they only want boy-fags in there. Let's stay here." The feast was on the street. There was no need to pay the entrance fee. No need to subject ourselves to the doorman's selection. There was cheaper alcohol, free music, and lots of fags on the street. We stayed outside.

Natasha waved to a friend across the street. We crossed Rua Almerinda Freitas to join her, gathering in front of a dark blue door, number 39. About five minutes later, Natasha announced that she wanted to go for a walk around the block. "Sure! Let's go!" I agreed.

"I'm going, fag . . . You're staying! I'm just going around the corner to piss." She laughed and left us.

"This fag is plotting something," Bira remarked.

Vavá and Nivaldo were busy buying drinks from a street cart selling caipirinha: Brazilian cachaça mixed with lime, ice, and sugar. Meanwhile, I talked to Natasha's friend. She was wearing a blond wig, plastic eyelashes, and a silver dress. "How do you know Natasha? Do you live in Rocinha?" I asked.

"Rocinha? No, not me. The first time I met her was in Lapa, I think," she told me.

"Do you like Lapa too?" I asked.

"I used to do sex work [*fazer programa*] in Lapa. But I've been away for a while. This is the first time I've gotten out of my house in ages," she said.

"Why? What happened?" Vavá got curious and joined the conversation.

"Fag! I've not been feeling very well . . ." Natasha's friend said.

"Babe, what is it? Don't tell me you got the Freddy [*pegou a Freddy*]?" Vavá laughed. I knew that Freddy was one of the Pajubá words for HIV and got concerned.[27]

"Freddy? Me? No . . . It's complicated, fag! I'm getting psychological help," she said.

"What is it?" Vavá insisted.

"I want to have a sex-change operation," she confessed. All of us went quiet for a while.

"Really? I think this is cool," Bira said.

"I think you're crazy! You are a travesti, not a woman!" Vavá commented.

"Crazy?" I asked.

"I'm not crazy, Vavá! The psychologists at SUS told me I am not. I am normal, but I am not a man. I am a woman!" Natasha's friend affirmed. I was aware that SUS (Sistema Único de Saúde) was a reference to the Public Universal Health System in Brazil, which had started to offer care to trans people.

Vavá's response was to laugh out loud again. "Will you really have an operation?" he asked her.

"Someday, I hope! I can't afford a private clinic. There is a long waiting list for that type of surgery at SUS. Maybe they will call me, and my dream will come true."[28]

At that exact moment, an old black Fiat Uno slowly drove through the busy road, displacing the crowds. The driver didn't look at us. On the passenger side, Natasha put half of her body out of the window and shouted: "Don't wait for me!"

Bira laughed out loud. "I told you she was plotting something!" he yelled, looking at me. "Don't worry, Moisés! You stay with us, and we'll go back to Rocinha together, okay?" Bira continued, laughing. "I know this car! I've been with this guy . . . It's a client!"

Rocinha to Rome

A couple of months passed without me learning any significant information on the supposed sex-trafficking scheme in Rocinha. I realized that Auro liked to exaggerate—in his stories, his facial expressions, and even his perfume. Perhaps he was trying to keep me entertained? I gave up on

CHAPTER SIX

openly asking him questions on the topic. Auro avoided the issue too. When I asked other people about it, almost everyone told me they had no idea of what I was talking about. Natasha was the only one who had offered me more information, but in the end, it was all inconclusive. Should I go speak to Shelly? I was afraid that she would be upset to know I was researching an "illegal" scheme of which she could be part. It was not until I met up with Auro's best friend again that I got back on track.

Marcus invited Auro and me for a cup of tea at the house he rented in the upper part of the favela. As we walked in, he was playing loud music. Listening to the lyrics, I could identify the name of Iemanjá, the Orixá of waters. It was the voice of the Brazilian singer Maria Bethânia, who was initiated in Candomblé. She was one of Marcus's favorites. "This tea came from London, darling. This is the advantage of working at the airport. If clients like you, they give you all sorts of gifts!" Marcus said. "By the way, Auro, I managed to schedule my next trip to Europe!" he continued.

"Fag! Wow, good for you. Where are you going this time?" Auro asked him.

"London," Marcus replied.

"London? Again?" Auro asked.

"Well, you know the airline I work for has a direct route to London, right? It was much easier for me to get a ticket on that flight. From London, I might go somewhere else. Maybe Rome or Milan, to visit the girls?" Marcus said.

"The travestis in Italy? Take Moisés with you. He has been very curious about them!" Auro laughed. I felt exposed.

"I'm not even sure if the girls are still there. I haven't talked to them in a while," Marcus remarked. Then he continued, "Oh, the Mattatoio in Rome! I have been there once. Remember I told you, Auro? They were all out there, working in the middle of the winter. The leather coats. Those beautiful Italian shoes. So elegant . . . You are giving me ideas. I will go back there someday!" I decided not to say anything. However, I did register the name of the prostitution venue in Rome—the Mattatoio.

While I was concerned that favela dwellers in Europe were being forced into slavery, Italy also seemed to figure as a territory of promises, dreams, and fables for travestis. Don Kulick, in his ethnographic research on this topic in Brazil, found a similar trope:

In addition to prostituting themselves on the streets of Salvador and other cities throughout Brazil, a large number of travestis leave the country to spend time working in Italy. Italy is to travestis what El Dorado was to the Spanish conquistadores of the

New World. It is the land of fabled riches to which one travels in order to make one's fortune and return with enough money to realize one's dreams.[29]

Did the ethnographic evidence that I encountered in Rocinha refer to a legitimate form of migration or a human-trafficking scheme? This question seemed to revert to different liberal positions. I decided that, rather than aiming for an easy resolution, I needed to further explore the issue on the ground. To either support sex work as a legitimate form of labor in a free market or to renounce it as a form of slavery a priori seemed like a false dichotomy. Instead, I chose to take another route. On September 9, 2010, at 5:45 p.m., on flight BA 0556, I landed in Rome with the hope of finding a more grounded perspective on the matter.

The Mattatoio

I arrived in Italy with no clear plan, other than to talk to Brazilian travestis working in the streets of Rome. Although what I really hoped was to meet Rocinha migrants, in part as a form of reconnection to the favela. By mid-2010, I had concluded the main period of extended fieldwork living in Rio de Janeiro, moved out of my house in Favela da Rocinha, and returned to St Andrews, in Scotland, to conclude my doctoral degree. However, the transition out of fieldwork had not been smooth. I was attached to people and their lives in the favela. I kept in regular contact with friends through phone, e-mail, and other means, but it wasn't enough. The slavery issue in Rome had put hooks into me; it was an open question that wouldn't let me disconnect from my fieldwork. Since I was temporarily based in Europe, it wasn't too hard to find an opportunity to gather the bits and pieces I had collected in Rio de Janeiro and trace them back to Rome. It was only my second time in the Italian capital. I didn't know my way around and certainly didn't know much of the Italian language—despite its common Latin roots with Portuguese. Luckily, I had friends working for the Brazilian Ministry of Foreign Affairs in Rome. And I had the name of the place where Brazilian sex workers supposedly worked in the Italian capital: the Mattatoio.

After settling in at the cheap hotel room I rented, I contacted my friends at the Brazilian embassy and scheduled to meet them at Piazza Navona toward the end of their working day. Over an early autumn dinner, I told them the details of my visit to Rome. "What? Travestis? Are you serious?" one of them said, surprised at my concern for the topic.

CHAPTER SIX

"We need to find out what is going on," I replied.

"Sorry, prostitution is not one of my responsibilities in the embassy," he replied.

"But there might be a human-trafficking scheme between Brazil and Italy. This is a serious matter. Shouldn't the Brazilian embassy be concerned?" I asked.

"Sure, but it is not my job to investigate this. Shouldn't the travestis contact the embassy if they need it? Instead of us going after them?" he pondered.

"The thing is, if they are really working under a slavery scheme, how could they seek for help? They are probably under the control of powerful groups, the Mafia, who knows?" I replied.

"Exactly! There are too many unknowns. And if you suspect that this is a serious criminal scheme, I would advise you to stay out of it. The Italian Mafia is no joke! Try to protect yourself," he warned me.

I went back to my hotel room to digest that conversation. I spent the rest of the evening searching for information on the Mattatoio and made a plan to go there the next day. The address that I had found on the internet was quite central in Rome: Piazza Orazio Giustiniani. I also realized that *mattatoio* in Italian literally translated to "slaughterhouse" in English. Was that just an unfortunate coincidence? Perhaps the slaughterhouse (Mattatoio) reference that I had heard in Rocinha had been some sort of joke that I didn't get at the time? But, I thought, at least a place called Mattatoio did exist in Rome. I had found it on the map. I planned my route and went to bed, resolute to visit the area the following day.

The next night, when I got to the location, at around 9 p.m., the Mattatoio was closed. I waited and walked around, wondering if I had been wrong. Or perhaps it was too early for sex workers to be out on the streets in Rome? I reached for my phone and realized that the Mattatoio that I had located was indeed the *former* slaughterhouse area of Rome. It was now operating as some sort of gentrified cultural center, and the actual slaughterhouse had been moved to the outskirts of the city. After a little longer, I returned to the hotel. I decided to try my luck in Italian, venturing an internet search using the words *mattatoio* and *prostituzione*. The results led me to a location called Centro Carni, and I also found an article in the *Guardian*, dated November 20, 2009, regarding the murder of a Brazilian travesti:

Italian police are investigating the murder of a Brazilian transsexual caught up in a drugs and prostitution scandal that forced the resignation of one of Italy's top politicians last month. The soot-encrusted corpse of the victim—known only as Brenda—was found this morning after a fire in her basement flat. She was one of two prostitutes at the heart of a case involving the blackmail of Piero Marrazzo, the former governor of Lazio, the region around Rome. A leading figure in the centre-left opposition to Silvio Berlusconi's government, Marrazzo was found to have been blackmailed by four members of the paramilitary carabinieri who filmed him while he had sex and took cocaine with one of the transsexuals. He resigned and fled to a monastery near Rome.[30]

The newly found location was more than an hour away from my hotel. I wouldn't be able to afford a taxi ride all the way there, and there was no easy access using public transport; I would have to make two connections on the bus. Moreover, there was no guarantee whatsoever that I was on the right track. Regardless, I left at around 6 p.m. the next day, hoping to get to Centro Carni before it got too dark. The moment I got on the bus, however, I was overcome with fear. I was acutely aware of being all alone in a large unknown city, in the dark, trying to trace a human-trafficking ring that might include cruel pimps, sex slaves, the powerful Italian Mafia, and even corrupt politicians. All I had in hand was some cash for the bus, a screenshot of a map of Rome saved on my phone, and some Italian words written on a notebook in my pocket. I worried that the situation could get out of control for me and, even worse, create unnecessary problems for the travestis. Before I left, I had called my friends at the embassy again to ask them about the place. They said they had never heard of Centro Carni and strongly advised me not to try to find it all alone.

On the third bus of the night, I thought of Natasha, KB7, and Auro. I missed them. I told myself that if Marcus had visited this place in the past, it should be okay for me to go too. I got off at a stop that I assumed was near the location, then approached an older Italian woman and asked her for directions in broken Italian: "Dove Mattatoio?" (Where Mattatoio?) She looked at me and said something I didn't understand. With her hands, she indicated that I should get back on the bus. I followed her instructions and boarded again. I tried to ask the bus driver for help, who seemed to indicate that I should be patient and remain on the vehicle. The journey was much longer than I had anticipated. Was I lost? At some point, the driver abruptly stopped the bus. He made a sign that I should get off. It was pitch-dark outside. I stepped down and watched the bus pull away, the red lights dimming into darkness.

I took a deep breath and looked all around. Lost. As my eyes turned, I noticed the figure of a blond travesti, with a clutch bag, standing on the pavement near the bus stop. She was leaning against a wall, and smiling at me. I approached her, almost in desperation, and abruptly said: "Ciao! Brasiliana?" (Hi! Brazilian?)

She replied, disappointed, "Non!" I continued babbling in bad Italian: "Dove Brasiliana?" (Where Brazilian?)

She turned her back to me and pointed toward a place that looked like a vast car park, completely in the dark. "Continua a camminare!" (Keep walking!) she ordered. I thanked her and slowly moved ahead. I couldn't even see where I was stepping. At that moment, I started to notice dim car headlights on the horizon. After a couple of minutes walking, my fear had been replaced with pure adrenaline. A phantasmagoric figure appeared in the distance. A car slowly passed, projecting some light onto her image: black hair, black dress, and black skin. Was this one of the enslaved travestis who had been haunting me all this time? The car drove away, and darkness prevailed again. "Brasiliana?" I asked, still from a distance.

"Sì!" I heard a voice replying. I kept moving closer.

"Da dove?" (Where from?) I asked almost instinctively, filled with joy.

"Rio de Janeiro," she said.

"Rocinha?" I asked, right in front of her, not even considering the unlikeliness that she would be from there.

"Como você sabe?" (How do you know?) she replied in Portuguese, and smiled.

"Eu não sabia!" (I didn't know!) I answered, as surprised as she was.

The woman, whose name, fittingly, was Angel, took me by the hand and asked me questions about Rocinha. Who did I know in the slum? How did I end up in Rome? "Shelly Sword? Do you know Shelly?" she inquired.

"Yes, I do! We are not really friends, but I know her," I replied.

"She is one of my closest people in the favela! We were born in the same area in Rocinha, called Macega,[31] have you heard of it?" she asked excitedly.

"Sure! I know Macega!" I replied. As we continued talking, Angel introduced more Pajubá words into the conversation. I didn't shy away. After all the time I had spent in Rocinha, my knowledge of the dialect had greatly improved. Angel seemed genuinely happy to meet me. I felt I had just encountered an old friend. I had heard the name Angel from Auro or Marcus—I wasn't sure. I mentioned their names to her, and Angel recognized them. After a while, I remembered the experience with KB7 in Praça do Ó and asked Angel: "Is it okay for you to talk, or should I let you work?"

She replied, "Please, stay. It's still early in the evening, and it's so good to meet someone from back home!"

After talking for a while about Rocinha, laughing, and gossiping, I moved on to tell her I was an anthropologist researching liberalism in Rocinha. Angel lost a bit of her enthusiasm: "When I saw you, I first thought you were a client. But then, a client without a car at a car park? I also realized you were a fag. Then, you told me about Rocinha. I thought, what does this fag want? Looking for work? Now you are saying this is a research. Is that it?"

I told Angel about the friends I had left in Rocinha—all the stories I had heard about travestis going to Europe for work. I also told her about the loneliness of my life writing up a thesis back in Scotland. I got slightly emotional and said, "I had to come here!"

Angel softened. "Next time that I call Brazil, I will tell the fags that you visited me. They will be happy to hear it. Now what exactly do you want to know for your research? Go ahead!"

She ended up helping me more than I seemed to be able to help her. Angel confirmed what I had heard from Natasha. She had been on female hormones for a while, then got some liquid silicone injected to enlarge her thighs, but she had no money for professional plastic surgery. "Then, I borrowed money from a friend. I didn't take much at once. I am not stupid. I did the basic implants, you know? Tits, bum, and all . . . and then I traveled. I thought my debt was not too high, but it was hard to pay it back. Actually, I am still paying it back because I borrowed more money recently to visit my family in Brazil. Oh, and I changed the size of my tits too! Look at this," she said, lowering her dress to show me her amazingly large breasts. "Next, I will get my teeth fixed!" She laughed, pointing to a tooth that was missing.

A dark blue car parked near us. Angel ignored him, but I told her not to worry about me. I was happy to have met her and would not lose her contact. She went to talk to the driver for a while, showing the volume of her tits first, then the size of her bulge. The driver closed the window and drove away, stopping several meters ahead to talk to another sex worker. "He is not serious, this guy! I know his car. A lot of men just come to see our bums, our tits, our dicks, and then drive away," she explained.

"The bigger, the better?" I asked.

"You're clever! Sure, the bigger, the better: tits, bum, and dick! Most of these men like dick. Tits are easier to enlarge than dicks. And by the way, liquid silicone can be a disaster. There are lots of travestis that I know who have totally deformed their bodies," she told me, laughing.

"They deformed their bodies having surgery to please the clients?" I asked.

She quickly corrected me: "What? No, not just to please the clients. To please ourselves! I always wanted to have the body that I have today. When I look at myself in the mirror, it's like a dream come true. But I did everything right. I'm not deformed, I am beautiful, right? Do you see me?"

Sex and Beauty

In his research on beauty, sex, and plastic surgery, Alexander Edmonds writes that for Brazilians, "female beauty often emerges as a key sign of the modern—as lure, moral threat, or even liberation." The author continues:

Beauty can be seen in relation to larger contradictions in modernity: between new freedoms and desires unleashed in consumer capitalism and the constraints on freedom experienced by "liberated" subjects as they are exposed to the hazards of generalized exchange.[32]

Edmonds emphasizes the power of aesthetics as a form of value that cannot be simply subsumed under other markers of difference. In fact, in his argument, it is exactly because there is a gap between aesthetics and other forms of social classification that beauty can become a route of social ascent when other, more formal, routes of social mobility are blocked. "While beauty is unfair in that it appears to be 'awarded' to the morally undeserving, it can also grant power to those excluded from other systems of privilege based in wealth, pedigree, or education."[33]

Angel's statement about her beauty refuted the idea that aesthetics was simply commodified and packaged for sale in the market for sex workers. There was more to it; the female body achieved through plastic surgery—even if dependent on debt—was not for the pleasure of the client only. It was first and foremost a matter of promoting bodily transformations that would be liberating to the travestis themselves. Of course, some might argue that only a perverse requirement of external validation, based on low self-esteem, could produce such travesti desires in the first place. Instead of resorting to psychologization, or even a false consciousness critique, I preferred to take Angel's truth as truth. Sex work was a form of life that enabled a specific type of queer liberalism, the achievement of the necessary freedom to undergo bodily transformations and to enjoy the pleasures to be found in sex itself.

When another car interrupted my conversation with Angel, she was clear about the pleasures of her queer positionality. "Fag! Did you see that one?" she asked.

"No, I couldn't see him very well. The light was blinding me," I lamented.

"Well, your loss! He was *troppo bello* [very handsome]! He made me frisky. What a hottie! This is a danger here . . . Italian men are too sexy. In Brazil, we are lucky to find a hot one over a whole day working. The better ones only want our money! Here? We are paid to go to bed with all these hunks! What else can I ask for?" she said, laughing. Angel wanted me to be a witness to the beauty of a potential client. Going to bed with men she considered extremely sexy was part of the pleasure of working there; it enriched her experiences in Europe. Italy seemed to deliver pleasures that were extremely satisfying to her. She had the aesthetic pleasure of having the men she desired, hunks who valued and worshipped her travesti body. In his work, Kulick has called attention to this particular form of queer pleasure:

As important as it is, however, money is not the entire story of why travestis prostitute themselves. Whenever travestis talk with one another about their activities on the street, another dimension, aside from the purely monetary one, frequently gets foregrounded and elaborated: pleasure. Travestis derive pleasure from their work as prostitutes. They enjoy this work. It reinforces their self-esteem, and it provides them with sexual satisfaction.[34]

However, there were also dangers associated with these clients. While Angel was speaking, I remembered what the anthropologist Erica Williams would call "ambiguous entanglements" of race and sexuality.[35] Most likely, some of these Italian men had a very different understanding regarding the nature of their relations with travestis. For instance, some of them might have been exoticizing these bodies, even more if these were Black Brazilian bodies, just like Angel's. Though she considered many of her clients beautiful, there were other sensitive issues that Angel revealed to me:

I don't really trust them, darling! They are hot and all, but most are mischievous. Some are just strange, very rude. Look, I'm a crazy bitch! I am. But the other day, I got into this car, right? This sexy guy, who looked like an Arab,[36] took me to a place nearby.

CHAPTER SIX

Before we started everything, he sniffed something [drugs] and offered me some. He said he was happy to share it for free. I don't know what he sniffed nor what he gave me, but I know that I passed out.

I followed her words with the utmost attention. She went silent for a second.

"Angel, and what happened?" I couldn't help but ask her.

She took a deep breath and continued: "I woke up, and he had pushed me out of his car. He left me on the bare asphalt. I couldn't even stand up. I kept my eyes open, but I was totally out of it. Really. I almost died that day. I'm sure about that. I think he tried to kill me on purpose." She got emotional, went silent again, and concluded: "But who knows what happened? Drugs here are too strong, different from Brazil. You be careful!"

The conversation was flowing as if I really had known Angel before. I thought it was an adequate moment to openly ask her more about trafficking. "Do you have a pimp? How does it work? Can you go back to Brazil whenever you want? Or are you under surveillance?" I rushed through questions that ideally would take a lot more intimacy to ask.

Angel refused to engage in depth. But she replied: "Yes! I go to Brazil. Whenever I pay down my debt, I'll go to Brazil again. There is someone in charge, but I don't use this word pimp [*cafetina*]. She is my friend, but I have to keep an eye on her because, all of a sudden, my debts will increase. I'm free to go when I pay my debts."

At that moment, I doubted her liberty. I didn't say anything, but it was very hard for me to believe that given her situation it would be so easy to just free herself from the whole scheme. But how could I know better than Angel? I asked her: "And why would you want to leave?"

She said, "I am getting old and tired of this life in Europe. We work a lot more here than in Brazil. Now it's okay, it's warm. But, fag! Imagine us standing here all night long during the winter. We get sick and all. And I can't get sick because I have to work, you know?" I couldn't help but to feel sorry for Angel. Perhaps she noticed something because she soon added: "But it's luxurious too! You should see me. I come here wearing a heavy fur coat that I bought at a secondhand store! Guess what do I do? I put on the coat and nothing underneath. When clients stop by, I simply open up the coat and show them everything they want to see!" She laughed.

I insisted on asking more about the conditions of her work. "But in terms of money, all the money you make goes to this person you have a loan with?"

She replied, "No! Not all the money. I need money for my things, my drugs and stuff, you know?" Different forms of drug use were common among most of my travesti friends. In this regard, Natasha was an exception. In fact, Natasha was often judgmental about other travestis in this aspect. "I better quit these damn drugs because they cost me a lot!" Angel vented and continued: "Also, in the past, I used to make a lot more money than now. There are too many travestis in Italy these days. When I arrived here, I made so much money that I paid all the debt and still saved some to buy a house for my mother in Rocinha! Those were good times, fag . . . I paid all my debts and went back to Rio." I listened to her and thought about Rocinha. I imagined her mother's happiness, even if I didn't know the woman. As Kulick has remarked, going to Italy is often a strategy that Brazilian travestis deploy to help them realize their dreams. Among these dreams, he also observes, giving a home to their mothers was a common priority.[37] I congratulated Angel. She replied: "I wish I had stayed in Rio, but I changed my silicone implants and returned. For now, I am here. But I'm going back to Brazil as soon as I pay the remainder of the loan."

I tried to probe some more: "And where do you live here? Do you have your passport to travel if you need?"

She looked at a car coming and told me: "Me? I'm with other fags from Brazil. Not far from here. We all live together. There were other two from Rocinha, but they moved to Spain, because they said that things were better there these days."

I kept trying: "And the passport?" Angel didn't reply. She was no longer paying attention to me. She had been following the lights of a vehicle from a distance. It was a black car that kept driving in circles.

All of a sudden, her tone changed. She warned me: "Fag! See that car? It is the carabinieri, the police. See where they are now? If they start to drive toward us, we will have to run, okay?"

I got scared. "Run? Run where?" I asked her.

"You see these bushes behind us?" she said. "We will hide in the bushes. I'll show you!" I imagined us running and hiding in the darkness. I thought of my friends in the Brazilian embassy and all the warnings they had given me.

"Do I have to run too?" I asked.

"Yes, if you don't run, they will take you. They will say you were involved in some illegal activity and take you, or both of us!" I realized that my whole body was trembling.

The police drove in circles for a while longer and then went away. Soon, Angel was back to asking me for news from Rocinha as if nothing

CHAPTER SIX

had happened. In fact, nothing did happen. Angel had gone through much worse. Another car approached us. I overheard Angel asking for fifty euros. The driver left. "This one thought we were together!" Angel told me. I was disrupting her night, and I hadn't gotten over the shock of the police threat. I told her it would be better that I left. Angel replied that she was enjoying spending time with me. Once again, I felt awkward that I would just walk away whenever I wanted, while Angel would spend most of her time at that car park in Rome's Centro Carni. "We will see each other in Rocinha, okay? If you come back to Italy, make sure you come to see me!" Angel said, hugging me tightly. I walked away into the darkness again, but now with a much warmer heart.

Rebuilding Relations

The amount of money that Angel had made through this international sex work scheme would have been difficult for her to make otherwise. Life in Brazil was not easy for queer favela dwellers. Nevertheless, Angel made it clear that it was not all about money or oppression. Writing on sex work in Kenya, anthropologist George Paul Meiu argues that sex workers from small villages valued the opportunity to make quick money in larger urban centers. Sex work and the extra income afforded them several opportunities and some challenges. In particular, "They struggled to reimagine what respectability and belonging meant, and how money produced through ethno-erotic exchanges could be converted into valuable relations and attachments."[38] Often, these resources were used exactly to strengthen kinship ties and belonging with their home communities.

Inspired by Meiu's observations in relation to sex workers in Kenya, I suggest that for Brazilian travestis who perform sex work in Europe, buying a house for their mothers offers the possibility to mend the very complicated relations that travestis tend to have with their blood families. If a libertine lifestyle made sex workers lose respectability, buying property—not for their own sake, but in the name of their families—seemed to reverse that effect to some extent. This transaction could be said to fit more with the valorization of private property (along with normative liberalism) than any form of minoritarian freedom. Nevertheless, in Rocinha, one could rarely own property in a formal sense, due to the generalized absence of legal property titles. Perhaps, this travesti investment in healing kinship relations would be better understood in dialogue with family values of peasant liberalism, as a movement away from individualism. Just when the "blood" mothers of many travestis—such as Dona Rosário—are devasted because their daughters seem enticed by the "false liberties" of modernity and capitalism, kinship ties (collectivities) reemerge under the form of a gift: a home for the family.

The construction of the travesti body in the name of sex work can be understood as a form of queer "care of the self"[39]—an ethic and aesthetic exercise rather than a normative liberal commercial transaction. The adventures afforded through prostitution, the attention that travestis receive in the streets, the unknown possibilities of pleasure, the capacity to heal broken kinship relations—all of these aspects speak to a form of liberation beyond normative liberalism. As I have quoted in the opening lines of this chapter: "It is not the product of his or her labor that the worker has a right to, but to the satisfaction of his or her needs, whatever may be their nature."[40] For travestis, like Angel, this form of liberation was the effect of a process of disidentification. Angel didn't seem to conceive of herself either as a modern slave or as a commodity in a free market. Instead, she was striving toward a liberalism that she could explore as a non-normative subject, living the pain and pleasures of her queer dreams.

Taking Liberties with Natasha

Back in Rocinha, I took the liberty to have a very direct conversation with Natasha. "But Natasha, how can you put up with it? It must be horrible! What about these men that don't shower and then pay to have sex with you? Is it not humiliating?" I debated with her.

"No!" she replied.

"Why not?" I asked.

"No! I don't go bed with men like that. Maybe you do?" she said, trying to provoke me.

"What? Now only the sexy ones come to you in the Asphalt?" I teased her.

"No. It's not like that, fag! I just say no. Are you crazy? Who told you that if I'm a prostitute, I have to go to bed with anyone who wants me? I go to bed with the ones I want to!" Natasha changed my perspective on the issue again.

"But aren't you afraid? What if the men get violent?" I continued.

"Let them try it! I know how to deal with them. I like the adventure of meeting new guys. When I am prostituting, I have the freedom to do things that I don't do even in Rocinha." She opened her big smile, smacked her lips, and gasped loudly.

CHAPTER SIX

If there was a certain heterotopic freedom to be had in the slum, leaving the territory of the favela could enable other minoritarian freedoms, too. After all, the Asphalt was not just a homogenized territory for normative liberalism. For my travesti friends, sex work offered a way to deterritorialize the Asphalt. From a normative liberal perspective, prostitution seems to present a binary: either sex workers are free or they are slaves, who necessarily have to be "saved" (territorialized) by normative liberalism. I argue that transgender sex workers are operating on both sides of this binary at once—working within the cracks that contradiction enables. Queer sex workers from the favela weren't liberal empowered agents who freely chose the beauty technologies that they wanted to consume and then chose to sell their services in a free market. Neither were they simply the exploited victims of an immoral system of exchange, based on a human-trafficking scheme, which propelled them to go into debt to achieve a standard female body, enriching the beauty industry and exploiting travestis' low self-esteem. Presented with this overly simplistic binary possibilities, minoritarian subjects took the disidentification route that I have ethnographically described in this chapter, satisfying some of their desires.

I have already argued that for most of my queer friends in Rocinha, freedom was related to the potential of deterritorialization offered by certain bodily practices.[41] Angel was fully engaged in the prostitution enterprise in Italy. She used the opportunities provided through this "illegal" scheme to challenge other norms. Angel achieved her desired figure, even when the travesti body she wanted for herself was considered abject according to heteronormative ideals. She worked in a "market" that did not fit the idealized liberal understanding of a free market. The Mattatoio operated in the shadowy peripheries of Rome, circulating money that did not come from state-regulated financial activities only. Most clients certainly did not have the sanction of their families, wives, and churches—quite the contrary. From a heteronormative perspective, the majority of these habitués were practicing "deviant" acts in secret—many of them guided by passions, fantasies, pleasures difficult for them to rationalize. These men were looking for something that other female bodies could not typically offer them. These interconnected minoritarian acts enabled alternative modes of liberalism to emerge, in an extensive assemblage that connected Rocinha to Rome.

SEVEN

As If There Is No Tomorrow

Freedom as a demonstrable fact and politics coincide and are related to each other like two sides of the same coin. HANNAH ARENDT, *BETWEEN PAST AND FUTURE*

I still recall the smell of old mattress when I entered that small room to find Natasha in a regretful state in 2012, after having temporarily lost contact with her.[1] All of her vitality seemed faded on the day that I encountered my friend sick, feverish on top of a sweaty bed in Rocinha. Natasha had not done her hair. She didn't brag about her beauty or delight in her pleasure in being a liberated travesti. But her desire for pride was still there, even if manifested differently. Natasha wanted my trust, to be taken seriously. She seemed to want some recognition from me that she still had control over her situation, the pride of having her truths acknowledged. That day, Natasha had told me she had a common virus, not even deserving of a name—a generic virosis, a virus that we shouldn't care about. Perhaps she knew it to be the opposite, but the fact is that she chose not to surrender.

Was it me who had a problem dealing with that situation? I had close to no previous experience with death until I moved to Rocinha. I only remembered my paternal grandmother's passing up to that moment, with no other deaths among my close friends or colleagues. There were numerous casualties while I lived in Rocinha. During police operations in the favelas, it was common for bodies to be left scattered around. Amélia had told me that when there were conflicts between rival drug-dealing factions, the situation was even worse. "Some years ago, I used to get up to go to work on

CHAPTER SEVEN

Monday mornings and had to jump over dead bodies in Rua do Valão! A truck from the municipality would come to collect them in piles," she remembered. Rocinha introduced me to a different relationship to death. Nevertheless, I was still not ready to accept the fact that Natasha's life could be at risk.

December 11

The day after the encounter with my moribund friend at Vavá's house, I went back to see Natasha's cousin Nivaldo. I wished to find out more from him about the situation. I was welcomed at their house again, where I told them both about my shock over seeing Natasha in such a state. I wanted their help in thinking up a plan of action to rescue Natasha. This idea took hold of me even though I was, at that time, intellectually aware of the argument that acts of "rescue" have a long colonial genealogy.[2]

"There's nothing we can do, Moisés! I already spoke to her several times. She doesn't want to go to the hospital." Nivaldo told me, while smiling in a strange way.

"But do you think she is going to get better?" I asked.

"Who knows? I hear she is not well at all," Nivaldo replied.

"Do you know what exactly her illness is?" I continued.

"She seems to have nodules growing all over her throat," he explained.

"Yes . . . but why? What is causing it? Do you think it could be cancer or something else?" I insisted.

"You mean, Freddy?" he bluntly put it.

"Could it be HIV?" I asked, using a more technical language, imaging it would be more delicate.

"Sure, it could be! This thing could catch any of us. And do you know her stories, right?" he answered, making me curious.

"What stories?" I wanted to find out more.

"Well, there are many . . . but do you know what happened to her in Ceará? Just before moving here to Rio de Janeiro?"

"No, I don't. What was it?" I asked anxiously.

"Oh, my . . . It's a novella," he remarked, and made himself more comfortable on his sofa, after straightening the heavy glasses on his face.

Nivaldo slowly told me that Natasha had been affected by an illness a few weeks before she decided to migrate to Rio. She was losing weight and had a persistent fever while still living in Martinslândia. After a few days of her feeling these intense symptoms, Dona Rosário decided to take Natasha (or Clodoaldo at that time) to the public hospital in Guaraciaba do Norte with the help of one of her sons. Natasha was so weak when she checked in that the nurse who attended to her first suggested she should be put on intravenous fluids straightaway. Dona Rosário was very worried; she had lost other children before. Natasha's mother waited for a few hours until a doctor was available to give them a diagnosis. He examined Natasha carefully and suggested she had a severe case of the flu. He discharged her. Dona Rosário hoped to make it back to Martinslândia that same day. However, on her way out of the public hospital, Natasha collapsed. One of the nurses rushed to help her and called for the doctor again. This time, it was an emergency. Natasha was put on a flimsy hospital bed. The doctor barely looked at her and ordered the nurses to take Natasha in for the night and perform blood tests. Dona Rosário cried. She wanted to sleep at the hospital that night to be with her daughter, but Natasha's brother convinced her to go back to Martinslândia and return the following day.

Natasha stayed in the hospital for days. Dona Rosário took the D-20 between Martinslândia and Guaraciaba several times to visit her.[3] About two weeks later, Natasha seemed to be getting better. The doctors received all the results of her blood tests and informed Natasha of her diagnosis. On the day that Natasha received the results, Dona Rosário worked on her little farm (*roça*) that morning and went to the hospital in the afternoon. Upon her arrival, she heard from the nurses that Natasha had pulled the IV drip from her arm and, with blood still spurting from her vein, escaped from the hospital through the front door. Dona Rosário was angry at the hospital staff. She started a desperate search for her daughter, but she heard nothing for a couple of days. When Dona Rosário finally had news from Natasha, the first thing her daughter said was that she was going to move to Rio de Janeiro and do everything in life that she had ever wanted to do.

I found Nivaldo's story very strange. I thought, "Blood was gushing out as Natasha escaped from a hospital?" Then I asked Nivaldo, "What were the results of her blood tests in the first place?"

"Who knows!" he replied, shrugging.

"Certainly, Dona Rosário knows?" I insisted.

"I don't know if she does. I really don't! And if she did, why would she tell us?" I didn't have time to continue that conversation for much longer. I was booked on a flight out of Brazil the following day. I returned to my place in the favela to pack up my things, including all my confused feelings from those intense days in Rocinha.

A couple of months later, in November 2012, I had just started a fellowship in Cambridge, Massachusetts. On November 11, Natasha's sister

CHAPTER SEVEN

Marieta sent me a message asking me to pray for my friend. Natasha's situation had deteriorated, and she had been admitted to a public hospital in Vila Isabel, near a famous soccer stadium in Rio, called Maracanã. When I asked her for details about Natasha's illness, all her sister said was "cancer in her throat." After that call, I frantically tried to contact several other people in Rocinha, without much success. Amélia didn't know anything about Natasha but promised to try to contact her family. When I talked to Bira, he confirmed that Natasha had been hospitalized and her condition was severe. He told me that the doctors were very concerned. At the same time, he also complained that her family had been very protective of her. He was upset because the family would not authorize Natasha's friends from Rocinha to visit her in the hospital.

Natasha's flatmate, Vavá, replied to me a day later. He also confirmed that our mutual friend was very sick. "Hopefully, she will recover as I did," he said. He forwarded a photograph of Natasha in her hospital bed, shirtless, with her eyes closed, exposing a pair of skinny arms and an extremely swollen neck. White tape crossed her face from side to side, holding in place a tube that went inside her semi-open mouth. Despite everything, Natasha looked peaceful. I stared at the photo on my screen for a few minutes before I started crying.

A few days after Natasha's sister contacted me, she wrote again to inform me that Natasha had been recovering well during the previous twenty-four hours. The doctors said the signs were positive. I got excited and immediately shared the good news with Amélia and Samira.

About a month later, on December 11, 2012, Natasha's family informed me that my friend had passed away. The burial took place on the same day as her death. I was invited but couldn't make it from the United States to Brazil with such short notice.

Buried in Pants

The following week after Natasha's death, I returned to the favela. This was the soonest I could get there. Amélia hosted me in her house. Her son, Moreno, had moved out to live with his girlfriend, and Amélia offered me his bed. Conversations about Natasha inevitably marked that visit of mine to Rocinha. I tried to see as many of our mutual friends as possible. There was a general feeling of revolt among them. People accused Natasha's family of not letting them say farewell to their friend. According to these folks, mostly from PAFYC, Natasha's brothers told them that fags were not welcome to visit her in the hospital. Given this attitude, and the lack of information about the burial, most of Natasha's friends from Rocinha didn't attend the ceremony at Cemitério do Catumbi. In any case, this cemetery was located quite far away from Rocinha.[4] One of Natasha's closest travesti friends, Segata, vented:

You know what? I am happy that I didn't attend this funeral, Moisés. Because I've heard that they buried the fag in pants! The family dressed her up as a man to go to the grave! Can you imagine this scene? Ridiculous! If I were there, I would have gone crazy. I swear it. I would have given my own dress to put on her dead body. Even if I had to go naked in the middle of the cemetery, I would have done it. You know I would have done it!

I was moved by the sorrow in people's memories regarding Natasha's last days. Apparently, her family had, more than ever, revolted against all queerness. I wondered if Natasha's family had blamed her "libertinism" for such a premature death. I heard from Nivaldo that her brothers had even moved out from Rocinha and relocated to Rio das Pedras, a favela with no drug traffickers, but with an order imposed on different principles than Rocinha. Rio das Pedras was a favela controlled by paramilitary (*milícia*) groups, mostly constituted by current or former state agents (e.g., policemen, firemen, and politicians). As such, paramilitaries aligned themselves much more closely to the most violent aspects of state power. On the other hand, their operations were more "discreet" than that of drug dealers. They also imposed a certain normative order to the place that was not possible in Rocinha.

Nivaldo gave me Natasha's brother's phone number to call, but it was hard to find the courage to do so. To my surprise, Natasha's sister ended up contacting me before I reached out. Marieta had seen on social media that I was back in Rocinha and dropped me a message saying her mother was in Rio das Pedras and wanted to see me. My heart got very tight at the thought of encountering Natasha's family after her death, after hearing all the stories of homophobia and transphobia attributed to them. If they didn't want any fags visiting Natasha in the hospital and had even tried to "normalize" her gender in Natasha's last moments on this earth, why would they be interested in talking to me?

Still, I arranged to visit them on a Saturday. I took the same white van from Rocinha to Rio das Pedras that, a few times before, I had taken in Natasha's company. As I didn't know the other favela well enough, Marieta offered to wait for me at the van stop in Rio das Pedras. Upon my arrival, I was happy to see that Dona Rosário had come to meet me at the stop too. She hugged me even harder that day than when I got off the truck in front of her house in Martinslândia. Before any words were

CHAPTER SEVEN

exchanged, the older woman's eyes teared up. Marieta seemed glad to see me. She gave me two kisses on the cheeks and pointed toward the direction of her house. "We all moved out of Rocinha. My brothers are living in Rio das Pedras now. There is too much confusion in Rocinha! It is like living in hell there. I always preferred Rio das Pedras. It's more organized here," Marieta explained to me along the way. What she didn't mention was that such "organization" was only possible at the expense of some freedoms. Drug dealing, for example, which was a public activity in Rocinha, was severely repressed in Rio das Pedras.

Natasha's sister lived with her husband and a baby daughter in a large one-bedroom apartment. "These days, my mother has been sleeping here in the living room," Marieta said, pointing to a brown sofa bed. Dona Rosário nodded.

Natasha's mother was quieter than usual. She asked me finally, "Were you traveling? How are you?" I explained about the fellowship in the United States and tried to avoid talking about Natasha's death. I wasn't sure when we would be ready to get to that painful topic. Dona Rosário surprised me by jumping straight into the issue: "We missed you at Clodoaldo's burial. There was no funeral. We didn't have the money for it. It was all very basic, but I am sure he would have liked you to be there."

I replied, "I wish I could've been there too! I met with her a couple of weeks before she was hospitalized. I'm glad I got to talk to her one last time then." Dona Rosário started crying again. Marieta rushed to grab her a glass of water.

Soon, my eyes started to well up with tears, too. I walked to a nearby window and looked out at Rio das Pedras to hide my face. Once I caught my breath, I tried to change the conversation topic and asked: "Are you going to move to Rio to live with your daughter now, Dona Rosário?" She didn't answer.

I looked at Natasha's sister, hoping she would break the silence. "Mom doesn't like it in Rio! She is only here now because of everything that has happened," Marieta replied with a timid smile. Her tone was very mellow, different from most of her family.

Dona Rosário finished her glass of water and then told me: "Come here! I want you to see something." She grabbed her luggage from underneath the sofa bed and pulled out an old box stuck between some clothing. Marieta looked at me. Dona Rosário held the box on her lap, then opened the cardboard lid. I got a whiff of old photographs. "I know that you had an appreciation for Clodoaldo. You were sincere . . . unlike most of his other friends! Most people liked to be with him during the nights out. They were good friends for moments of fun and wrongdoings. But what about the difficult moments?" she said. "I know you cared for him. You even came to Martinslândia to see us, to see his family."

Dona Rosário handed me the photographs she thought I should see. Marieta sat by my side. We looked at pictures of Natasha in Guaraciaba do Norte as a child. Images of my friend laughing among her brothers. Photos of Natasha in her hospital bed, like the ones Vavá had already shown me. Scenes of the burial, the coffin always with the lid closed. In one of the pictures, Natasha was in Rocinha, starting to transition into her travesti self, smiling, wearing a red cropped T-shirt. "My sister was such a happy person!" Marieta remarked, using the feminine pronoun. "I miss her company. I miss her excitement. We will never forget her! She was extraordinary."

Dona Rosário added: "But the little thing suffered a lot. I can't even tell you, Moisés! I can't explain how I felt seeing him in that hospital bed. As thin as a needle, but his neck was so swollen that he couldn't breathe." She paused, then continued, "Then, there was a day they told me that Clodoaldo was getting better! We all got so excited. You should have seen us that day. I thought I would have my son back. I really did! A few weeks later, he was dead."

Looking at the coffin photos, I wondered if they had really dressed the body in male clothing for the final moment. I still wanted to know the official cause of Natasha's death, too. But I didn't ask any of these questions. It wasn't the right moment. Indeed, that moment would never come. The pain and the void created by Natasha's absence took over. Dona Rosário was trying to share with me what was left of Natasha's presence. Despite all the criticisms I had heard regarding the family and the way they had handled Natasha's last days, the family deeply cared for her. I was also thankful that Dona Rosário knew that I cared for her daughter too. Having said that, I thought she was mistaken in thinking that Natasha's other friends were not sincere. Some were very close to her, queer sisters who were not allowed to say goodbye to Natasha. That day as I left Marieta's house to go back to Rocinha, Natasha's mother asked me to never forget Clodoaldo.

Resignation

I continue to think of Natasha and still try to grapple with how to best honor her life and her appreciation of "deviant" liberties in the face of all prejudice, oppression, and violence. Her courage is perhaps what struck me the most in the experiences I had in her company. There were

CHAPTER SEVEN

plenty of moments in our relationship when I worried about Natasha's safety and her future. I told her all the time: "Look after yourself, Natasha!" I asked her repeatedly about whether she was protecting herself by using condoms. In her last weeks of illness, when I was almost sure that Natasha was HIV positive, I considered forcing her to take antiretrovirals. But I worried that I was stepping beyond a legitimate ethics of care and moving into patronizing her. Perhaps, worse, I was inadvertently imposing a normative liberal logic of self-care upon someone I feared lived life too freely. I did not want to reproduce the moralizing framework that connected HIV with sexual freedom, but I could not always help it.[5]

When Natasha did die, I felt guilty in a way I still find hard to explain. Maybe I felt that I should have done more to intervene. But Natasha wouldn't let me. She wouldn't even go to the hospital. In my grief, I felt that she had failed to look after herself. And I had failed too. During my mourning period, I questioned if I had enjoyed Natasha's existence to the fullest extent that I possibly could. The deep disconnect that I sensed the last time I met her in person had left me with a sour aftertaste.

Finally, I came to think that, if Natasha's "excessive freedoms" were part of her desire for a form of non-normative liberation, perhaps her death had not been the total failure that I assumed at first. Instead, Natasha's complex life paths could serve as evidence of her courage to embody a travesti existence till the end, even when disapproved of by others. That Natasha would not heed my liberal pleas for "self-care," or her mother's clamors for "decent" freedoms, shouldn't come as a disappointment. After all, Natasha never told me that she was interested in living a long life and dying of old age. She never said that she wanted to die young either; I don't think Natasha was trying to kill herself. On the contrary, she enjoyed life so much that she consciously accepted the consequences of living life to the fullest extent according to her own liberal ideals, despite the severe oppressions to which she was subjected.

The recent literature on queer sex, particularly those works focused on sexual practices known as "barebacking,"[6] supports such understanding of Natasha's attitudes as a legitimate life choice, without falling into the trap of normative liberal judgments. David Halperin, a remarkable theorist, has argued that LGBTQ subjects continue to occupy the "risk group" category, despite claims to the depathologization of queer sexuality. When faced with queer sexual practices, public health specialists tend to offer "psychological" explanations to behaviors they find hard to explain. For example, there are claims that queer folks would engage in "dangerous sex" due to self-hatred, internalized homophobia, lack of self-esteem, sexual compulsion, among other accusations. The rise of barebacking as a queer sexual practice has attracted even more accusations of this kind. For Halperin, however, such narratives must be contested. It's pressing for queer politics to challenge what is understood as "risk taking" in relation to queer lives. The author calls for an understanding that does not necessarily oppose an ideal responsible hypercognitive liberal subject to other "deviant" ones, often understood as cognitively deficient, psychologically ill, and, ultimately, unable to make the right choices.[7]

Literary critic Michel Warner has also proposed that what is considered LGBTQ "risk behavior" must be understood in a different register: not as an individual psychological issue, but as a collective (social) phenomenon. He suggests three possibilities that could serve as alternative forms to interpret barebacking sex (particularly, in situations in which seronegative subjects consent to "unprotected" sex with seropositive ones): solidarity with seropositive partners, an ambivalent attitude toward the importance of living a long life, and, finally, the refusal to live a "normal" life.[8]

I started to wonder if Natasha's death could be conceptualized as a challenge to normative liberalism. The wider ethnographic theory of minoritarian liberalism that I offer is faithful to Natasha's expressed desires and her politics. However, I wondered if such an interpretation would only serve to comfort the pain and guilt of not being able to save her life. On the worst days, I questioned if, rather than being truthful to Natasha's desires, I was uncritically accepting the inequalities and injustices that make some people live longer than others. Would Natasha have died if class difference, discrimination, and transphobia didn't exist? Would Natasha be dead if normative liberalism wasn't so nefarious?

I know that, given the conditions of possibility presented to a Brazilian travesti living in a large favela in Rio de Janeiro in those years, around 2010, Natasha didn't let the possibility of death take away her liberties. What seemed to me like a potentially lethal illness, something that deserved immediate treatment and hospitalization, was turned into a different issue for Natasha. Again, I don't think that Natasha was happy to die, but I felt from her a sense of resignation, the acceptance that comes from someone certain of her life choices. There was no self-pity or drama in her attitude during my last meeting with Natasha. There was only the desire that I would trust her words. I wish that I could have offered her a different kind of care and attention at that moment, one that surpassed my limitations of dealing with her imminent physical health.

CHAPTER SEVEN

This book is meant to honor Natasha Kellem's friendship in a way that I wasn't able to do before.

"No Future"

What I have been describing are alternative conditions of possibility for freedom in the life (and death) of favela dwellers, forms of liberalism that deviate from other established liberal understandings. Natasha's "excessive liberties" were not an exception in Rocinha; the crew of young queers in the favela, self-denominated as PAFYC, also took liberties that made me concerned for their future, health, formal education, and overall safety. All of those conversations I tried to have with them, which were really about protecting these kids for the future, revealed the difficulties I encountered when dealing with liberalisms other than my own.

In a book called *No Future*, Lee Edelman denounces the implicit orientation toward the future when it comes to the defense of human rights, private property, and longevity at any cost, including the liberal logic that includes the future of children as a fundamental consideration in any form of political reasoning. He calls this form of liberal normalization "reproductive futurism." In his argument, queer politics must challenge assumptions not just that humans must reproduce, but also that we must always think about a better future for "our" children as the ultimate political goal. In Edelman's words, "The true oppositional politics implicit in the practice of queer sexualities lies not in the liberal discourse and patient negotiation of tolerances and rights, important as these undoubtedly are to all of us still denied them, but in the capacity of queer sexualities to figure the radical dissolution of the contract." For Edelman, the "contract" is both a social contract and symbolic one, prescribing a (hetero)normative future orientation. Queerness shouldn't have to be incorporated into a "civil order" already determined, but should be able to redefine such notions, challenging "the foundational faith in the reproduction of futurity."[9]

Among the gay and lesbian bourgeoise, queer liberalism has come to signify the normalization of queer life in Europe and the United States, and also in nations considered more peripheric, such as Brazil and Mexico. According to the sociologist Rafael de la Dehesa, queer liberation in Latin America started to acquire more momentum in the 1970s, as an item added to the political agenda against "illiberal" forms of government, such as the military dictatorship in Brazil and the "one-party rule" of the Mexican PRI. In both cases, the normative liberal queer movement benefited from international liaisons with Europe and, most importantly, the United States. The international efforts to "democratize" Latin America opened up the region to other items in the international liberal agenda, such as the universalization of claims for human rights and the emphasis on notions of "modernity" derived from the Enlightenment. Along with these, there was also a push to expand civil rights to co-opt subjects who had been marginalized due to their non-normative desires and sexual practices.[10] More recently, these achievements have reached the point that it has become "normal" for homosexual couples not just to marry, but also to reproduce, having children both through adoption and other reproductive technologies.

For my friends in the favela, however, minoritarian modes of liberalism offered different possibilities. Favela dwellers challenged the liberal social contract in their unapologetic occupation of land, and they presented an even bolder challenge when they refused to live life according to the expectations of reproductive futurism. Their main concern was not necessarily related to a better future, getting legally married, living as long as possible, or saving resources for their offspring.[11] Instead, they cared much more about living life to the fullest, enjoying sexual pleasures disconnected from concerns with biological reproduction and even with one's "health." Instead of preserving their bodies for the future, they were more concerned with testing the limits of bodily transformations.

The Death Toll

Different modes of liberalism continue to emerge in Rocinha. Following LGBTQ life paths in the favela over the years, I kept witnessing several other histories that bring me back to Natasha's memories. The desire for alternative forms of liberation continues to exist, despite what the Brazilian Constitution guarantees, pressures for modernization, and the existence of a Universal Declaration of Human Rights. As the PAFYC crew members grew older, their life projects continued to be implicated in desires that often coalesced in what I have been calling minoritarian liberalisms, with ramifications that are difficult to accept for those living according to more normative ideals of freedom.

Apart from my former neighbors that I see more often, I kept in regular contact with Samira, Segata, and members of the PAFYC group, such as Pituca and Adilson. In April 2014, I noticed a post on social media announcing the death of a travesti named Kimberley Ambrósio, who was still in her teens.[12] Samira confirmed it when I called her. I had never been close to Kimberley, but I still grieved her death, in part because she reminded me of Natasha. When I asked how she died, Samira replied: "Water in her lungs, they said. I don't know anything else. You know how these things are, right? It's complicated." Yes, I told her. I understood it from past experiences.

In the following year, only seven days after my birthday, in January 2015, I heard that a friend from Rocinha, Anderson Dieckmann, had died. "Yes! It's true," Samira confirmed. "Anderson is dead. He died of tuberculosis. Maybe it was something he caught in jail?" Samira reminded me that Anderson had spent some time in jail when he was caught by the police trafficking drugs in the Asphalt. Anderson was very tall, with a pointy nose. His adopted surname, Dieckmann, was a reference to the Brazilian actress Carolina Dieckmann. They both had similar nose shapes. I tried to find out more from Anderson's family. I wished to talk to them and offer assistance. Nobody in Rocinha helped me in that endeavor. Again, there was a sense of resignation that I found hard to cope with.

Then, in late March 2015, an acquaintance named Dellon passed away too. He was not exactly a friend, but I knew him well from hanging out with mutual friends. The year before his death, he had been arrested, and the news was all over Brazilian media. The police accused him of participating in a sex work scheme involving underage teenagers from Rocinha. He was charged as a pimp. Dellon was a little older than other PAFYC members but not even twenty-one. When I asked Samira about his death, she replied, "Are you thinking what I am thinking? Every year at least one of our friends from PAFYC is dying. What do you think it is? Is it HIV?" I didn't know what to say. It seemed like a combination of factors. I had thought a lot about HIV and AIDS during Natasha's death, perhaps too much. As I went silent during our dialogue, Samira continued to talk. "Dellon had been sick for a while. He was skinny. Nobody openly said it was AIDS, though. I think it was."

As with previous deaths. People would pay homage to the dead mainly on their social media profiles. A few weeks later, the messages would stop, and life would go on until another death would take place. In March 2017, it was João Marcos who died. I barely knew João, but Samira still wrote me a message to let me know. She was upset about his death. João was also a member of PAFYC. "Cancer! A brain tumor took away his life, Moisés. At least, this is what I've heard. He was very young." I remembered Natasha's family informing people that Natasha had died of cancer, too. I tried to console Samira over the phone and said I wanted to meet her in person to talk about all these deaths. I still wondered if they were preventable. I wish there was more we could do than just witnessing death after death. At the same time, I didn't want to be patronizing either; I was trying to learn to cope with death in the way that my favela friends did.

Some months later, in October 2017, Samira and I met again in person in Beco do Foguete, PAFYC's usual rendezvous in Rocinha during the first years I lived there in 2009 and 2010. We had a long talk and discussed if there was anything we could have done to prevent all these deaths. Samira told me, "This is not due to a lack of advice, Moisés. I always talk to these kids and tell them to look after themselves, right?" She continued, "My friend Maria, you know Maria? Who is much older than us? She openly tells them to wear condoms and tells them to get tested for HIV. They agree to it, and then they lie about it! I know they don't want to get tested. Maybe they are afraid of the test results? Maybe they don't want to worry about it or even care? Why should we care if they don't care themselves?" I offered to think about some public health project or organization that would bring rapid HIV testing to the favela so we could get our PAFYC friends tested. Samira remarked: "Well, you can try . . . but it's not going to work, I'm telling you." I confessed that the desire to "save them" reemerged with every single death that took place, even when I was critical of reproducing a moralizing attitude like that of some Evangelicals I had met in Rocinha. Whenever I tried to act upon that desire for salvation, it was clear there was not much I could actually do.

Since then, as I write these final chapters of *Minoritarian Liberalism*, in 2020, two more deaths have occurred among the PAFYC group. The travesti Roberta, a good friend of mine, has passed. She was only about ten years old when I met her in Rocinha for the first time, and I kept in contact with her ever since. In 2013, she was caught with two others walking around Morro do Banco, a small favela on the other side of Morro da Gávea, west of Rocinha and closer to Barra da Tijuca. In that episode, traffickers from Morro do Banco, members of a rival faction to the traffickers in Rocinha, accused Roberta and her friends of espionage. They took her and the two friends to a hidden place in Morro do Banco and severely abused them. The photos of Roberta's head bleeding from pistol-whipping ended up all over the news. But Roberta had survived that episode. In 2020, she seemed to be doing really well. Her death was sudden. As I checked her photo albums online, I noticed that over the years Roberta had been wasting away. "Maybe drugs?" Samira asked me when I pointed that out. She continued, "I really don't know, Moisés. It is all very sad to me. But I know Roberta had been involved with drugs."

CHAPTER SEVEN

Just a few days later, it was Marcelo who died. He was about sixteen at the time of his death, so maybe he had been too young to remember when I lived in Rocinha. Over the years, as he grew up, he was often singled out among the PAFYC crew due to his good looks. He also tried to act more masculine than the others and kept his hair bleached blond, like a surfer. The combination of his youthfulness, physical attributes, and masculine attitude was very profitable for him. Marcelo had been working as a male sex worker (*garoto de programa*) for quite a while. I often saw photos of him taken in luxurious apartments in the South Zone of Rio de Janeiro, where he used to meet his male clients. I always worried that most of his partners were at least three times Marcelo's own age. Likely, a useless moralism from my part. Marcelo died in a hospital, after a few weeks in intensive care. Just like Natasha.

Once again, I turned to Samira, feeling devasted, guilty, and tired of all these deaths. I asked her upfront: "Was there something we could have done to prevent Marcelo's death?"

She replied, "They said it was cancer. But I think it was HIV. And you?"

I said, "I don't know! Not everything is HIV. But soon, all of our PAFYC friends will be gone. How is that possible?"

Samira replied, "Yeah, my dear! It seems that things only get worse with all these deaths. But what can we do? These kids only think about fucking around and enjoying life as if there is no tomorrow!"

Life, Ethics, and Freedom

There were several traits presented by Oscar Lewis as part of what came to be known as the "culture of poverty" approach in the 1960s and 1970s. At first sight, some of them would fit well with the situation of some dwellers of Brazilian favelas. Lewis mentions, for example, "confusion of sexual identification, a lack of impulse control, a strong present-time orientation with relatively little ability to defer gratification and to plan for the future."[13] As I have argued in the introduction to this book, the normative liberal basis of the "culture of poverty" approach presents a challenge to the understanding of life in territories of urban poverty. I wouldn't deny, for example, that "strong present-time orientation" seems an apt description of the attitude that most of the PAFYC members have. The assumption, however, that such time orientation is a (cultural) problem can only be made against an expectation of future orientation as the norm. What Lewis calls "confusion of sexual identification" is based on assumptions of a normative gender binarism.

I don't mean to be anachronic or repeat critiques that have already been made. What I want to suggest, using Lewis's observations from more than fifty years ago, is that alternative forms of liberalism might have existed in the so-called territories of urban poverty for much longer than we assume. In previous studies, however, these minoritarian freedoms would have been dismissed, if not erased—treated, for instance, as problems that "development" should be able to solve.

The short life span of queer favela dwellers is not only a matter of necropolitics.[14] At the core of the problem with LGBTQ "untimely" deaths is an assumption from a normative liberal standpoint that these subjects hold an *inability* to appreciate the value of life (versus death, and also versus non-life).[15] As *living* subjects, my friends were expected to go through all the different normative stages of life (birth, growth, reproduction) before reaching the final stage, which should be death. Instead, their queer insistence in non-reproduction, no future orientation, and their capacity to endure premature deaths and cultivate relations with spirits of the dead present a challenge to the normative liberal constitution of the ordering of life (biopower).[16] At the same time, they also question the ideal relationship between the living and other beings not supposed to have the capacity for life. Furthermore, queer favela dwellers present a problem for normative liberalism because they challenge the social contract requirement that one must offer obedience to the nation-state in exchange for the care and the protection of their lives. Minoritarian liberalisms and queer experiences in favelas reconfigure life and non-life in such a way that it becomes impervious to the profit maximization requirements of neoliberalism. This is not a simple issue to be fixed through further inclusion of this population into public health policies, development projects, or even an issue of Universal Human Rights alone. Nor could it simply be resolved with more benevolence from the part of drug traffickers or some new law of the Hillside.

James Laidlaw's notable article "For an Anthropology of Ethics and Freedom" called my attention to the promise that anthropology held in the face of a central human dilemma: the conditions of possibility for freedom. In Laidlaw's words, "Wherever and in so far as people's conduct is shaped by attempts to make of themselves a certain kind of person, because it is as such a person that, on reflection, they think they ought to live, to that extent their conduct is ethical and free."[17] My friends in Favela da Rocinha are well aware of their oppression and its consequences: economic exploitation, class difference, lack of access to public services, among others. However, they often respond to these most stifling dimensions of their lives in ways that are not obvious to others, partly because their diagnosis of the problem does not derive from a normative position. The analysis of liberalism that I've been proposing derives from multiple encounters with liberties and freedoms from Brazilian favelas that I could not have witnessed if it wasn't for the queer forms of life that my friends made for themselves. I celebrate Natasha's existence and that of all my friends from Rocinha who have already passed. May they continue to be free spirits.

Neither Bland nor Shy

For as long as the elite controls the possibilities for freedoms and liberties, the oppressed are bound to remain oppressed. Conceiving of an anthropology of liberation, Michael Singleton issued a warning to the effect that "the present generation, knowing the theology of liberation only by name, will come to replace it by a bland anthropology."[18] The efforts of the so-called "decolonial generation"[19] of anthropologists give us hope that this struggle will not be bland. But we may not need to let "anthropology burn"[20] to challenge the powers of normative liberalism.

In fact, minoritarian liberation demands a detailed ethnographic engagement to understand "disidentification": that is, how those outside the racial, sexual, and even adult mainstream negotiate with dominant powers not by aligning themselves with or against these exclusionary forces, but rather by transforming them for their own purposes.[21] An important contribution of queer slum dwellers' political work has been the constant production of "lines of flight" in the face of intertwined forms of oppression. One way they produce such lines is through deterritorialization and the mobilization of multiple modes of liberalism at once, which so often go unnoticed or are immediately maligned. Perhaps what we need is not to propel toward the end of anthropology, but to strive for an anthropology more connected to the minoritarian existences we claim to support. Anthropology has fallen short in its contributions to the cause of freedom because most anthropologists fear an alignment with normative liberalism. This book has shown that if we carry on with the urgent task of decolonizing liberalism, we should be able to better appreciate the differences between a (normative) liberal anthropology and a (minoritarian) anthropology for liberation.

Epilogue

> Only through serious play can one experience freedom both as a means and as an end of human existence because freedom is not merely an abstract goal but also an educational experience in shared humanity. SVETLANA BOYM, *ANOTHER FREEDOM*

In normative liberalism, the use of language is understood as a performance of a determined "right to freedom," often guarded by the rule of Law.[1] In a book entitled *There's No Such Thing as Free Speech*, however, philosopher Stanley Fish argues that the liberal idea of "free speech," as, for example, present in the American Constitution, is unattainable. This is because "in as far as the point of the First Amendment is to identify speech separable from conduct, and the consequences that come in conduct's wake, there is no such speech, and therefore nothing for the First Amendment to protect."[2] Although Fish's point may seem controversial, the argument refers to the idea that every utterance is in itself an act; speech itself is a form of conduct.[3] The limits between "free speech" and "hate speech" is the most accepted formulation that clearly demonstrates the problem of assuming free speech as a "universal right."[4]

In Rocinha, where the rule of law established by the Brazilian state didn't operate in the same way as in the Asphalt, the realization that "there's no such thing as free speech" seemed to be more evident than in other territories. Among the field annotations from my experiences in the slum, I count several occurrences of an expression that friends of mine, such as Mazinho, Kayanna, and Natasha, deployed frequently: "Quem te deu a liberdade de falar assim comigo, hein?" (Who gave you the freedom to speak to me like that, huh?) The expression was used when, within a given interaction, one of the parties somehow felt offended by the speech act of the other. Even if the expression is not exclusive to favelas, it was undoubtedly more prominent there than in other places where I had lived. In this final section, I would like to pose this common slum question back to myself and, by extension, to the field of anthropology: "Who gave you the freedom to speak about minoritarian liberalisms?"

Natasha used to "take liberties" with others, or *dar um it*.[5] At the same time, she also demanded respect. When the same question above was posed to her, the most common answer that Natasha would offer was simply saying: "Eu posso! Sou Natasha Kellem Bündchen!" (I can do it! I am Natasha Kellem Bündchen!) She knew that being a travesti living in a Brazilian favela carried some libertarian traction. As for me, I could presume that I needed no special permission to speak claiming that in the favela "anything goes." This would be wrong. Or else, I could invoke a constitutional right to speech, in the normative liberal fashion. Relying on normative liberalism to justify the conditions of possibility for this book, however, would be a self-defeating exercise, against my political intentions.

Instead, learning from my friends in Rocinha, while recognizing our unequal positions, I propose to make more explicit the conditions that I consider having allowed for this research (beyond the formal consents I received to this effect). I would like to highlight three aspects that have marked the anthropological endeavor that led to the publication of this book; demands that were posed to me in the field as emergent conditions for my speech on liberalism. First, Natasha and others demanded a dialogue based on the understanding of their truths as truths. Second, fieldwork showed me the importance of the distinction between a liberal anthropology and an anthropology for liberation—the latter proving to be more aligned with the interests of my queer friends. Third, in the face of these other conditions, writing became a particular ethic and political exercise, the tailoring of a narrative in support of minoritarian modes of liberation.

The concept of minoritarian liberalism introduced in this book is not meant to be simply a variation of liberalism within a pre-established framework of tolerance toward cultural "diversity." Instead, the concept is derived from fieldwork experiences and an anthropology "based on conscious political choices about standing on the side of struggle and transformation."[6] In this case, rather than merely looking to expand a catalog of freedoms, as some sort of anthropological "butterfly collection" exercise, I have suggested that the main point of taking minoritarian liberties seriously is to further the struggle of favela dwellers against forms of domination that are not the most evident and, for that same reason, more effective. Notably, I am referring to the colonization of liberal possibilities by normative liberalism. Many anthropologists, even those who claim to support freedom, have blind spots when it comes to liberalism. The realization that minoritarian modes of liberalism exist should serve to increase the heterogeneity (deterritorialization) of liberalism, not to further its universalization.

While in Rocinha, I experienced modes of minoritarian liberation that made me wonder if I ever really wanted to return to a form of life in which normative liberalism seemed more acceptable. The very possibility of choice in this case presented itself as a "liberal" problem to me. Who can choose what? As I was once reminded in Rocinha, as a middle-class Brazilian, I had the freedom to choose where to live, while most of the favela dwellers were trapped in the slum. Meanwhile, some neighbors of mine, mostly Evangelicals, proved that it was indeed possible to move out of Rocinha. In the latter's view, what often happened was that favela dwellers actually liked the "confusion" and "libertinism" of life in the favela.[7] From my part, I kept thinking: What did it mean to be trapped in a territory of alternative freedoms? Is that how favela drug lords must feel? All freedom and power within the slum while also entrapped in it? Are people in the Asphalt any freer or just living different forms of imprisonment than favela dwellers? It made me think of the lyrics from the popular Brazilian song "Minha Alma" (My soul): "The condominium bars are meant to bring protection. But they also raise the question of whether you are the one who is in prison." When walking down to the beach with my favela friends, we used to pass by several upper-middle-class condominiums along the way. While we laughed and explored the streets freely, condominium children looked at us through iron bars, their parents expressing fear toward us.

Jail and Otherwise

In the favela, different modes of liberalism exist in articulation with the power and governmentality of drug lords. These minoritarian experiences are mainly constituted based on the "disidentification" of favela dwellers with the normative liberalism of the Brazilian elites. As Natasha herself acknowledged, she had more freedom to be herself in Rocinha than in the Asphalt. Partly, this was due to the laws of the Hillside, some of which were particularly tailored for the LGBTQ population in the favela. For some northeastern migrants, the possibility of a different experience of freedom was a fundamental facet in their desire to migrate from places like the interior of Ceará state to Rio de Janeiro. As a sort of migrant too, I experienced the direct effects of some of the drug lord's policies regarding queer liberties. For example, this happened when I was in the company of my friend Auro and we were targets of an ultimately unsuccessful homophobic attack in the favela.[8]

The dependence that some modes of favela liberalism have on activities considered "illegal" by the nation-state, such as drug dealing, highlighted another set of relationships (and fractures) between the laws of the Hillside and the rule of law (also known as the laws of the Asphalt). Even though the police had little control over the favela territory on a daily basis, traffickers were still subjected to limitations on their freedom of movement outside the slum. Drug dealers had to continually pay bribes to the police to avoid arrests and armed conflicts. As such, the territory of the jail figured as a vital articulator of liberties in the life of favela dwellers. My friend Rose explained this connection to me during one of my visits to a favela called PPG.[9] Traffickers who went to jail ended up valuing the most diverse possibilities for freedom, even more than those who had never been to jail. Confirming the importance of state prisons as nodes in assemblages of freedom in the lives of favela dwellers, Amélia's partner, Bezerra, once confessed during a conversation with his son, Moreno: "I want to have my freedom, man! Those people go to jail and are humiliated in prison, big time!" They discussed the easy money that could be made through drug dealing, and Bezerra ended up voicing a common understanding in the favela: for the urban poor, not being in prison was equivalent to having freedom already.

The Brazilian jail system is infamous for being overcrowded and corrupt, with a disproportionate non-white population. Bourgeois Brazilians, when they go to jail at all, are known to receive official and "unofficial" privileges. For instance, in a country where access to higher education is still a prerogative of the elites, by law, prisoners with a college degree are granted the right to have their own individual cell and to be kept separate from "ordinary" prisoners.[10] Meanwhile, the underprivileged population commonly suffer the worst forms of abuse in jail. Those without previous association to organized crime often end up joining drug-trafficking factions to guarantee their survival.[11] Jails are part of the punitive apparatus of the (neo)liberal state geared toward the urban poor, be it through humiliation or physical punishment. Jails are also part of the normative apparatus of religion in Brazil. Neo-Pentecostal churches offer spiritual liberation from the traps (*armadilhas, laços*) of the devil, but not only that: there are strong connections between religious and state forms of prison. Many convicts in state jails end up converting to Christianity in order to achieve one or both forms of liberation.

At the same time, the profound contradictions that exist among modes of normative liberalism and minoritarian liberalism were highlighted to me once again in 2020, while watching a TV show from Brazil. The program, aired on Brazilian television on Sundays, was presented by the medical doctor Drauzio Varella. He brought a camera into a Brazilian prison to explore different life stories of the incarcerated travesti population. In one scene, the presenter introduced the case of a travesti called Lolla, who had recently been authorized to leave the jail and go back home. Contrary to viewers' expectations, the fact that Lolla was free from prison did not bring her fulfillment. In Varella's words: "Living with her father, Lolla revealed that because she was back in society, she was no longer free to express her female gender identity as she wished to." Then he interviewed Lolla directly, who affirmed: "In jail, I had more freedom!"[12]

For travestis like Lolla, there were more minoritarian liberalisms to be enjoyed in jail than living outside of it, in "society," with her family, under a patriarchy. This serves as a reminder that kinship relations can both oppress "deviant" subjects and, at times, promote their liberalism, as it was the case in the PAFYC sisterhood.[13] Among queer groups, friendship can be such an important form of relationality that sometimes it turns into kinship. Therefore, critically examining the oppressive dimension of kinship relations is not the same as affirming that minoritarian liberalism should necessarily depend on individualism as an alternative. As the PAFYC case demonstrated, the freedom of their crew of "liberated fags," as a collectivity, was a matter of greater importance to them than individual liberation (although they also tested the more individual possibilities for liberation at the UCKG). At times, kinship relations "by blood" were also valued, and some travestis went to great lengths to mend them, *despite* the fact that they remained a source of oppression.

Outside the family sphere, most favela dwellers had stories to tell regarding their experiences with the nation-state. These went beyond their encounters with police officers and institutions like jails; favela residents engaged with state power whenever they obtained national identification cards or a workbook (Carteira de Trabalho),[14] received electricity at their homes, or were treated at public hospitals. A successful income redistribution program called Bolsa Família operated under President Lula's leftist government in 2009 and 2010.[15] Nevertheless, it was the nation-state policing apparatus that most marked the life of Rocinha

EPILOGUE

residents. There was a constant threat of police "invasions" into the favela territory (with shootings, arrests, and stray bullets). There were also fears related to the body searches at the entrance of the slum and, above all, the fear of going to prison (or the reality of having friends, sons, daughters, and other relatives in jail).

In a book called *Freedom with Violence*,[16] queer theorist Chandan Reddy highlights that, for minoritarian populations, liberalism seldom means freedom from violence. On the contrary, most (normative) narratives of liberty attach the possibility of rights and citizenship of privileged (dominant) groups to a supposedly necessary and legitimate use of violence, often perpetrated by the nation-state against Black folks, queer people, undocumented migrants, and others. Reddy's observations are based on the realities of the US state. Although *Minoritarian Liberalism* is not focused on an explicit comparative analyses, it's still possible to consider the differences and similarities established through the operations of liberalism in different nation-states.[17] What seems to be evident in both the United States and Brazil is that the normative liberal assemblage in these two territories is greatly dependent on the perpetration of state violence (mainly through police violence and incarceration), which deeply affects the underprivileged populations of these countries. It shouldn't come as a surprise, therefore, that the recognition of alternative forms of liberalism becomes a political project that is urgent and extremely relevant to the life projects of Lolla and others in minoritarian groups.

Liberation Beyond Humanism

The relationship between the nation-state and different religious phenomena has also become evident through this ethnography of liberalism. The Catholic Church, the Neo-Pentecostal churches, and Afro-Brazilian religions all offered their own forms of liberation to favela dwellers. Combined with the state failure to support slum dweller's life projects, "religion" proved to be a valuable domain in the provision of liberties, be it through collective work (*mutirões*), exorcisms, or through trance and witchcraft. Religious liberation mattered to my friends from Rocinha in ways that secular liberalism could not address. For example, the transformations experienced by queer people through possessions and exorcisms were directly connected to the flexibility of their bodies, which allowed for a variety of non-human entities (deities, demons, and spirits) to penetrate and exist in (or instead of) them.

In the Universal Church's particular case, while I conducted fieldwork on their liberation services, an episode took place that made me connect again with the nation-state apparatus of liberalism.[18] I will never forget that I ended the night at a police station in Gávea, where I filed a legal case against the church. As such, one could think that the church and the nation-state are organizations that work through different modes of freedom. However, the Universal Church's efforts at exorcism and spiritual liberation also operated as an apparatus for the normalization of freedoms in the life of those favela friends who aimed to deterritorialize their bodies, desires, and sexual practices. In some sense, the UCKG and the nation-state were both agents that operated against minoritarian freedoms, but from different sides of the normative liberal fold.

Afro-Brazilian religions attracted most queer folks I met in Rocinha and challenged normative liberalism by promoting the deterritorialization of the self-possessed individual. I only recently heard from friends that even Natasha, who was more skeptical about these rituals, sought the help of a particular Pomba-gira in Rocinha when she needed it. These friends struggled with norms that could be defied through encounters with spirits and divinities, who advised on issues related to love, sex, and prostitution—challenging understandings of life and non-life and, by literally possessing human bodies, transformed their bounded existences.[19]

Importantly, if humans suffer from state violence, spirits are obviously not susceptible to the same punitive state apparatus, to policing, and to jail. At least, not in the normative liberal sense. Some of the Exus and Pomba-giras that were celebrated in Rocinha were considered criminals in previous lives. Some were sex workers, libertines, or formerly enslaved folks; humans that encountered the most brutal forms of state violence and were not the typical beneficiaries of normative liberalism during their lives. In other-than-human form, however, they managed to free themselves from the abuses of normative liberalism. Aware of this situation, the Neo-Pentecostal churches seem to have found an important "niche" of operation as agents in the regulation and oppression of these "deviant" spirits and their minoritarian freedoms, fulfilling the role of the state from a different side of the fold.

Times of Violence and Times of Fun

Even though I moved out of the favela in 2010, I was able to buy a one-bedroom apartment near Amélia's house a couple of years afterward.[20] Since the shack had no official deed to transfer, I signed a piece of paper produced by the previous owner acquiring the "rights" (in the sense of the laws of the Hillside) over the property. My permanent location in the favela is in the exact same alleyway where I lived in 2009 and 2010, just a few buildings closer to the Friends United School (FUS). As such, I have a home in Rio de Janeiro and keep my connections with most people I met during fieldwork. When I am not in Rocinha, Amélia and other neighbors help me to look after the *barraco* (shack).

In November 2010, the government of Rio de Janeiro decided to "occupy" the complex of favelas called Complexo do Alemão (the German Complex), located in the North Zone of Rio de Janeiro, not far from Rio's international airport. Complexo do Alemão can be best understood as a large conurbation of different favelas. As opposed to Rocinha's "Owner of Hillside," Complexo do Alemão had a much more complicated power arrangement, different "Owners," and different drug-trafficking factions throughout its fragmented territory. The decision to occupy such a complex was a clear sign of a new, more ambitious, and ever more violent form of "public security" policy in Rio de Janeiro.

The police operation was part of a broader program aimed at fighting drug trafficking and at bringing "order" to the favelas of Rio, as Brazil prepared to host the World Cup in 2014 and the Olympic Games in 2016. Because the police's occupation was strongly resisted in Complexo do Alemão, the Brazilian government decided to bring in the national army to fight against favela dwellers. The media coverage of the event included a lot of blood. The army justified their brutal display of force against those resisting the occupation by vehemently arguing that such a war was necessary to bring *liberdade* to the population living in that favela. A commandant of the police group that took part in the operation was cited in many newspapers as saying: "Vencemos. Trouxemos a liberdade à população do Alemão." (We won. We brought liberty to Alemão's population.)[21]

In the early hours of November 13, 2011, it was Rocinha's turn to be occupied by the police, in collaboration with the Brazilian army. The operation was announced on television days in advance by the high echelon of the Rio de Janeiro government, leaving my friends in Rocinha anxiously (and fearfully) waiting for the war to come. As before, the government and the national media continued to justify the nation-state occupation through claims that it would bring liberty to the favela population. After the initial occupation, the professed plan was to install what the local government was calling UPPs (Unidades de Polícia Pacificadora, or Pacifying Police Units) in Rocinha. Up to that moment, police operations consisted mostly in the "invasion" of state forces into the favelas, searching for drugs, arresting people, and then leaving. The UPPs were based on a different logic, the main principle was that nation-state agents would not only invade, but also *occupy* favela territories, bringing a much larger contingent of state representatives to the slums, and establishing new police stations inside the communities.

It was not very clear to anyone how the traffickers in Rocinha would react to such an "attack" by the government, though. Some thought that—bearing in mind the bloody conflicts that happened at Complexo do Alemão in 2010—the traffickers in Rocinha would simply run away and avoid direct confrontation with the police. However, many other people had quoted Nem—the Owner of the Hillside at the time—who swore that he and his group would fight the police to the death. A close friend of mine also told me that, at a big party a few days before the scheduled occupation, Nem made an emotional speech, promising to put on a big bloody fight against the national forces in Rocinha. The violent scenes of the historical Canudos War came to mind once again in their historical parallelism to the favelas.[22]

On November 10, 2011, two days before the occupation was supposed to start, I was in Cambridge, Massachusetts, chatting on the internet to Armando, the FUS director. At one point in our conversation, he told me that he was shaken and could not believe what he had just seen on television. TV Globo had just interrupted its regular schedule to show some breaking news about Rocinha. My heart started to beat fast, I asked him what was going on and if he could hear fireworks. He told me no, but he wouldn't say more. Traffickers commonly used fireworks to signal imminent trouble in the favela. After a lot of back-and-forth, my friend finally told me: "TV Globo said that the police caught Nem!" It was my turn to go silent; I did not know what to say. Almost immediately, messages started to pop up on the internet about the possibility that Nem had been caught. My friends from Rocinha started to post frenetically on Facebook. Was it true that Nem had been arrested? Armando asked me to stay online and told me that he would try to keep me informed. He was still a bit doubtful of the news himself. Minutes later, my friends on Facebook started to post links to news articles that confirmed that Nem had been captured by the police while trying to flee Rocinha inside the trunk of a diplomatic car.

The reaction from the part of my queer friends in the favela was extremely negative. One of them kept publishing her views online. At one point she stated: "Liberdade Pro Nem da rocinha :) *_* vai toma no cú (UPP)," (Freedom To Nem of rocinha :) *_* go fuck yourself (UPP).) Overall, the negative mood was dominated by uncertainties about the future of the favela and, in particular, what the episode meant for the protection of queer liberties in Rocinha.

In many of my frequent subsequent visits, I heard complaints from my queer friends about how much things had changed. They missed all the fun parties. They missed the attention they used to receive from the traffickers. Above all, they mentioned that homophobia was increasing in the alleyways of Rocinha. "Who can we appeal to now? To the homophobic police officers?" asked one of my travesti friends. It turned out that even the Rocinha Gay Pride Parade, a new event that had emerged right after I moved out of the favela in 2010—and separate from the one that took place in the Asphalt—was under threat. It now depended on the formal authorization of the police to take place and, even worse, without the support of traffickers, there would not be funds to finance the event. Those first years of the UPP presence in Rocinha remained some of the worst for the minoritarian liberties of my favela friends. No significant changes took place in terms of introducing more normative liberties, either.

Since 2014, the UPP project fell apart in Rio. Without the required financial resources, the technical capacity, or the political will to put an end to profitable "illegal" activities, a dual and unstable system of power has become more apparent in favelas. New traffickers have been slowly encroaching upon the Hillside. Lately, there has been heightened excitement among my queer friends in Favela da Rocinha that the "times of fun" will prevail.

Acknowledgments

There are relationships that survive death. I celebrate all friends (dead or alive) that I have made in Favela da Rocinha and everything they have shared with me during the years I spent in the slum—and beyond. These comrades know who they are even when I prefer not to disclose their actual names. I will be forever grateful to each one of them.

During the long journey since my initial fieldwork, I have also learned a lot from students and colleagues at several institutions. The Federal University of Bahia (UFBA), where I am tenured, is a public institution that provides the best *free* education we possibly can to people who are, to a great extent, Black or working class in Brazil. My experiences with them have profoundly influenced the political positions I hold. UFBA's support for a paid sabbatical leave was fundamental for the production of this manuscript.

Still at UFBA, I am grateful to Marcelo Moura Mello, Guillermo Vega Sanabria, Núbia Bento Rodrigues, and Cecilia McCallum. From the group of colleagues working in other public Brazilian universities, I would like to thank the contributions received from Maria Elvira Diaz Benitez, Corinne Davis Rodrigues, and Paulo Victor Leite Lopes. Márcio Goldman generously hosted me at Museu Nacional during the initial period of my fieldwork in Rio de Janeiro. Antônio Carlos de Sousa Lima has been a loyal friend.

At the London School of Economics (LSE), I would like to acknowledge the support received from Olivia Harris (*in memoriam*), Michael Scott, and Gustavo Barbosa. In Scotland, at the University of St Andrews, Joanna Overing and my adviser, Huon Wardle, were fundamental for the success of my doctoral research. Mark Harris, Peter Gow (*in memoriam*), Nigel Rapport, Máire Ní Mhórdha, Daniel Billinge, Jan Grill, Daniela Castellanos, Veronika Groke, Giovanna Bacchiddu, and Ian Amaral were all supportive in different ways. My research program in both institutions in the UK would not have been possible without the financial support received from the IJURR Foundation (previously Foundation for Urban and Regional Studies) and different scholarships offered by the LSE and the University of St Andrews.

Steven Caton, the external examiner for my doctoral thesis, challenged and inspired me. It was at his invitation that I took my first postdoc position in the United States. Monica Munson offered me emotional and bureaucratic support while I was at Harvard. From a postdoctoral fellow in the Department of Anthropology under Professor Caton's supervision, I moved to Brandeis University, where I worked for a couple of years as an adjunct professor. I would like to thank all my colleagues from Brandeis, especially, Elizabeth Ferry, Jonathan Anjaria, Sarah Lamb, Pascal Menoret, Anahi Russo Garrido, and Mrinalini Tankha.

I am fortunate to have had the support of several other people. All my appreciation to Adedoyin Olosun, Nancy Scheper-Hughes, James Laidlaw, Loïc Wacquant, Fares Alsuwaidi, Jane Guyer, Veena Das, Camila Teixeira, Baba Pecê, Cassandra White, Joshua Reason, Suneeta Gill, John Beardsley, Daniele Gomes, Christian Werthmann, Balraj Gill, George Paul Meiu, George Marcus, Ieva Jusionyte, and Svetlana Boym (*in memoriam*). I must also thank the International Social Science Council (ISSC) for awarding me a World Social Science Fellowship, which has been a great resource.

When time came to look for a press, Priya Nelson was the first editor to see potential in my work, and I will never forget her encouragement. I must also thank Emily Sekine and Alan Thomas for adopting me and giving me developmental advice until Mary Al-Sayed took over as the anthropology editor at Chicago. Along with Tristan Bates, Erin DeWitt, and Kristen Raddatz, they all guided me to the successful launch of this book.

I have been working on this research project since 2009. However, much of the actual manuscript was only written in 2019 and 2020, while I took a visiting fellowship at Harvard University. Gareth Doherty has been the most supportive partner during all these many years. Ivone Pereira de Andrade, my mother, has offered me unconditional love. Natasha Kellem Bündchen has been an endless source of inspiration. I miss my brave and dear friend with all my heart. Together, in minoritarian liberation, we stand.

Notes

PREFACE

1. In most cases, I use pseudonyms in this book to afford more privacy to the lives of those I depict. In a few instances, interlocutors have explicitly asked me to use their real names. Natasha is among the latter.
2. According to the Brazilian National Association of Travestis and Transsexuals (ANTRA), travestis can be defined as "people who live a female gender construction opposite to the sex assigned at birth, along with a permanent female physical construction, and who identify in social, family, cultural, and interpersonal life through such an identity" (my translation). Source: https://antrabrasil.org/sobre/.
3. Fernando Meirelles and Kátia Lund, dirs., *City of God* (Miramax Films, 2002).
4. For the anthropologist Loïc Wacquant, "neighborhoods of urban relegation" refer to marginalized urban territories that, for this very reason, turn out to be central in the operations of the neoliberal state. Wacquant, "The Militarization of Urban Marginality," 58.
5. As discussed by Pitkin, "Are Freedom and Liberty Twins?"
6. "Contractualism" is used here to refer to the argument that some sort of "social contract" should be necessary for the achievement of rights and liberty. Thomas Hobbes, John Locke, and Jean-Jacques Rousseau would be among well-known contractualists from the Enlightenment. This is not to say that there is a homogeneous approach among these three classic figures. Hobbes and Rousseau, for example, are almost at odds with each other regarding the ideal model of government and how much power a sovereign should have.

NOTES TO PAGES xi–2

See Hobbes, *Leviathan*; Locke, *Two Treatise of Government*; and Rousseau, *The Social Contract*.

7. For a more extended discussion on the normative definition of "liberalism," see Cassin et al., *Dictionary of Untranslatables*, 570.
8. Sometimes, the political and economic aspirations of liberalism are at odds with each other. In more contemporary times, discussions over economic liberalism (and neoliberalism) have dominated the liberal agenda. Also, it is important to highlight that there have been instances of European liberal thought taking issue with normative liberalism, e.g., in the work of Karl Marx and Antonio Gramsci. These latter critiques have led to alternative reflections on liberalism by various thinkers outside of Europe, including Bhimrao Ambedkar, Aimé Césaire, and Paulo Freire.
9. At the same time, as Arjun Appadurai argues, "no modern nation, however benign its political system and however eloquent its public voices may be about the virtues of tolerance, multiculturalism, and inclusion, is free of the idea that its national sovereignty is built on some sort of ethnic genius." Appadurai, *Fear of Small Numbers*, 3.
10. As I explain in the introduction, "minoritarian" here is derived from Deleuze and Guattari, *Kafka*.
11. Tyler Stovall argues that liberty has been a privilege of whiteness in nations such as France and the United States. ". . . to an important extent, although certainly not always, ideas of freedom in the modern world have been racialized. In particular, many have considered whiteness and white racial identity intrinsic to modern liberty." Stovall, *White Freedom*, 5.
12. Muñoz, *Disidentifications*, 31.

INTRODUCTION

1. The Treaty of Tordesillas between Portugal and Spain, dividing the Americas (and the world) between the two kingdoms, dates from 1494.
2. Pacheco de Oliveira, *O Nascimento do Brasil e Outros Ensaios*.
3. Inconfidência Mineira was a prominent libertarian movement in Brazil in the late eighteenth century. Their motto, in Latin, affirmed: "Libertas Quæ Sera Tamen" (Liberty Even If Late). The "Independence" events that took place in 1822, led by a Portuguese prince regent, did not have the liberal effects that some Brazilians expected.
4. As discussed, for example, by Chalhoub, *Visões da Liberdade*.
5. The abolition of slavery in Brazil was not followed by economic policies to assist this population. Migration to urban centers became necessary in their search for livelihood.
6. As discussed by Valladares, *A Invenção da Favela*. Licia Valladares also states that both in the 1948 and 1950 census, Black folks and Mestizos were by far the most dominant ethnic groups living in favelas.
7. An argument made by Valladares, *A Invenção da Favela*.

NOTES TO PAGES 3–5

8. Da Cunha, *Os Sertões*.
9. Valladares, *A Invenção da Favela*, 35. *Favella* (arch.) or *favela* is also the name of a plant (*Cnidoscolus quercifolius*) that grew over the hills in Canudos (Bahia).
10. Da Cunha, *Os Sertões*.
11. Importantly, these genealogies of the favela are not mutually exclusive. Lorraine Leu's work on race and space in Rio de Janeiro effectively argues that despite the fact that favelas ended up being home to poor populations of various races, these are clearly "Blackened" space within the wider geography of the city. See Leu, *Defiant Geographies*.
12. Valladares, *A Invenção da Favela*.
13. Lima, *Um Grande Cerco de Paz*.
14. The work of the Brazilian educator Paulo Freire has also been a great inspiration for collective liberation in Latin America. See, for example, Freire, *Pedagogia do Oprimido*.
15. For references on the topic of *mutirões*, see, for example, Marciato, *A Produção da Casa (e da Cidade) no Brasil Industrial*. Also Boff, *O caminhar da Igreja com os Oprimidos*.
16. According to the Brazilian Institute of Geography and Statistics (IBGE), only 9% of Brazilians declared themselves to be Evangelicals in the national census of 1991. In 2010, this number had gone up to 22.2% of the population.
17. Something that I explore in further detail in chapter 5.
18. Pacheco de Oliveira, *O Nascimento do Brasil e Outros Ensaios*.
19. For example, Brazil's Gini coefficient increased from 0.574 in 1981 to 0.625 in 1989, which indicates a worsening in inequality. See Ferreira, Leite, and Litchfield, "Brazil."
20. It could be argued that the election of President Lula (Luiz Inácio Lula da Silva) in 2002 meant a slight deviation from this trend.
21. For an extended discussion on the logic of neoliberalism, see Brown, *Undoing the Demos*.
22. As João Pacheco de Oliveira points out, it is not a coincidence that recent state policies to "integrate" Rio de Janeiro favelas to the "formal" city in the early years of the twenty-first century have received the same designation as previous efforts to integrate the Amerindian population into the Brazilian nation: "Pacificação" (Pacification). See Pacheco de Oliveira, *O Nascimento do Brasil e Outros Ensaios*.
23. Poverty could be understood here as a condition with quasi-psychological "cultural traits" of its own, which were perpetuated intergenerationally. Introduced by the sociologist Michael Harrington, this approach was popularized through the work of the anthropologist Oscar Lewis. See Harrington, *The Other America*; and Lewis, *The Children of Sanchez*.
24. The medical anthropologist Paul Farmer explains that the concept of structural violence dates back at least to the 1960s when it was first used by

Latin American liberation theologians to refer to "sinful social structures characterized by poverty." He then sums up by saying that "the concept of structural violence is intended to inform the study of the social machinery of oppression." Farmer, *Infections and Inequalities*, 307. Nancy Scheper-Hughes and Philippe Bourgois also adopt the concept of an oppressive social machinery in relation to the question of "structural violence," but add another dimension to it, namely, the problem of its invisibility. Scheper-Hughes and Bourgois, *Violence in War and Peace*, 13.

25. Sen, *Development as Freedom*, 3–4.
26. See, for example, Valentine, *Culture and Poverty*; and Katz, *The Undeserving Poor*.
27. See, for example, Scheper-Hughes, "The Primacy of the Ethical."
28. Farmer, *Infections and Inequalities*, xxv.
29. Whitt, "The Problem of Poverty and the Limits of Freedom in Hegel's Theory of the Ethical State," 258.
30. There is great diversity to what is collectively known as favelas. These are not only differences in physical form, but also in mechanisms of power. To that extent, my findings in Rocinha are not automatically translatable to the realities of all Brazilian favelas.
31. Foucault, *Technologies of the Self*, 15.
32. UN General Assembly, *Universal Declaration of Human Rights* (217 [III] A, Paris: UN, 1948).
33. Povinelli, "A Flight from Freedom," 145.
34. Following Michel-Rolph Trouillot, I understand "the West" more as a power project for domination than an actual homogeneous geographic location. See Trouillot, "Anthropology and the Savage Slot."
35. Mahmood, *Politics of Piety*, 5.
36. Povinelli, "A Flight from Freedom," 162.
37. Chakrabarty, *Provincializing Europe*, 4.
38. This is despite the fact that European thinkers, such as Friedrich von Hayek, continue to be central to neoliberalism. Von Hayek, *The Road to Serfdom*.
39. Wacquant quoted in Hilgers, "The Three Anthropological Approaches to Neoliberalism," 357.
40. Hilgers, 359.
41. As an example of this approach, Mathieu Hilgers cites the work of the Comaroffs. See Comaroff and Comaroff, "Millennial Capitalism."
42. According to Hilgers, "The Three Anthropological Approaches to Neoliberalism," the work of Loïc Wacquant could be classified in this category. Wacquant argues that "what is 'neo' about neoliberalism [is], namely, the remaking and redeployment of the state as the core agency that actively fabricates the subjectivities, social relations, and collective representations suited to making the fiction of markets real and consequential." Wacquant, "Three Steps to a Historical Anthropology of Actually Existing Neoliberalism," 68.

43. The works of Aihwa Ong and James Ferguson could be cited in this group. See Ong, *Neoliberalism as Exception*; and Ferguson, *Global Shadows*.
44. Wacquant, *Urban Outcasts*.
45. Povinelli, "A Flight from Freedom," 146.
46. Mazzarella, "The Anthropology of Populism," 53.
47. Jobson, "The Case for Letting Anthropology Burn," 259.
48. As a concept, an "anthropology for liberation" has been previously put forward by Harrison, *Decolonizing Anthropology*, 10.
49. Shange, *Progressive Dystopia*, 8.
50. Regarding the existential conditions of African Americans, Du Bois has argued that there is a "double consciousness" in operation. "Two souls, two thoughts, two unreconciled strivings; two warring ideals in one black body, whose dogged strength alone keeps it from being torn asunder." At the same time that this tension causes unrest, it also provides African Americans with the potential for "second-sight," the ability to see the world differently from others. See Du Bois, *The Souls of Black Folk*, 17.
51. Harrison, *Decolonizing Anthropology*, 90.
52. I praise the wealth of crucial initiatives toward decolonization, including not just efforts from the queer and Black movements, but also Amerindian struggles toward sovereignty. In *Society Against the State*, for example, Pierre Clastres discusses a mode of minoritarian politics that could be conceived as an "indigenous liberalism."
53. This definition includes what is often described as "libertarianism."
54. As explained in the preface, following José Esteban Muñoz, I use the concept of "disidentification" to refer to creative strategies through which minoritarian populations engage with dominant forces to produce their own truths. See Muñoz, *Disidentifications*.
55. Shange, *Progressive Dystopia*, 8.
56. Deleuze and Guattari, *Kafka*.
57. In an interview recorded by Claire Parnet, Felix Guattari affirms: "It's not simply a greater quantity [of people] that vote for something, but the majority presupposes a standard. In the West, the standard that every majority presupposes is: 1) male, 2) adult 3) heterosexual, 4) city dweller. . . ." Felix Guattari, *G Comme Gauche* (interview, 1988).
58. Not because Black people are less important than white, but because racism in Brazil prescribes whiteness as the standard that should be universally desired (if not achieved).
59. See Deleuze and Guattari, *Kafka*, 18.
60. Hobsbawm, *Echoes of the Marseillaise*.
61. Deleuze and Guattari, *A Thousand Plateaus*. See also the discussion in Holland, "Deterritorializing 'Deterritorialization.'"
62. DeLanda, *A New Philosophy of Society*, 13.
63. See, for example, Eng, *The Feeling of Kinship*.

64. Issues of translation also speak to the difficult commensurability of different conceptions of liberalism. "Too much liberty becomes libertinism!" (*Excesso de liberdade é libertinagem!*), Amélia once explained to me, as she referred to the need to control her daughter's sexual life, making sure she remained a virgin.
65. The genealogy of the term *travesti* refers back to colonial encounters in Latin America. Originally, in reference to what was understood as native "cross-dressing" practices, given the colonizer's inability to transcend gender binaries. The originally pejorative adjective has been re-signified in Latin America and adopted as a gender identity that implies gender variance and a more permanent transition (from masculine to feminine) but not necessarily a desire for sex reassignment. For a more detailed history of the term, see Campuzano, "Reclaiming Travesti Histories."
66. In Franz Boas's essay "Liberty among Primitive People," he argues that "freedom is a concept that has meaning only in a subjective sense. A person who is in complete harmony with his culture feels free" (51). Criticizing Boas for taking a "subjective" approach to the topic, Bronisław Malinowski comments: "As far as I know, however, no anthropological contribution to freedom has yet been made. An article by Professor Franz Boas recently published cannot be considered as in anyway satisfactory." Instead, Malinowski, choosing to emphasize freedom as an objective fact through the (public) concept of culture, says: "Culture—the complex instrumentality of social organization, mechanical invention and spiritual values—is the real context in which human freedom is born and by which it is specifically limited. Culture gives freedom to man in that it allows him to control his destinies. Man frames his purpose in terms of cultural instrumentalities." Malinowski, *Freedom and Civilization*, vii, 319.
67. For specific references and a more detailed account of the history of freedom in anthropology, see the introduction of Lino e Silva and Wardle, eds., *Freedom in Practice*.
68. Humphrey, "Alternative Freedoms." In her text, Caroline Humphrey intentionally brackets off philosophical discussions of freedom in favor of ethnographic ones. The fact that the American Philosophical Society still awarded a prestigious prize to Humphrey for that essay is an indication of how important an anthropological approach to the theme of freedom could be for other fields of knowledge.
69. Humphrey, 2.
70. Humphrey, 3.
71. Peter Loizos has criticized the fact that anthropology has had an awkward engagement with the concepts of freedom and liberty, particularly when compared with the prolific production on these themes by philosophers and political scientists. Loizos argues that, instead, anthropology "has rewritten freedom-questions under other conceptual headings. These include the study of unfree statuses as they impinge upon groups; the study of

resistance to power structures and ideological pressures, both by groups, and by individuals; and the study of socialization as it limits both collective and individual autonomy." Loizos, "Anthropology's Engagement with Freedom-Questions," 88–89.

72. On the nuances of sovereignty and violence in Brazilian favelas, anthropologist Jaime Alves states, "The city's necropolitical governance strategy is produced at the intersections of racialized bodies, criminalized geographies, and police killing practices." Alves, "From Necropolis to Blackpolis," 324.
73. As Saba Mahmood has already indicated in *Politics of Piety*. For a comprehensive review, see Baehr, *Varieties of Feminist Liberalism*.
74. Hobbes, *Leviathan*.
75. Thomas Hobbes was fond of the idea that liberty should rest in the hands of a strong sovereign government. Debates over the extent to which individual autonomy matters in liberalism have varied among different currents. Particularly in the Anglo-Saxon tradition, those that were most influenced by Immanuel Kant's philosophy tend to highlight the importance of human autonomy and rationality as key liberal aspects.
76. A Marxist reference discussed in Holland, "Deterritorializing 'Deterritorialization,'" 58.
77. Pateman, *The Sexual Contract*, 2–6.
78. See Kulick, *Travesti*.
79. Eng, *The Feeling of Kinship*.
80. Eng, 2–3.
81. D'Emilio, *Sexual Politics, Sexual Communities*.
82. Stryker, "Transgender History, Homonormativity, and Disciplinarity."
83. Spivak, *A Critique of Postcolonial Reason*.
84. As Nicholas Rose has already argued in *Powers of Freedom*.
85. Mahmood, *Politics of Piety*.
86. Oksala, *Foucault on Freedom*, 209. I have also discussed this point previously: Lino e Silva and Wardle, *Freedom in Practice*.
87. Pitkin, "Are Freedom and Liberty Twins?"
88. Quine, *Theories and Things*, 2.
89. Deleuze defines "assemblages" as "a multiplicity constituted by heterogeneous terms and which establishes liaisons, relations between them." See Deleuze, *Dialogues II*, 52.
90. McFarlane, "Assemblage and Critical Urbanism."
91. Povinelli, "A Flight from Freedom," 147.
92. For a detailed discussion on "socialist" forms of liberalism, see Humphrey, "Alternative Freedoms."
93. Wacquant, "Three Steps to a Historical Anthropology of Actually Existing Neoliberalism," 70.
94. Deleuze and Guattari, *A Thousand Plateaus*, 246.
95. Regarding the importance of uncertainties and slowness in the production of knowledge, see Stengers, *Another Science is Possible*.

CHAPTER ONE

1. On this topic, Michel Foucault states: "We must cease once and for all to describe the effects of power [only] in negative terms: it 'excludes,' it 'represses,' it 'censors,' it 'abstracts,' it 'masks,' it 'conceals.' In fact, power produces; it produces reality; it produces domains of objects and rituals of truth." Foucault, *Discipline and Punish*, 194.
2. The state must not be idealized either. Corruption, for example, is one of the mechanisms that could lead to traffickers' freedom even in the formal city.
3. *Caguete* was another term used in the favela to refer to snitches, spies, and double-crossers.
4. The concepts of negative liberty (absence of constraints) and positive liberty (possibility of action) resonate here. See Berlin, "Two Concepts of Liberty," in *Four Essays on Liberty*.
5. As scholars have often pointed out, racial categories are complex in Brazil. Affirmative action skeptics have historically asked: "Who is Black in Brazil?" Black activists have consistently responded: "Ask a Brazilian policeman, he'll know!" For further discussions on the intricacies of racial issues in the country, see, for example, Guimarães, *Classes, Raças e Democracia*.
6. At the time, one US dollar was the equivalent of 2.23 Brazilian reais.
7. According to Brazilian Rule of Law, freedom of movement is a constitutional guarantee, as stated in article 5, XV, of the Federal Constitution of Brazil of 1988.
8. This is indicated in the very subtitle of Kulick's book: *Travesti: Sex, Gender, and Culture among Brazilian Transgendered Prostitutes*. Nevertheless, not all travestis that I met were actually prostitutes.
9. This is her chosen name in full, which makes a reference to a desired kinship with Gisele Bündchen, a blond Brazilian model and actress internationally renowned for her beauty.
10. *Matesca* is a derivation of the word *mato* in Portuguese, which could be translated as "bush" or "the wild."
11. Having said this, Roy Wagner states that "surely we have no right to expect a parallel theoretical effort, for the ideological concern of these people puts them under no obligation to specialize in this way, or to propound philosophies for the lecture room." Wagner, *The Invention of Culture*, 31.
12. The term *halfie* has been used in anthropology to refer to hybrid identities. See, for example, Abu-Lughod, "Writing Against Culture."
13. For further discussions on the issue of language and queer status, see Leap and Boellstorff, *Speaking in Queer Tongues*.
14. In her ethnographic research in Rio das Pedras (a favela in the West Zone of Rio), Silvia Aguião also encountered the same identification category of bicha-boy in operation. However, for one of Aguião's informants, the category bicha-boy was different from the category gay not just in terms of class, but also because bicha-boys were considered more feminine than

gays. I didn't come across the same considerations in Rocinha. See Aguião, "'Aqui nem todo mundo é igual' Cor, Mestiçagem e Homossexualidades numa Favela do Rio de Janeiro."
15. This sizable medical emergency center had been inaugurated during the presidency of Getúlio Vargas (1934–37). It was located about five kilometers away from the favela going through the Zuzu Angel Tunnel, on the Lagoa-Barra Highway, toward Lagoa Rodrigo de Freitas. During my entire fieldwork, this hospital was one of the main health-care providers for Rocinha residents.
16. Vavá was hospitalized for a long time at no cost to him. Miguel Couto was a public hospital, and antiretrovirals were made available free of charge under Lula's government (and since Fernando Henrique Cardoso's term). Natasha once said she liked President Lula, because he was a migrant from the Brazilian Northeast, too.
17. George Marcus is critical of the fact that "the most common mode [of ethnographic research] preserves the intensively-focused-upon single site of ethnographic observation and participation while developing by other means and methods the world system context." Marcus, "Ethnography in/of the World System," 96.
18. A conceptualization inspired by the work of Roberts, *Freedom as Marronage*.
19. Michel Foucault offers a historical analysis of diverse mechanisms of power that "defined how one may have a hold over others' bodies, not only so that they may do what one wishes, but so that they may operate as one wishes, with the techniques, the speed and the efficiency that one determines." See Foucault, *Discipline and Punish*, 138.
20. "The important thing here, I believe, is that truth isn't outside power, or lacking in power: contrary to a myth whose history and function would repay further study, truth isn't the reward of free spirits, the child of protracted solitude, nor the privilege of those who have succeeded in liberating themselves. Truth is a thing of this world: it is produced only by virtue of multiple forms of constraint. And it induces regular effects of power." Foucault, *Power/Knowledge*, 131.

CHAPTER TWO

1. Smith, *An Inquiry into the Nature and Causes of the Wealth of Nations*, 316.
2. Jaguaribe, "Favelas and the Aesthetics of Realism," 329.
3. Marx, "Debates on the Law on Thefts of Wood," 228.
4. Article 6 of the Federal Constitution of Brazil: "Social rights are: education, health, food, work, housing, transport, leisure, security, social welfare, maternity and childhood protection, assistance to the helpless, in the form of this Constitution."
5. Refer to Keisha-Khan Perry's important work on the role of Black women as protagonists in the struggle for land and housing rights, against the erasure

NOTES TO PAGES 46–60

of favelas, in the context of another important Brazilian urban center, Salvador da Bahia. Perry, *Black Women against the Land Grab*.

6. In *O Mito da Marginalidade*, Janice Perlman describes one of these crimes of arson against favela dwellers that took place in Praia do Pinto in 1969.
7. Article 25, UDHR (UN General Assembly, 1948).
8. Lino e Silva and Doherty, "Formally Informal."
9. A similar argument is made by Wacquant, "The Militarization of Urban Marginality."
10. Pandolfi and Grynszpan, *A Favela Fala*, 22 (my translation).
11. Derrida, *Writing and Difference*.
12. Wacquant, "The Militarization of Urban Marginality," 71.
13. This is a well-known historical trend in Rio de Janeiro. According to Eduardo Campos de Lima, in 2019, "between January and October, 1,546 people were killed by police in the State of Rio de Janeiro, most of them during operations in favelas, or poor, often-hillside neighborhoods of precarious houses and shacks that are home to at least 1.4 million Rio residents. The increasing number of fatal acts of police are among the emerging concerns addressed by the Pastoral of Favelas, an archdiocesan commission created 42 years ago to respond to the needs of Rio's slum dwellers." Campos Lima, "Police Are Killing Poor Civilians in Brazil's Favelas."
14. In a study conducted in Brazil, Nancy Scheper-Hughes describes contexts in which violence is so pervasive that mothers were not able to weep over the death of their children. Scheper-Hughes, *Death without Weeping*.
15. Clothing merchants, stationery stores, supermarkets, building material traders, butchers, and restaurants all operated in the favela. Some large Brazilian banks also had branches there—Banco do Brasil, Banco Bradesco, and Caixa Econômica Federal. National chains of household appliances sometimes sold more in favelas than in most Asphalt locations.
16. As described in the preface.
17. Alessi, "Subiu o Morro como Antônio, Desceu como Nem da Rocinha."
18. Rua do Valão is a relatively wide street that directly connects with the Lagoa-Barra Highway. It is one of the main battlefields between the police and traffickers in Rocinha. Bandits are more exposed in the Valão area, but the higher profits from selling drugs in an easily accessible location seemed to offset the increased risks.
19. Certainly, drug use took place in areas like Flamengo too, but under different conditions and concerns. At Kyle's party that day, I didn't observe any "illegal" drugs being consumed.
20. *Macumba* is often a derogative term when used by those outside the Afro-Brazilian religious context. Sometimes it could be translated as witchcraft. However, among my queer friends, it was used more as a colloquial term to refer to their own religious practices.
21. Several legal decisions in Brazil, including from superior courts, have exposed diverging understandings of "consent" by adolescents older than

fourteen. In any case, the law states that any kind of sexual practice with a child younger than fourteen years, even without violence and with "consent," should be classified as rape (Art. 217-A Penal Code).
22. There were not many female drug dealers, but some women were known as "bandits' wives." Top-ranked bandits demonstrated their power by parading around with good-looking, richly adorned women. This is certainly a reminder that also in the minoritarian favela territory, male gender constituted a dominant force (despite other minoritarian facets of these men). Male traffickers would "own and display" women as a token of such power inequalities.
23. For a more in-depth analysis of masculinity as a consideration in the life of Brazilian travestis and their lovers, see Pelúcio, *Abjeção e Desejo*.
24. Heterotopia could be defined "as a sort of simultaneously mythical and real contestation of the space in which we live in. . . ." Foucault, "Of Other Spaces, Heterotopias," 4.
25. As discussed in the introduction. See Pateman, *The Sexual Contract*.
26. In terms of racism, however, I was not aware of any "laws of the Hillside" tailored to protect Black folks as a minoritarian group. Perhaps, because favelas were already considered "Blackened" spaces. See Leu, *Defiant Geographies*.
27. Walter Benjamin affirms that "the world dominated by its phantasmagorias, is—to use an expression from Baudelaire—modernity." Benjamin, *Das Passagen-Werk*, 77.

CHAPTER THREE

1. Valladares, *A Invenção da Favela*.
2. As discussed in the introduction.
3. Brazilian Demographic Census of 2010.
4. The farther one goes into the interior of Brazil, the greater the chances to see a D-20. The flatbed truck manufactured by the Brazilian subsidiary of General Motors was launched in Latin America around 1985.
5. The Brazilian expression *pau de arara* could be translated into English as "macaw's perch." One of the narratives to explain the meaning of the term comes from the fact that these birds were often tied to a pole for sale while being transported. This same image was applied to humans, by analogy, in reference to the uncomfortable means of transportation in flatbed trucks, like the D-20. The expression also applies to torture devices used during the Brazilian military dictatorship. Teresa Caldeira further discusses the torture device in *City of Walls*.
6. For example, some northeastern products also circulated in abundance between the Northeast and Rio de Janeiro—foods such as *rapadura*, biscuits, green beans, and a special type of cassava flour (*farinha d'água*) could always be seen for sale in Rocinha. Cheap clothing from Fortaleza was a common presence in the favela markets too.

NOTES TO PAGES 67–87

7. In 2010, the state of Ceará had at least 1,502,924 residents living in households with a monthly income of less than 70.00 Brazilian reais per capita (Source: IBGE, 2010). This would be the equivalent of approximately 16 US dollars (conversion rate used: 1 USD = 4.3 BRL in January 2020).
8. Weston, *Families We Choose*.
9. Rubin, "The Traffic in Women."
10. Schneider, *American Kinship*.
11. Kulick, "Can There Be an Anthropology of Homophobia?"
12. Perhaps this could help explain Natasha's concern with wearing pants when going out to Kyle's party.
13. For a more extended discussion on this issue, see Lino e Silva, "Red Brick in Rio."
14. The Brazilian Northeast is known for its high infant mortality rates. For example, see the discussion of Scheper-Hughes, *Death without Weeping*.
15. As Saba Mahmood had previously noticed. Mahmood, *Politics of Piety*.
16. Pateman, *The Sexual Contract*.
17. Source: PNAD, IBGE, 2015.
18. DaMatta, *A Casa & a Rua*.
19. Woortmann, "Com Parente Não se Neguceia," 23 (my translation).
20. Woortmann, 22.
21. *Alforria* (manumission) is part of a vocabulary of freedom inherited from colonial slavery times.
22. According to ANTRA, Brazil has been the leading country in murders motivated by transphobia. See https://antrabrasil.org/category/violencia/.
23. For a more detailed discussion regarding the role of silence in contexts of extreme violence, see Das, *Life and Words*.
24. *Comadre* is the godmother of one's son or daughter.
25. Seyferth, "As Contradições da Liberdade," 91 (my translation). In a similar vein to Seyferth, Pina-Cabral and Silva report that their interlocutors in another northeastern context, in the south of Bahia state, display an "insistence on the freedom of the person on the land, on their essential mobility and on how the person is the ultimate agent of responsibility." Cabral and Silva, *Gente Livre*, 77 (my translation).
26. Velho, *Capitalismo Autoritário e Campesinato*, 221 (my translation).
27. TV Record is a Brazilian TV channel owned by Edir Macedo, the leader of the Universal Church of the Kingdom of God (UCKG), the largest Evangelical group in Brazil.
28. *Mala* is Pajubá for penis, or the volume produced by the penis, i.e., "bulge." For example: "Aqüenda, mona! Aqüenda esse bofe com a mala odara!" A possible translation would be: "Look, woman! Look at this man with a wonderful bulge!" Of these, only the words *esse*, *com*, and *a* would be considered standard Portuguese.
29. Kulick, *Travesti*, 6.

30. "Those fucking cracks! Just because they have a pussy? They disrupt our lives," Natasha complained. It was a provocative way of referring to what, for Natasha, defined a type of female body: there were cracked and non-cracked female bodies, and the cracked ones were ridiculed almost in a defective sense. "Cracks" were enemies in the hunt for males, for "real" men.
31. In *Travesti*, Don Kulick makes a similar observation regarding the special significance of the penis for travestis in Salvador.
32. See also Hubert Dreyfus and Paul Rabinow, eds., *Michel Foucault: Beyond Structuralism and Hermeneutics* (London: Routledge, 2016).
33. See chapter 2.

CHAPTER FOUR

1. PAFYC is an acronym formed by the initial letters derived from each of the names of the group's founding members. I explain more in the next pages.
2. As further explained in Benveniste, *Indo-European Language and Society*.
3. For expanded considerations on this issue, see Schlemmer, *The Exploited Child*.
4. See Arendt, *Between Past and Future*. At the same time, I observed during fieldwork that motherhood could also be conceived as a condition that led to restrictions on freedom.
5. For example, the repression of incestuous desires. See Freud, *Five Lectures on Psychoanalysis*.
6. Foucault, *The History of Sexuality*, vol. 1.
7. Street children could be understood as homeless children. For a research focused on this topic in Brazil, see Hecht, *At Home in the Street*.
8. For further discussion on this topic, see Carade, "Entre a 'Síndrome do Pato' e o 'Efeito Mateus.'"
9. UN General Assembly, *Universal Declaration of Human Rights*.
10. Arendt, *Between Past and Future*.
11. See chapter 3.
12. Joyce, *The Rule of Freedom*, 11.
13. Park and Burgess, *The City*, 4.
14. As discussed in the introduction.
15. For a critical review of the forma/informal binary, see Lino e Silva and Doherty, "Formally Informal."
16. Secretaria Municipal de Habitação, *Política Habitacional da Cidade do Rio de Janeiro* (Rio de Janeiro, 1995).
17. PAFYC members were usually between six and sixteen years old, born and raised in the slum (*crias do morro*).
18. A version of this short vignette appears in Lino e Silva, "Queer Sex Vignettes from a Brazilian Favela."
19. The concept of "moral region" emerges in classic urban sociology and, despite the different context of its insurgence, still proves to be a valuable

contribution for the understanding of life in Rocinha. "A moral region is not necessarily a place of abode. It may be a mere rendezvous, a place of resort. In order to understand the forces which in every large city tend to develop these detached milieus in which vagrant and suppressed impulses, passions, and ideals emancipate themselves from the dominant moral order, it is necessary to refer to the fact or theory of latent impulses of men." Park and Burgess, *The City*, 43.
20. Moncorvo Filho, *História da Proteção à Infância no Brasil, 1500–1922*, 128 (my translation).
21. The issue of religion proved to be more complicated than I supposed. See chapter 5.
22. "To be incubated" was the PAFYC way to refer to someone who was repressed, or in the closet (although, as I discuss ahead, an easy translation here could be problematic).
23. See chapter 3.
24. D'Emilio, *Sexual Politics, Sexual Communities*, 11.
25. D'Emilio, 11.
26. For an extended analysis regarding the relationship of LGBT groups and the Brazilian state in terms of rights and the constitution of identities, see Aguião, "Fazer-se no 'Estado.'"
27. As discussed in the preface and introduction.
28. Meunier, *Os Moleques de Bogotá*.
29. Amado, *Capitães da Areia*.
30. About the expression "to give an it," see the preface.
31. Carlos Decena has argued that "taking for granted that all LGBTQ people should come out of the closet is consistent with a neoliberal interpretation of coming out characteristic of the current political climate in the United States." Decena, "Tacit Subjects," 339.
32. Manalansan, *Global Divas*.
33. Manalansan, 23.
34. At the same time, the constitution of any type of "family" can also serve as a strategy to counter the exploitation of normative liberalism. See chapter 3.
35. Benveniste, *Indo-European Language and Society*.
36. As Eduardo Viveiros de Castro argues, "Here seems to me to lie an important mistake, which is that of taking bodily 'appearance' to be inert and false, whereas spiritual 'essence' is active and real. . . . I argue that nothing could be further from the Indians' minds when they speak of bodies in terms of 'clothing.' It is not so much that the body is a clothing but rather that clothing is a body.'" Viveiros de Castro, "Cosmological Deixis and Amerindian Perspectivism," 482.
37. Don Kulick describes some of the deleterious effects of injecting industrial silicone into travestis' bodies in *Travesti*.
38. Sex at the beach and sex in the alleyways were also dimensions of a "street life."

39. Kulick, *Travesti*.
40. See chapter 2.

CHAPTER FIVE

1. "Secularism here is understood not simply as the doctrinal separation of the church and the state but the rearticulation of religion in a manner that is commensurate with modern sensibilities and modes of governance." Mahmood, "Religious Reason and Secular Affect," 837.
2. Asad, *Genealogies of Religion*, 115.
3. Taussig, *The Devil and Commodity Fetishism in South America*, 42.
4. Jesuits were most active in Brazil from the sixteenth to the eighteenth century. Having said that, their efforts in the educational sector continue to be strong; several Brazilian universities are currently owned and operated by Jesuits, for example.
5. Taussig, *The Devil and Commodity Fetishism in South America*, 41.
6. *Macumba* can be a derogatory term to refer to Afro-Brazilian religious practices. However, the word has also been re-signified by practitioners, such as Auro, as a term of empowerment.
7. De Almeida, *A Igreja Universal e seus Demônios*, 57 (my translation).
8. This number is a personal estimate.
9. Vânia Cardoso remarks that Exu and Pomba-gira are often understood as "trickster" spirits. Pomba-giras are also referred to as the spirits of "deviant" women, such as prostitutes. Collectively, Exu and Pomba-gira are known under the spiritual category of "people of the streets" (*povo da rua*). In life, these were subjects who occupied positions of marginalization. A large part of Afro-Brazilian rituals, known as *macumba*, consists in pleasing these spirits, asking for their assistance to "open the pathways" (*abrir caminhos*) toward the solution of difficult problems. See Cardoso, "Narrar o Mundo" (my translation).
10. Taussig, *The Devil and Commodity Fetishism in South America*, 43.
11. Kardecists (followers of Allan Kardec) and Buddhists were not a common presence in Rocinha at all but were used as exemplars of "other" faiths. According to my Evangelical friends, however, the favela was infested with witchcraft. This latter issue was often used to explain why the place was "poor" and why people had so much trouble in their lives.
12. AMABB was established in the 1970s to represent the collective interests of Favela da Rocinha residents, mostly as it concerned their struggle against forced removals. Bairro Barcelos is situated very close to Autoestrada Lagoa Barra, and most of its streets are laid out on a straight line and wide enough to fit a car—whereas most other alleyways are only wide enough for motorcycle and pedestrian traffic.
13. For a more detailed discussion on the marginalization of funk music, see, for example, Facina and Passos, "Funk Pacificado?"

14. When I asked Laiza about fainting, she was eager to differentiate it from spirit possession. She explained that humans could feel the presence of the Holy Spirit, but could never get possessed by it. People would pass out just from being in God's presence; if God were to actually possess them, they would die.
15. For a detailed account on the historical roots of Afro-Brazilian religions, see Parés, *The Formation of Candomblé*.
16. See Lino e Silva, "Ontological Confusion."
17. The deity manifests in Yorubaland as a river deity, and in Afro-Brazilian religions mostly as a deity of the seas.
18. Ogum is a masculine warrior Orixá (deity), related to brute force, metals, technology, and all forms of violence. Iansã is a female warrior Orixá, the goddess of winds, hurricanes, and related to fire.
19. This more "scientific" tradition of dealing with spirits became popular among the white middle classes in Brazil. For information on their basic religious doctrine, see, for example, Kardec, *The Spirits' Book*.
20. In most Afro-Brazilian rituals, Caboclos are acknowledged and worshipped as native Brazilian spirits. In the Portuguese language, the term also means a person of mixed Amerindian and European ancestry.
21. For a more detailed discussion focused on Pomba-giras, see Hayes, "Wicked Women and Femmes Fatales."
22. Exu João Caveira had been described to me as a spirit that lives in cemeteries.
23. For a complete account of the facts briefly described in this passage, see Lino e Silva, "Ontological Confusion."
24. For example, UCKG prescriptions did not tolerate most forms of minoritarian freedoms related to sexuality, the use of drugs, and even the baile funk.
25. See chapter 1.
26. The epigraph to this chapter presents one of the meanings of slavery in the Bible.
27. The Vatican itself had been divided between liberation theologists and those who were against it. This interpretation of freedom as a class struggle was more prevalent in Latin America than in other parts of the world.
28. Ronaldo de Almeida has made a similar observation regarding the UCKG in *A Igreja Universal e seus Demônios*.
29. To put it in a simplified way, as Paizinha once explained to me, in prosperity theology the more one pleases God, and the more God likes them, the more financial success that person should have in their life.
30. Johnson, *Spirited Things*.
31. Foucault, *Technologies of the Self*.
32. See chapter 4.
33. Luz and Lapassade, *O Segredo da Macumba*, xvi. According to these authors: "Macumba is rejected by all institutions because it is a specific form of counter-institution, a counter-culture that expresses a counter-society" (xxi; my translation).

NOTES TO PAGES 135-150

34. Taussig, *The Devil and Commodity Fetishism in South America.*
35. Geschiere, *The Modernity of Witchcraft,* 5.
36. There had been a complicated precedent of a journalist who had infiltrated Rocinha. See Ludemir, *Sorria, Você Está na Rocinha.*
37. Rocinha dwellers assured me this would not be necessary. They had not asked for permission to live in Rocinha either. In my case, it had been Babi who initially arranged a place for me in the favela. Her brother had been married to a colleague of mine, an urban sociologist.
38. Article 146 of the Brazilian Penal Code states that forcing (*constrangimento ilegal*) someone, "through violence or grave threat, or after having reduced by any other means his or her ability to resist, not to do what the law permits, or to do what the law does not command," is punishable with imprisonment from three months to one year, or a fine.
39. Asad, *Genealogies of Religion.*
40. O'Sullivan, "Fold."
41. Comaroff and Comaroff, "Millennial Capitalism."
42. Crosson, "What Possessed You?"

CHAPTER SIX

1. See chapter 5.
2. "None of the daughters of Israel shall be a prostitute, and none of the sons of Israel shall be a prostitute. You shall not bring the fee of a prostitute or the wages of a dog into the house of the Lord your God in payment for any vow, for both of these are an abomination to the Lord your God." Deuteronomy 23:17–18 (English Standard Version).
3. For a more global mapping of travesti movement, migration, and sex work, see Vartabedian, *Brazilian Travesti Migrations.*
4. The nouveau riche neighborhood of Barra da Tijuca (West Zone) was perceived as more affluent than the more traditional neighborhood of Copacabana, in the South Zone of Rio de Janeiro.
5. A park from colonial times situated near the famous Maracanã soccer stadium in Rio de Janeiro.
6. Vila Mimosa is one of the oldest and best-known areas for sex work in Rio de Janeiro. It is not located too far from Quinta da Boa Vista.
7. Néstor Perlongher argues that gestural and discursive performances of masculinity are a requirement for most male prostitutes. Perlongher, *O Negócio do Michê.*
8. Madureira can be described as a popular and relatively poor suburban neighborhood located in the northwest part of Rio de Janeiro.
9. Via Ápia was the name given to one of the most famous roads that existed in the Roman Empire.
10. Matos and Ribeiro, "Territórios da Prostituição nos Espaços Públicos da Área Central do Rio de Janeiro," 60 (my translation).

11. See Lino e Silva, "Queer Sex Vignettes from a Brazilian Favela," 7.
12. Park and Burgess, *The City*. See also chapter 4.
13. Day, "The Re-emergence of 'Trafficking,'" 817–18.
14. For discussions on the particular challenges of queer sex work, see Laing et al., *Queer Sex Work*.
15. Pateman, "What's Wrong with Prostitution?," 57.
16. Gabriela Leite passed away in 2013. For a complete biography, see Leite, *Filha, Mãe, Avó e Puta*.
17. Patterson, "Trafficking, Gender, and Slavery," 323. See also Patterson, *Slavery and Social Death*.
18. Patterson, "Trafficking, Gender, and Slavery," 324.
19. Brazilian Penal Code (1940).
20. Not all forms of violence can be classified as "human rights violations." See Piscitelli, "Entre as 'Máfias' e a 'Ajuda,'" 58 (my translation).
21. Pateman, "What's Wrong with Prostitution?," 54.
22. Something also observed by Kulick, *Travesti*.
23. Article 233 of the Brazilian Penal Code.
24. See chapter 3.
25. See chapter 2.
26. White bread with a fried egg (*pão-com-ovo*) is a classic cheap snack in Brazilian bakeries, even if a bit tasteless. By analogy, the lowest-status fags in the favela were called bread-and-egg faggots, easy to get and bland. Coca-Cola was also very easy to get, but had a bit more prestige than bread-and-egg.
27. One of the explanations I heard from my friends in Rocinha was that the term "Freddy" referred to Freddy Krueger, a fictional character representing a serial killer in movies such as *A Nightmare on Elm Street* (1984).
28. On the complexities of this subject in Brazil, see Franklin, "Surgical Subjects and the Right to Transgender Health in Brazil."
29. Kulick, *Travesti*, 166.
30. John Hooper, "Brazilian Prostitute in Italian Political Scandal Found Murdered," *Guardian*, November 20, 2009, https://www.theguardian.com/world/2009/nov/20/transsexual-murder-brenda-piero-marrazzo.
31. Macega is one of the most destitute areas of Rocinha.
32. Edmonds, *Pretty Modern*, 30, 33.
33. Edmonds, 20.
34. Kulick, *Travesti*, 183.
35. Williams, *Sex Tourism in Bahia*.
36. There could be some prejudice against Arabs in that context that I didn't quite understand at the time.
37. Kulick, *Travesti*, 178.
38. In his work, George Paul Meiu examines the intersections between sex work and ethnicity in Kenya. See Meiu, *Ethno-Erotic Economies*, 243.
39. The concept here derives from Michel Foucault and could be defined as "those intentional and voluntary actions by which men [sic] not only set

themselves rules of conduct, but also seek to transform themselves, to change themselves in their singular being, and to make their life into an oeuvre that carries certain aesthetic values and meets certain stylistic criteria." Foucault, *History of Sexuality*, vol. 2, 10.
40. Déjaque, "L'Echange," 6.
41. See chapter 4.

CHAPTER SEVEN

1. As described in chapter 1.
2. As discussed by Comaroff and Comaroff in the edited volume *Modernity and Its Malcontents*.
3. As discussed in chapter 3, D-20 is a flatbed truck still used for public transport in some places in the Brazilian Northeast. It's a very uncomfortable vehicle but often the only option for those who can't afford other means of transportation.
4. Cemitério do Catumbi (also known as Cemitério de São Francisco de Paula) is located about ten miles northeast of Rocinha.
5. For further discussions on this issue, see, for example, Bersani, *Is the Rectum a Grave?*
6. Sex performed without a condom.
7. Halperin, *Que Veulent les Gays?*
8. Warner, *The Trouble with Normal*.
9. Edelman, *No Future*, 117, 16, 17.
10. For a more detailed account of the LGBTQ rights struggle in Latin America, see Dehesa, *Queering the Public Sphere in Mexico and Brazil*. For the Brazilian historical context in particular, see Green, *Beyond Carnival*.
11. As far as I noticed, capital accumulation was not a priority. I discuss an exception to this general observation in chapter 6; some queer sex workers expressed a desire to save enough to buy a house for their "blood" mothers. The reasons why they desired to do so are not necessarily related to the accumulation of wealth per se, but to repair (often compromised) family relations.
12. Just as Natasha had adopted the Bündchen surname in reference to the supermodel's beauty, Kimberley had chosen another Brazilian top model for a surname. Ambrósio was a reference to Alessandra Ambrósio.
13. Lewis, *La Vida*, 53.
14. Mbembe, *Necropolitics*.
15. Elizabeth Povinelli has argued that a focus on biopower alone seems to have served the economic interests of Western elites. Beyond an exclusive concern with life and death, Povinelli suggests that our politics must focus on the wider problem of life versus non-life. Povinelli, *Geontologies*.
16. Foucault, *The History of Sexuality*, vol. 1.
17. Laidlaw, "For an Anthropology of Ethics and Freedom," 327.

18. Singleton, "Pour une Anthropologie de la Liberation," 54 (my translation).
19. Allen and Jobson, "The Decolonizing Generation," 137.
20. Jobson, "The Case for Letting Anthropology Burn."
21. Muñoz, *Disidentification*.

EPILOGUE

1. Hanssen, *Critique of Violence*.
2. Fish, *There's No Such Thing as Free Speech*, 106.
3. Austin, *How to Do Things with Words*.
4. Butler, *Excitable Speech*.
5. See the preface.
6. Harrison, *Decolonizing Anthropology*, 88.
7. Lino e Silva, "Ontological Confusion."
8. I described this in detail in chapter 2.
9. Also in chapter 2.
10. This law has been in place since 1941. See the Brazilian Penal Code (Código de Processo Penal Brasileiro, Decreto-Lei 3.689)
11. As Rose explained, most of these factions have explicit values related to a minoritarian form of liberalism. For an ethnography of life in one of these jails, mainly from the perspective of the largest Brazilian trafficking faction (PCC), see Biondi, *Junto e Misturado*.
12. https://www.uol.com.br/universa/noticias/redacao/2020/03/07/acharam-a-lolla-trans-retratada-por-drauzio-vai-receber-ajuda-de-campanha.htm?cmpid=copiaecola.
13. See chapter 4.
14. This is the official document one must hold in order to have a "legal" job in Brazil (*trabalho de carteira assinada*). The document looks like a passport, and different employers are responsible for stamping its pages. As such, it creates a record of employment history that can be verified.
15. Created through the Presidential Decree No. 5.209, on September 17, 2004, the program was based on conditional cash transfers to the Brazilian population below the "poverty line" (a quantitative measure of monthly income). One of the conditions to receive the state benefit was sending children to school, for example. This unified and expanded other cash programs created in the previous government.
16. Reddy, *Freedom with Violence*.
17. See, for example, the work of Wacquant, *Urban Outcasts*.
18. See chapter 5.
19. In Umbanda, a male body could become a female entity through spirit possession, for example.
20. This section contains excerpts from my chapter in Lino e Silva and Wardle, *Freedom in Practice*.

21. See the original news on Globo's G1: http://g1.globo.com/rio-de-janeiro/rio-contra-o-crime/noticia/2010/11/veja-frases-sobre-o-combate-ao-crime-no-rio-de-janeiro.html.
22. In the introduction, I explain the connection between Brazilian favelas and the Canudos War.

References

Abu-Lughod, Lila. "Writing Against Culture." In *Recapturing Anthropology: Working in the Present*, edited by Richard Fox. Santa Fe: School of American Research Press, 1991.

Aguião, Silvia. "'Aqui nem todo mundo é igual' Cor, Mestiçagem e Homossexualidades numa Favela do Rio de Janeiro." Master's thesis, UERJ, 2007.

Aguião, Silvia. "Fazer-se no 'Estado': uma etnografia sobre o processo de constituição dos 'LGBT' como sujeitos de direitos no Brasil contemporâneo." PhD diss., Unicamp, 2014.

Alessi, Gil. "Subiu o Morro como Antônio, Desceu como Nem da Rocinha." *El País*, December 28, 2016.

Allain, Jean. *The Legal Understanding of Slavery: From the Historical to the Contemporary*. Oxford: Oxford University Press, 2012.

Allen, Jafari, and Ryan Jobson. "The Decolonizing Generation: (Race and) Theory in Anthropology since the Eighties." *Current Anthropology* 57, no. 2 (April 2016): 129–48. DOI: 10.1086/685502.

Alves, Jaime A. "From Necropolis to Blackpolis: Necropolitical Governance and Black Spatial Praxis in São Paulo, Brazil." *Antipode* 46, no. 1 (2014): 323–39. https://doi.org/10.1111/anti.12055.

Amado, Jorge. *Capitães da Areia*. São Paulo: Companhia de Bolso, 2009.

Anshen, Ruth Nanda, ed. *Freedom: Its Meaning*. London: George Allen and Unwin, 1942.

Appadurai, Arjun. *Fear of Small Numbers*. Durham, NC: Duke University Press, 2006.

Arendt, Hannah. *Between Past and Future*. New York: Penguin, 1961.

Asad, Talal. *Genealogies of Religion: Discipline and Reasons of Power in Christianity and Islam*. Baltimore: Johns Hopkins University Press, 1993.

Austin, John L. *How to Do Things with Words*. Oxford: Clarendon Press, 1962.

Baehr, Amy, ed. *Varieties of Feminist Liberalism*. Lanham, MD: Rowman and Littlefield, 2004.
Benjamin, Walter. *Das Passagen-Werk*. Frankfurt: Suhrkamp, 1982.
Benveniste, Émile. *Indo-European Language and Society*. Miami: Miami Press, 1973. Available online at http://nrs.harvard.edu/urn-3:hul.ebook:CHS_Benveniste.Indo-European_Language_and_Society.1973.
Berlin, Isaiah. *Four Essays on Liberty*. London: Oxford University Press, 1969.
Bersani, Leo. *Is the Rectum a Grave?* Chicago: University of Chicago Press, 2009.
Biondi, Karina. *Junto e Misturado: Uma Etnografia do PCC*. São Paulo: FAPESP, 2010.
Boas, Franz. "Liberty among Primitive People." In *Freedom: Its Meaning*, edited by Ruth Nanda Anshen. London: George Allen and Unwin, 1942.
Boff, Leonardo. *O caminhar da Igreja com os Oprimidos*. Petrópolis: Editora Vozes, 1981.
Boym, Svetlana. *Another Freedom: The Alternative History of an Idea*. Chicago: University of Chicago Press, 2010.
Brown, Wendy. *Undoing the Demos: Neoliberalism's Stealth Revolution*. Brooklyn: Zone Books, 2015.
Butler, Judith. *Excitable Speech: A Politics of the Performative*. London: Routledge, 1997.
Caldeira, Teresa. *City of Walls: Crime, Segregation, and Citizenship in São Paulo*. Berkeley: University of California Press, 2000.
Campos Lima, Eduardo. "Police Are Killing Poor Civilians in Brazil's Favelas: The Church Offers Protection." *America: The Jesuit Review*, January 20, 2020. https://www.americamagazine.org/politics-society/2019/12/23/police-are-killing-poor-civilians-brazils-favelas-church-offers.
Campuzano, Giuseppe. "Reclaiming Travesti Histories." *IDS Bulletin* 37, no. 5 (2006): 34–39.
Carade, Hildon. "Entre a 'Síndrome do Pato' e o 'Efeito Mateus': Juventude e Políticas Sociais na Periferia de Salvador." PhD diss., UFBA, 2016.
Cardoso, Vânia. "Narrar o Mundo: Estórias do 'Povo da Rua' e a Narração do Imprevisível." *MANA* 13, no. 2 (2007): 317–45.
Cassin, Barbara, et al., ed. *Dictionary of Untranslatables: A Philosophical Lexicon*. Princeton, NJ: Princeton University Press, 2014.
Chakrabarty, Dipesh. *Provincializing Europe*. Princeton, NJ: Princeton University Press, 2000.
Chalhoub, Sidney. *Visões da Liberdade: Uma História das Últimas Décadas da Escravidão na Corte*. São Paulo: Companhia das Letras, 2011.
Clastres, Pierre. *Society Against the State: Essays in Political Anthropology*. New York: Zone Books, 1987.
Comaroff, Jean, and John Comaroff. "Millennial Capitalism: First Thoughts on a Second Coming." *Public Culture* 12, no. 2 (2000): 291–343.
Comaroff, Jean, and John Comaroff. *Modernity and Its Malcontents: Ritual and Power in Postcolonial Africa*. Chicago: University of Chicago Press, 1993.

REFERENCES

Crosson, J. Brent. "What Possessed You? Spirits, Property, and Political Sovereignty at the Limits of 'Possession.'" *Ethnos* 84, no. 4 (2019): 546–56. DOI: 10.1080/00141844.2017.1401704.

Da Cunha, Euclides. *Os Sertões*. Rio de Janeiro: Laemmert, 1902.

DaMatta, Roberto. *A Casa & a Rua: Espaço, Cidadania, Mulher e Morte no Brasil*. Rio de Janeiro: Rocco, 1997.

Das, Veena. *Life and Words: Violence and the Descent into the Ordinary*. Berkeley: University of California Press, 2006.

Day, Sophie. "The Re-emergence of 'Trafficking': Sex Work Between Slavery and Freedom." *Journal of the Royal Anthropological Institute* 16 (2010): 817–18.

De Almeida, Ronaldo. *A Igreja Universal e seus Demônios*. São Paulo: Terceiro Nome, 2009.

Decena, Carlos. "Tacit Subjects." *GLQ: A Journal of Lesbian and Gay Studies* 14, nos. 2–3 (2008): 339. DOI: 10.1215/10642684-2007-036.

Dehesa, Rafael de la. *Queering the Public Sphere in Mexico and Brazil: Sexual Rights Movements in Emerging Democracies*. Durham, NC: Duke University Press, 2010.

Déjaque, Joseph. "L'Echange." *Le Libertaire*. New York, 1858.

DeLanda, Manuel. *A New Philosophy of Society: Assemblage Theory and Social Complexity*. London: Bloomsbury, 2006.

Deleuze, Gilles. *Dialogues II*. New York: Columbia University Press, 2007.

Deleuze, Gilles, and Félix Guattari. *Kafka: Toward a Minor Literature*. Minneapolis: University of Minnesota Press, 1986.

Deleuze, Gilles, and Félix Guattari. *A Thousand Plateaus: Capitalism and Schizophrenia*. London: Continuum, 2004.

Deleuze, Gilles, and Félix Guattari. "What Is a Minor Literature?" *Mississippi Review* 11, no. 3 (2001): 13–33.

D'Emilio, John. *Sexual Politics, Sexual Communities*. Chicago: University of Chicago Press, 1998.

Derrida, Jacques. *Writing and Difference*. London: Routledge, 1981.

Dreyfus, Hubert and Paul Rabinow, eds. *Michel Foucault: Beyond Structuralism and Hermeneutics*. London: Routledge, 2016.

Du Bois, W. E. B. *The Souls of Black Folk*. Greenwich, CT: Fawcett, 1961.

Edelman, Lee. *No Future: Queer Theory and the Death Drive*. Durham, NC: Duke University Press, 2004.

Edmonds, Alexander. *Pretty Modern: Beauty, Sex, and Plastic Surgery in Brazil*. Durham, NC: Duke University Press, 2010.

Eng, David. *The Feeling of Kinship: Queer Liberalism and the Racialization of Intimacy*. Durham, NC: Duke University Press, 2010.

Facina, Adriana, and Pâmella Passos. "Funk Pacificado? Reflexões Sobre a Implementação das Unidades de Polícia Pacificadora (UPPs) e seus Impactos Culturais." In *Direitos Humanos e Neoliberalismo*, ed. Antônio Pele et al., 1–16. Rio de Janeiro: Lumen Juris, 2018.

REFERENCES

Farmer, Paul. *Infections and Inequalities: The Modern Plagues.* Berkeley: University of California Press, 1999.

Ferguson, James. *Global Shadows: Africa in the Neoliberal World Order.* Durham, NC: Duke University Press, 2006.

Ferreira, Francisco, Phillippe Leite, and Julie Litchfield. "Brazil: The Search for Equity." *Revista* (Spring 2007).

Fish, Stanley. *There's No Such Thing as Free Speech, and It's a Good Thing, Too.* New York: Oxford University Press, 1994.

Foucault, Michel. *Discipline and Punish: The Birth of the Prison.* New York: Vintage, 1995.

Foucault, Michel. *The History of Sexuality.* Vol. 1, *An Introduction.* London: Vintage, 1990.

Foucault, Michel. *The History of Sexuality.* Vol. 2, *The Use of Pleasure.* New York: Vintage, 1986.

Foucault, Michel. *Power/Knowledge.* New York: Vintage, 1980.

Foucault, Michel. "Of Other Spaces, Heterotopias." Translated from *Architecture, Mouvement, Continuité*, no. 5 (1984): 46–49.

Foucault, Michel. *Technologies of the Self: A Seminar with Michel Foucault.* Amherst: University of Massachusetts Press, 1988.

Fox, Richard, ed. *Recapturing Anthropology: Working in the Present.* Santa Fe, NM: School of American Research Press, 1991.

Franklin, Joshua. "Surgical Subjects and the Right to Transgender Health in Brazil." *TSQ* 5, no. 2 (May 2018): 190–206. https://doi.org/10.1215/23289252-4348629.

Freire, Paulo. *Pedagogia do Oprimido.* São Paulo: Paz and Terra, 2013.

Freud, Sigmund. *Five Lectures on Psychoanalysis.* New York: Penguin, 1995.

Geschiere, Peter. *The Modernity of Witchcraft.* Charlottesville: University of Virginia Press, 1997.

Green, James. *Beyond Carnival: Male Homosexuality in Twentieth-Century Brazil.* Chicago: University of Chicago Press, 2001.

Guimarães, Antônio. *Classes, Raças e Democracia.* São Paulo: Editora 34, 2009.

Halperin, David. *Que Veulent les Gays?: Essai sur le Sexe, le Risque et la Subjectivité.* Paris: Amsterdam Press, 2010.

Hanssen, Beatrice. *Critique of Violence: Between Poststructuralism and Critical Theory.* London: Routledge, 2000.

Harrington, Michael. *The Other America: Poverty in the United States.* New York: Macmillan, 1962.

Harrison, Faye. *Decolonizing Anthropology: Moving Further toward an Anthropology for Liberation.* Arlington, VA: American Anthropological Association, 1997.

Hayes, Kelly. "Wicked Women and Femmes Fatales: Gender, Power, and Pomba Gira in Brazil." *History of Religions* 48, no. 1 (2008): 1–21. DOI:10.1086/592152.

Hecht, Tobias. *At Home in the Street: Street Children in Northeast Brazil.* Cambridge: Cambridge University Press, 1998.

Hilgers, Mathieu. "The Three Anthropological Approaches to Neoliberalism." *ISSJ* 61 (2002): 351–64.

Hobbes, Thomas. *Leviathan*. Menston: Scolar P, 1651.
Hobsbawm, Eric. *Echoes of the Marseillaise: Two Centuries Look Back on the French Revolution*. New Brunswick, NJ: Rutgers University Press, 1990.
Holland, Eugene. "Deterritorializing 'Deterritorialization': From the *Anti-Oedipus* to *A Thousand Plateaus*." *SubStance* 20, no. 3, issue 66 (1991): 55–65.
Humphrey, Caroline. "Alternative Freedoms." *Proceedings of the American Philosophical Society* 151, no. 1 (2007): 1–10.
Jaguaribe, Beatriz. "Favelas and the Aesthetics of Realism: Representations in Film and Literature." *Journal of Latin American Cultural Studies* 13, no. 3 (2004): 327–42.
Jobson, Ryan. "The Case for Letting Anthropology Burn: Sociocultural Anthropology in 2019." *American Anthropologist* 122, no. 2 (2020): 259–71.
Johnson, Paul. *Spirited Things: The Works of Possession in Afro-Atlantic Religions*. Chicago: University of Chicago Press, 2014.
Joyce, Patrick. *The Rule of Freedom: Liberalism and the Modern City*. London: Verso, 2003.
Kardec, Allan. *The Spirits' Book*. Miami: FEB, 2018.
Katz, Michael. *The Undeserving Poor: From the War on Poverty to the War on Welfare*. New York: Pantheon, 1989.
Kulick, Don. "Can There Be an Anthropology of Homophobia?" In *Homophobias: Lust and Loathing Across Time and Space*, ed. David Murray. Durham, NC: Duke University Press, 2010.
Kulick, Don. *Travesti: Sex, Gender, and Culture among Brazilian Transgendered Prostitutes*. Chicago: University of Chicago Press, 1998.
Laidlaw, James. "For an Anthropology of Ethics and Freedom." *Journal of the Royal Anthropological Institute* 8, no. 2 (2002): 311–32.
Laing, Mary, et al., eds. *Queer Sex Work*. London: Routledge, 2016.
Leap, William, and Tom Boellstorff. *Speaking in Queer Tongues*. Chicago: University of Illinois Press, 2003.
Leite, Gabriela. *Filha, Mãe, Avó e Puta*. São Paulo: Editora Objetiva, 2009.
Leu, Lorraine. *Defiant Geographies: Race and Urban Space in 1920s Rio de Janeiro*. Pittsburgh: University of Pittsburgh Press, 2020.
Lewis, Oscar. *The Children of Sanchez: Autobiography of a Mexican Family*. New York: Random House, 1961.
Lewis, Oscar. *La Vida*. London: Panther, 1968.
Lima, Antônio Carlos de Souza. *Um Grande Cerco de Paz. Poder Tutelar, Indianidade e Formação do Estado no Brasil*. Petrópolis: Vozes, 1995.
Lino e Silva, Moisés. "Ontological Confusion: Eshu and the Devil Dance to the Samba of the Black Madman." *Social Dynamics* 41, no. 1 (2015): 34–46. DOI: 10.1080/02533952.2015.1032507.
Lino e Silva, Moisés. "Queer Sex Vignettes from a Brazilian Favela: An Ethnographic Striptease." *Ethnography* 16, no. 2 (June 2015): 223–39. DOI: 10.1177/1466138114534335.
Lino e Silva, Moisés. "Red Brick in Rio." *New Geographies* 3, no. 1 (2011).

Lino e Silva, Moisés, and Gareth Doherty. "Formally Informal: Daily Life and the Shock of Order in a Brazilian Favela." *Built Environment* 37, no. 1 (2011).

Lino e Silva, Moisés, and Huon Wardle, eds. *Freedom in Practice: Governance, Autonomy, and Liberty in the Everyday*. New York: Routledge, 2016.

Locke, John. *Two Treatise of Government*. London: Whitmore and Fenn, 1821.

Loizos, Peter. "Anthropology's Engagement with Freedom-Questions: Achievements and Agenda." In *LSE on Freedom: A Centenary Anthology*, edited by Eileen Barker. London: LSE Books, 1995.

Loomba, Ania, et al. *Postcolonial Studies and Beyond*. Durham, NC: Duke University Press, 2005.

Ludemir, Julio. *Sorria, Você Está na Rocinha*. São Paulo: Editora Record, 2004.

Luz, Marco Aurélio, and Georges Lapassade. *O Segredo da Macumba*. Rio de Janeiro: Paz e Terra, 1972.

Mahmood, Saba. *Politics of Piety*. Princeton, NJ: Princeton University Press, 2011.

Mahmood, Saba. "Religious Reason and Secular Affect: An Incommensurable Divide?" *Critical Inquiry* 35 (2009): 837.

Malinowski, Bronisław. *Freedom and Civilization*. New York: Roy Publishers, 1944.

Manalansan, Martin. *Global Divas: Filipino Gay Men in the Diaspora*. Durham, NC: Duke University Press, 2003.

Marciato, Ermínia, ed. *A Produção da Casa (e da Cidade) no Brasil Industrial*. São Paulo: Editora Alfa Ômega, 1979.

Marcus, George. "Ethnography in/of the World System: The Emergence of Multi-Sited Ethnography." *Annual Review of Anthropology* 24 (October 1995): 95–117. https://doi.org/10.1146/annurev.an.24.100195.000523.

Marx, Karl. "Debates on the Law on Thefts of Wood." In *Collected Works* by Karl Marx and Friedrich Engels. Vol. 1. New York: International Publishers, 1989.

Matos, Rogério, and Miguel Ribeiro. "Territórios da Prostituição nos Espaços Públicos da Área Central do Rio de Janeiro." *Revista Geográfica* 15, no. 1 (1994): 57–79. https://doi.org/10.5216/bgg.v15i1.4327.

Mazzarella, William. "The Anthropology of Populism: Beyond the Liberal Settlement." *Annual Review of Anthropology* 48 (2019): 45–60. https://doi.org/10.1146/annurev-anthro-102218-011412.

Mbembe, Achille. *Necropolitics*. Durham, NC: Duke University Press, 2019.

McFarlane, Colin. "Assemblage and Critical Urbanism." *City* 15, no. 2 (2011): 204–24. DOI: 10.1080/13604813.2011.568715.

Meirelles, Fernando, and Kátia Lund, dirs. *City of God*. Miramax Films, 2002.

Meiu, George Paul. *Ethno-Erotic Economies: Sexuality, Money, and Belonging in Kenya*. Chicago: University of Chicago Press, 2017.

Meunier, Jacques. *Os Moleques de Bogotá*. Rio de Janeiro: DIFEL, 1978.

Moncorvo Filho, Carlos. *História da Proteção à Infância no Brasil, 1500–1922*. Rio de Janeiro: Editora Pongetti, 1926.

Muñoz, José Esteban. *Disidentifications: Queers of Color and the Performance of Politics*. Minneapolis: University of Minnesota Press, 1999.

Murray, David, ed. *Homophobias: Lust and Loathing across Time and Space*. Durham, NC: Duke University Press, 2010.

Oksala, Johanna. *Foucault on Freedom*. Cambridge: Cambridge University Press, 2005.

Ong, Aihwa. *Neoliberalism as Exception*. Durham, NC: Duke University Press, 2006.

Ong, Aihwa. "Neoliberalism as a Mobile Technology." *Transactions of the Institute of British Geographers*, n.s., 32, no. 1 (2007): 3. http://www.jstor.org/stable/4639996.

O'Sullivan, Simon. "Fold." In *The Deleuze Dictionary*. Edinburgh: University of Edinburgh Press, 2005. Also available at https://www.simonosullivan.net/articles/deleuze-dictionary.pdf.

Pacheco de Oliveira, João. *O Nascimento do Brasil e Outros Ensaios: "Pacificação," Regime Tutelar e Formação de Alteridades*. Rio de Janeiro: Contra Capa, 2016.

Pandolfi, Dulce, and Mário Grynszpan. *A Favela Fala*. Rio de Janeiro: Editora FGV, 2003.

Parés, Luis Nicolau. *The Formation of Candomblé: Vodun History and Ritual in Brazil*. Chapel Hill: University of North Carolina Press, 2013.

Park, Robert and Ernest Burgess. *The City*. Chicago: University of Chicago Press, 2019.

Pateman, Carole. *The Sexual Contract*. Redwood City, CA: Stanford University Press, 1988.

Pateman, Carole. "What's Wrong with Prostitution?" *Women's Studies Quarterly* 27, nos. 1/2 (Spring–Summer 1999): 53–64.

Patterson, Orlando. *Slavery and Social Death: A Comparative Study*. Cambridge, MA: Harvard University Press, 1982.

Patterson, Orlando. "Trafficking, Gender, and Slavery: Past and Present." In *The Legal Understanding of Slavery: From the Historical to the Contemporary*, ed. Jean Allain. Oxford: Oxford University Press, 2012.

Pele, Antônio, et al. *Direitos Humanos e Neoliberalismo*. Rio de Janeiro: Lumen Juris, 2018.

Pelúcio, Larissa. *Abjeção e Desejo: uma Etnografia Travesti sobre o Modelo Preventivo de Aids*. São Paulo: Annablume, 2009.

Perlman, Janice. *O Mito da Marginalidade. Favelas e Política no Rio de Janeiro*. Rio de Janeiro: Paz e Terra, 1977.

Perlongher, Néstor. *O Negócio do Michê: A Prostituição Viril em São Paulo*. São Paulo: Brasiliense, 1987.

Perry, Keisha-Khan. *Black Women against the Land Grab: The Fight for Racial Justice in Brazil*. Minneapolis: University of Minnesota Press, 2013.

Pina Cabral, João, and Vanda Silva. *Gente Livre: Consideração e Pessoa no Baixo Sul da Bahia*. São Paulo: Terceiro Nome, 2013.

Piscitelli, Adriana. "Entre as 'Máfias' e a 'Ajuda': a Construção de Conhecimento sobre Tráfico de Pessoas." *Cadernos Pagu* 31 (2008): 29–63.

Pitkin, Hanna. "Are Freedom and Liberty Twins?" *Political Theory* 16, no. 4 (November 1988): 523–52. DOI:10.1177/0090591788016004001.

REFERENCES

Povinelli, Elizabeth. "A Flight from Freedom." In *Postcolonial Studies and Beyond*, edited by Ania Loomba et al. Durham, NC: Duke University Press, 2005.

Povinelli, Elizabeth. *Geontologies: A Requiem to Late Liberalism*. Durham, NC: Duke University Press, 2016.

Quine, W. V. *Theories and Things*. Cambridge, MA: Harvard University Press, 1981.

Reddy, Chandan. *Freedom with Violence: Race, Sexuality, and the US State*. Durham, NC: Duke University Press, 2011.

Reiter, Rayna, ed. *Toward an Anthropology of Women*. New York: Monthly Review Press, 1975.

Roberts, Neil. *Freedom as Marronage*. Chicago: University of Chicago Press, 2015.

Rose, Nicholas. *Powers of Freedom*. Cambridge: Cambridge University Press, 1999.

Rousseau, Jean-Jacques. *The Social Contract*. New York: Hafner, 1947.

Rubin, Gayle. "The Traffic in Women: Notes on the Political Economy of Sex." In *Toward an Anthropology of Women*, ed. Rayna Reiter. New York: Monthly Review Press, 1975.

Scheper-Hughes, Nancy. *Death without Weeping*. Berkeley: University of California Press, 1989.

Scheper-Hughes, Nancy. "The Primacy of the Ethical: Propositions for a Militant Anthropology." *Current Anthropology* 36, no. 3 (June 1995): 409–40.

Scheper-Hughes, Nancy, and Philippe Bourgois. *Violence in War and Peace*. Oxford: Blackwell, 2004.

Schlemmer, Bernard. *The Exploited Child*. London: Zed Books, 2000.

Schneider, David. *American Kinship: A Cultural Account*. Chicago: University of Chicago Press, 1980.

Sen, Amartya. *Development as Freedom*. Oxford: Oxford University Press, 1999.

Seyferth, Giralda. "As Contradições da Liberdade: Análise de Representações sobre a Identidade Camponesa." *Revista Brasileira de Ciências Sociais* 7, no. 8 (1992): 78–95.

Shange, Savannah. *Progressive Dystopia: Abolition, Antiblackness, and Schooling in San Francisco*. Durham, NC: Duke University Press, 2019.

Singleton, Michael. "Pour une Anthropologie de la Libération." *Recherches Sociologiques et Anthropologiques* 1 (2011): 54.

Smith, Adam. *An Inquiry into the Nature and Causes of the Wealth of Nations*. London: Strahan and Cadell, 1778.

Spivak, Gayatri. *A Critique of Postcolonial Reason*. Cambridge, MA: Harvard University Press, 1999.

Stengers, Isabelle. *Another Science Is Possible*. New Jersey: John Wiley and Sons, 2017.

Stovall, Tyler. *White Freedom: The Racial History of an Idea*. Princeton, NJ: Princeton University Press, 2021.

Stryker, Susan. "Transgender History, Homonormativity, and Disciplinarity." *Radical History Review* 1, no. 100 (January 2008): 145–57. https://doi.org/10.1215/01636545-2007-026.

REFERENCES

Taussig, Michael. *The Devil and Commodity Fetishism in South America*. Chapel Hill: University of North Carolina Press, 2010.

Trouillot, Michel-Rolph. "Anthropology and the Savage Slot: The Poetics and Politics of Otherness." In *Recapturing Anthropology: Working in the Present*, edited by Richard Fox, 17–44. Santa Fe: School of American Research Press, 1991.

Valentine, Charles. *Culture and Poverty: Critique and Counterproposals*. Chicago: University of Chicago Press, 1968.

Valladares, Licia do Prado. *A Invenção da Favela: do Mito de Origem a Favela.com*. Rio de Janeiro: Editora FGV, 2005.

Vartabedian, Julieta. *Brazilian Travesti Migrations: Gender, Sexualities, and Embodiment Experiences*. London: Palgrave, 2018.

Velho, Otávio. *Capitalismo Autoritário e Campesinato: um Estudo Comparativo a partir da Fronteira em Movimento*. Rio de Janeiro: Editora Centro Edelstein, 2009.

Viveiros de Castro, Eduardo. "Cosmological Deixis and Amerindian Perspectivism." *JRAI* 4, no. 3 (1998).

Von Hayek, Friedrich. *The Road to Serfdom*. London: Routledge, 2001.

Wacquant, Loïc. "The Militarization of Urban Marginality: Lessons from the Brazilian Metropolis." *International Political Sociology* 2 (2008), 56–74. DOI:10.1111/J.1749-5687.2008.00037.x.

Wacquant, Loïc. "Three Steps to a Historical Anthropology of Actually Existing Neoliberalism." *Social Anthropology* 20 (2012): 66–79.

Wacquant, Loïc. *Urban Outcasts: A Comparative Sociology of Advanced Marginality*. Malden, MA: Polity, 2007.

Wagner, Roy. *The Invention of Culture*. Chicago: University of Chicago Press, 2016.

Warner, Michael. *The Trouble with Normal: Sex, Politics, and the Ethics of Queer Life*. Cambridge, MA: Harvard University Press, 2000.

Weston, Kath. *Families We Choose: Lesbians, Gays, Kinship*. New York: Columbia University Press, 1997.

Whitt, Matt. "The Problem of Poverty and the Limits of Freedom in Hegel's Theory of the Ethical State." *Political Theory* 41, no. 2 (2013): 257–84.

Williams, Erica L. *Sex Tourism in Bahia: Ambiguous Entanglements*. Chicago: University of Illinois Press, 2013.

Woortmann, Klaas. "Com Parente Não se Neguceia." O Campesinato Como Ordem Moral, *Anuário Antropológico* 87 (1990), 11–73.

Index

Africa, 60, 136, 141
African Americans: double consciousness of, 205n50; second sight, 205n50
Afro-Brazilian religions, 109, 117–18, 122, 124–25, 131, 135, 142–44, 194, 216n17, 216n20; deities, 134; deities, and the devil, 127, 130; empowerment, 136; initiation, concept of, 126; normative liberalism, challenging of, 195; queer people, 130, 195
agency, 65, 93; and poverty, 5; and women, 74
Aguião, Silvia, 208–9n14
AIDS, 128, 184
alterity, 38; alterity regimes, 1
alternative freedoms, 14–15
Alves, Jaime, 207n72
Amado, Jorge, 101
Ambedkar, Bhimrao, 202n8
Ambrósio, Alessandra (supermodel), 219n12
Ambrósio, Kimberley, 184, 219n12
American Philosophical Society, 206n68
Amerindians, 4, 18, 44, 85, 105, 117, 203n22
Amigo dos Amigos (A.D.A./Friends of Friends), 33, 55, 64
Angola, 60
anthropology, x, 9–11, 15, 24, 41, 43, 206–7n71; butterfly collection exercise, 190–91; and liberalism, 13; of liberation, 188
anthropology for liberation, 10, 188
Appadurai, Arjun, 202n9
Arendt, Hannah, 91, 173; freedom, vision of, 92
Asad, Talal, 116, 140

Asphalt (formal city), 21–23, 26, 38–39, 46–49, 53–54, 62–63, 66–67, 95, 98, 100, 107, 157, 171–72, 184, 189, 198, 203n22, 208n2; drugs, illegal in, 57; "gay," as marker of identity, 108; law of, 153–54; modern urban infrastructure, 94; moral zones, 151; normative liberalism of, 89; queer politics, 89. See also Rio de Janeiro
assemblages, 20–24, 100, 116, 126, 151, 154; as defined, 207n89; minoritarian modes of liberalism, 101
Australia, 52
autonomy, xi, 11, 94, 99; of favela dwellers, 5, 100; indigenous, 4; individual, 19, 141, 206–7n71, 207n75; personal, 132; and poverty, 5

Bantu, 60
Bar & Mar (club), 52
Baudelaire, Charles, 211n27
Benin, 59
Benjamin, Walter, 211n27
Benveniste, Émile, 90, 103
Berlusconi, Silvio, 163
Bethânia, Maria (singer), 160
bicha-boys, 39, 108, 145, 208–9n14
biopower, 42, 187; Western elites, 219n15
Black population, 4–5, 18, 44; cortiços, 2; housing issues, 2
Boas, Franz, 14, 206n66
Bogotá, Colombia, 101
Bolsa Família program, 193
Bolsonaro, Jair, 141
Bourgois, Philippe, 203–4n24

233

INDEX

boy-fags, 39, 52, 61, 68–70, 86, 88–89, 98, 104–5, 110, 145, 158
Boym, Svetlana, 189
Brazil, 21, 24, 30, 48, 60, 65, 88, 109, 115–18, 150, 156–57, 159–60, 165, 168, 170, 176, 182–83, 193–94, 202n3, 220n14; atavistic migratory instinct, 84–85; and beauty, 166; Black population, 2, 18; Catholic social movements, 4; child rearing, as domestic sphere, 73; church and state, 141; "colonial encounter," 1; and consent, 210–11n21; demons and deities, struggle between, 117; dictatorship in, 4–5; elite in, 44; Evangelicals, rise in, 4; Gini coefficient, 203n19; households, headed by single women, 74; independence of, 1–2; Italy, human-trafficking scheme between, 162; jail system, as corrupt and non-white, 192; Jesuits in, 117, 215n4; laws in, as contradictory, 45; liberalism in, xi, 7; liberty, and social movements, 1–2; peasantry, 84; poverty line, 220n15; race and class, 11; racial categories, 208n5; racism in, 205n58; religion in, 192; slavery, abolition of, 202n5; Spain, human trafficking between, 152; transphobia, and murder, 212n22; tutelary regime, 4; whiteness, as universally desired, 205n58
Brazilian Criminal Code, 139
Brazilian Democratic Movement, 4
Brazilian National Association of Travestis and Transsexuals (ANTRA), 201n2, 212n22
bread-and-egg faggots, 218n26
Bündchen, Gisele (supermodel), 208n9, 219n12
Bündchen, Natasha Kellem, xii, 6, 11–12, 18, 23–24, 28–29, 31–34, 36, 43, 48, 51–54, 57–58, 60–62, 64–69, 71, 74, 77–78, 86, 95, 108, 125, 133, 136, 139–42, 154, 156–57, 159–60, 163, 165, 169, 171, 178, 182–83, 188–89, 195, 201n1, 212n12, 219n12; becoming herself, process of, 102; as center of attention, 102; clothing, emphasis on, 104; cruising, 106; death of, 176, 179–80, 184; death of, as challenge to normative liberalism, 181; devil, privileged relations with, 131; disorientation, potential for, 102;

as empowered, 87; entrapped, feelings of, 85; Evangelicals, hatred toward, 115, 117; favela liberalism, interest in, 89; freedoms of, 88–89, 191; funeral of, 176–77; governmentality, as outsider to, 107; illness of, 40–42, 173–76, 180; libertinism of, 75, 131, 177; liberty, assertion of, 76, 99, 100; as outspoken, 30; racism of, 59; religion, 115–16; respect toward, 190; as risk-taker, 89; self-defense, 72; sense of humor, 42; sexual prowess, 106; sexual violence, 79–80; as target of violence, ix, 89; as travesti, 14, 17, 22, 30, 80, 87–88, 99, 102, 180, 190
Burgess, Ernest, 94

Caboclo Pena Branca (spirit), 125, 127, 216n20
Cafeteria Riots, 18
caguete, 208n3
Campos de Lima, Eduardo, 210n13
Candomblé (religion), 124–25, 160
Canudos, Brazil: liberty, as representative of, 3
Canudos War, 2–3, 65, 197
capitalism, 63, 84, 171; consumer, 166; favela liberalism, 89
Cardoso, Fernando Henrique, 209n16
Cardoso, Vânia, 215n9
Catholic Church, 3, 49–51, 109, 130, 132, 194
Catholic social movements, 4
Caveira, João (Exu), 129, 216n22
Ceará, Brazil, 21–23, 28, 30–33, 49–50, 52–53, 61, 65–68, 71, 75–77, 79–80, 83–89, 92–93, 99–100, 108, 131, 174, 192, 212n7
Césaire, Aimé, 202n8
Chakrabarty, Dipesh, 8
Chicago, Illinois, 94
Chicago School, 94
children: disidentification, 92; favela kids, 92; forced labor, 92; freedom of, 91; home confinement, 94; as incomplete beings, 92; and newness, 91; paid labor, 92; as potentially dangerous, 92; street kids, 92
Christianity, 117–18, 128, 138; demonization of minoritarian deities, 135; liberation services, 130; and whiteness, 127
City of God (film), x

INDEX

Clastres, Pierre, 205n52
Cold War, 133
Collor de Mello, Fernando, 4
Colombia, 116
colonialism, x, 16, 117; and liberalism, 2, 7–9
colonization, 5, 130; and enslavement, 116–17
Comaroff, Jean, 141
Comaroff, John, 141
Communist Party, 4; popular democratic committees, 3; urban poor, 3
Compton's Cafeteria Riots, 18
Congo, 60
Conselheiro, Antônio, 3
contractualism, 48, 201–2n6; contractualist philosophy, xi
cortiços, 2
culture of neoliberalism, 141
culture of poverty, 5–6, 186

Da Cunha, Euclides, 3
Davida (NGO), 152
Day, Sophie, 151
De Almeida, Ronaldo, 118, 216n28
Decena, Carlos, 214n31
decolonization, 205n52; decolonial anthropology, 11; decolonial generation, 188; decolonial liberalism, 10
Dehesa, Rafael de la, 182
Déjaque, Joseph, 143
DeLanda, Manuel, 13
Deleuze, Gilles, 12–13, 24–25, 202n10, 207n89
D'Emilio, John, 100–101
deterritorialization, xii, 13, 16, 62, 64, 92, 172, 188, 195; of liberalism, 135
D-20 flatbed truck, as mode of transportation, 66–69, 81, 175, 211n4, 211n5, 219n3
devil, 31, 68, 77, 97, 111, 114, 130–32, 135, 140–41, 192–93; agency of, 136; devil worship, 118–19; different forms of, 127; as dirty, 120, 127; as evil, 136; fear of, 116–17; slave owners, 123. See also exorcism; possession; witchcraft
Dieckmann, Anderson, 184
Dieckmann, Carolina (actress), 184
disease, and sexuality, 68
disidentification, xii, 16, 101, 188, 191, 205n54; and children, 92; and liberation, 171; as political form of minoritarian politics, 14
Doherty, Gareth, 46
domestic work, as form of exploitation, 77
drug trafficking, 5, 25, 29, 33, 54, 57–58, 107, 184, 187, 196; payments of bribes, 192. See also human trafficking; traffickers
Du Bois, W. E. B., 10, 205n50

economic liberalism, 202n8; free-market ideology, 44–45
Edelman, Lee, 182
Edmonds, Alexander, 166
Egypt, 8
elites, xi, 4, 6, 17, 27, 38–39, 44–49, 54, 62, 66–67, 92, 94–95, 100, 103–4, 115, 141, 158, 188, 191–92, 219n15
encubada, 99, 102
Eng, David, 17–18
Enlightenment, 1, 8, 183, 201–2n6
ethnographic theory, xi
Eurocentrism, 8, 19, 157
Europe, 1, 7–8, 11, 13, 16, 21–22, 38, 100, 115, 155–57, 160–61, 165, 167–68, 170, 182–83, 202n8
Evangelical churches, 20, 118–19, 133–34; Afro-Brazilian religion, as counter to, 117; conversion and baptism, 126; liberation services, 114–15, 120–21, 123, 137; and possession, 122–23; unfreedom, sense of, 123
Evangelical Congregation of Liberation, 115
Evangelicals, 4, 86, 95, 98, 108, 113–16, 118, 126, 139, 185, 191, 203n16; devil, manifestation of, 127; mode of liberation in favelas, 133; unfreedom, 123
exorcism, 24, 144, 194–95. See also devil; possession; witchcraft
Exu (spirit), 118, 124, 127–28, 135, 195
Exu Cachaceiro (spirit), 127–28

Farmer, Paul, 6, 203–4n24
favela (plant), 203n9
favela children, 94
Favela da Rocinha, ix–x, xii, 4–7, 12, 19–24, 30–32, 34–37, 39–40, 46, 49–50, 52–53, 59–60, 63–67, 71–72, 76–77, 79, 81, 84–85, 87–90, 93–94, 99, 101, 111–13, 133, 138–39, 143, 150, 153, 161, 164–65, 169–74, 176–78, 182, 184–88, 190, 195,

INDEX

Favela da Rocinha (*cont.*)
197, 204n30; alterity in, 38; Catholic Church in, 132; drug traffickers, 25–26, 33, 55–56, 80, 82; drug traffickers, as protectors, 198; drug traffickers, as tyrants, 54; drug-trafficking governmentality, 25; and freedom, 91; "Great Ditch," 26; kinship ties, as threat to liberties, 74; as liberal, 15; as liberal heterotopia, 62, 147, 154; liberation services in, 115–17, 122, 127; minoritarian liberation in, 103; modes of liberalism in, 57, 183; modes of minoritarian liberation, 191; moral region, concept of, 213–14n19; occupation of, 196; Owner of Hillside, 54; PAFYC in, 95–96, 104; police and traffickers, 210n18; policing apparatus, 193–94; prostitution, 80; queer liberalism in, 135; queer liberation in, 105; queers, treatment of in, 58; Red Command, 128; rule of law, 189; sex-trafficking scheme, 159; slavery of motherhood, rebellion against, 74; snitches as X-9, designation of, 26; unfreedom, 135; women, lack of freedom, 73–74; young queers, as attention seekers, 102

favelado, 39

Favela do Vigidal, 49

favela dwellers, 109, 111, 160, 182–83, 191; Catholic Church, 132; devil's presence, 130; and elites, 45, 47; elites, tactics against, 46; lack of choice, 191; modes of liberalism, 48; national army, 196; and nation-state, 193; normative liberalism, 47; property rights, 47; and religion, 116; rule of law, 47; sex work network, 150–51; social contract, challenging of, 183; state power, and killing of, 48; stigma against, 46; Umbanda practices, 124–25. *See also* favelas

favela liberalism, 12, 23, 54, 57, 68, 88, 192; and capitalism, 89; LGBTQ expression, protection of, 102–3; peasant liberalism, as minoritarian alternative to, 89; principles of, 62; types of freedom, 63

favelas, ix–x, 9, 12–13, 16, 25, 29–30, 37, 43, 67, 79, 83, 99, 128, 138–39, 157, 183, 186, 188, 190, 192, 195, 202n6, 210n15; Afro-Brazilian religions in, 130; Asphalt and Hillside, territorial dynamic between, 107; autonomy, 100; *bicha-boy burguesa*, 39; birth of, 2–3; as "Blackened" space, 203n11; Black freedom, 42; bourgeois and favelado, distinction between, 38–39; and bourgeoisie, 63; boy-fags, 52; bringing order to, 196; coming out, 105; confusion of in, 191; deterritorialization, 62; diversity of, 204n30; and elites, 27, 38–39; elites, as enemy to, 45; Evangelical churches in, 115; favela slang, and queer life, 58–59; foreign nationals, tolerance toward, 38; forms of power, xi; freedom, lack of, 5, 14, 74; freedom, types of, 61–64; gay, synonyms for, 39; as heterogeneous, 62; hinterlands, connections between, 65, 84–85; and humiliation, 77; inability to be monitored, 107; irrational urbanity of, 106; lack of formal addresses, 107; lack of liberty, 94; landmarks of, 27; laws of the Hillside, 107; laws of the Hillside, and queer freedoms, 88; liberalism in, 64, 89; liberdade, xi–xii, 6–7, 18, 32; libertinism in, 191; liberty in, 54; modes of liberalism, 191; morals, 111; military policies toward, 4; minoritarian freedoms, 172; as morally degraded territories, 98; mortality rate, 62; narco-traffickers, 54; natality rate, 62; nation-state, 48, 63; neoliberal state, as central to, 47–48; Neo-Pentecostal Christians, 117; No Limite, 27, 150; normative liberalism, 108–9; occupation of, 45, 196–97; outside public, closed to, 63; Pacificação (pacification) policy, 5, 45; as peripheral territories, 47; police killings in, 210n13; private land, "illegal" occupation of, 45; property laws, violation of, 94–95; queer kinship in, 103; queer liberalism, 100, 154; queer liberation in, 100–101, 104; queer life in, 23, 58; racism in, 42; rule of law, 46; "security force," 63; state, ambiguous relationship with, 47; state forces into, 196–97; as state of nature, 17; teenage pregnancy, 74; territoriality of, 61–62; travestis in, 17, 52, 62; urban centers and hinterlands, comparison between, 65; as violators of property rights, 44; as violent, 46–47; violent removals, 4; as zones of violence and poverty, 45. *See also individual favelas*

INDEX

Favela Tours, 39
Ferguson, James, 205n43
Filipino migrant communities, 102
First Amendment, 189
Fish, Stanley, 189
Fortaleza, Brazil, 66, 83
Foucault, Michel, 1, 92, 208n1, 218–19n39; biopower, 42; on power, 209n19, 209n20; and universalisms, 7
France, 155, 202n11; *banlieue* in, 48
freedom, ix–xii, 2–3, 8, 10–11, 13, 16, 19–24, 43, 45; and children, 91; civil, 17; as commodity, 63; concept of, 14; as difference, 92; forms of, as undesirable, 98; lack of, 14; liberalism, forms of, 48; limitations on, 75, 85, 94; peasant conceptions of, 65; possibility for freedom, 187; and power, 25; as practice, 18; Russian concept of, 14–15; as state of being, 9; and subjection, 17; and unfreedom, 5–6, 14, 123, 135; universalization of, 7, 17; and violence, 47
free speech, 189
Freire, Paulo, 203n14
French Revolution, xi, 13
Freud, Sigmund, 92
Friends United School (FUS), 52–53, 66–67, 74, 108, 110, 113, 119, 132, 138, 196–97
Fulani, in West Africa, 14
funk, 122

gay, as word, 39
Gay Pride at Copacabana, 132
gender: and liberalism, 16; and sexuality, 22, 88
Geschiere, Peter, 135–36
"Girl from Ipanema, The" (song), 49
Globo (TV channel), 136, 139
Glorious Revolution, xi
governmentality, 1, 8, 23–25, 48, 57, 62, 100, 191; and surveillance, 107
Gramsci, Antonio, 202n8
gringo behavior, 38
Grynszpan, Mário, 47
Guaraciaba do Norte, Brazil, 66–68, 73, 79–80, 82, 85, 92–93
Guattari, Félix, 12–13, 24–25, 202n10, 205n57

halfie, 208n12
Halperin, David, 180–81

Harrington, Michael, 203n23
Harrison, Faye, 10–11, 205n48
hate speech, 189
Hayek, Friedrich von, 204n38
heterogeneity, 149
heteronormative gender structures, 74–75
heterotopia, 211n24
heterotopic freedom, 172
Hilgers, Mathieu, 8
Hillside: favela, 21–22, 26, 38–39, 46, 54, 56, 108, 198; laws of, 57–58, 64; queer population of, 55
hinterlands, 3, 23, 30, 33, 65, 68, 78, 89; escape from, 85; favelas, as counterpoints to, 84–85; freedom of, 92; women's morality, as protected by lack of freedom, 73–74
HIV, 40, 42, 68, 159, 174, 180, 184–86
Hobbes, Thomas, 16, 201–2n6, 207n75
Hobsbawm, Eric, 13
homophobia, 23, 68, 89, 177, 198; internalized, 180–81
humanism, 7–8, 10
human trafficking, 152–53, 155, 161–63, 172; and slavery, 24. *See also* drug trafficking; traffickers
Humphrey, Caroline, 14–16, 206n68

Iansã (Orixá), 124, 216n18
Iemanjá (Orixá), 123–24, 126–27
income redistribution program, 193
Inconfidência Mineira movement, 202n3
incubated fags, 99, 104, 111
Independence Hill, 4. *See also* Morro do Borel
indigenous people: indigenous autonomy, 4; indigenous liberalism, 205n52; spiritual protection, 72
individualism, 9, 11, 17, 44–45, 84, 88–89, 99, 103, 151–53, 170–71, 193
individuality, 88, 152; normative liberalism, 89, 99–100
Ipanema, Brazil, 49, 78, 128
Italy, 156–57; Brazil, human-trafficking scheme between, 162; Brazilian sex workers, 24; Brazilian travestis in, 160–62, 169

Jaguaribe, Beatriz, 45
Jain, 14
Jesuits, 117, 215n4

237

INDEX

Jobim, Antônio Carlos, 49
Jobson, Ryan, 9–10
Joyce, Patrick, 93

Kant, Immanuel, 94, 207n75
Kardec, Allan, 124, 215n11
Kenya, sex workers in, 170
Kikongo, 60
kinship, 68, 73, 75–76, 103–4, 157; and liberalism, 193; and oppression, 193; as threat to liberties, 74; travesti, 170–71
kosi, 59
Kulick, Don, 30, 87, 160, 167, 169, 208n8, 213n31, 214n37

labor, 56, 68, 75–76, 83, 92, 143, 171; commodification and exploitation of, 84; forced, 92, 152; sex work as, 152–53, 161; as slavery, 77
Laidlaw, James, 14, 187
land ownership, 45, 68, 75–76
Lapassade, Georges, 135
Latin America, 1, 117, 133, 203n14, 206n65, 216n27; Christianity in, 118, 132; colonization of 130; queer liberation in, 182–83; power struggles, 115; slums of, 5
laws of the Asphalt, 192. *See also* rule of law
laws of the Hillside, 100, 107, 138, 187, 191–92, 195–96; rapists, treatment of, 89; stealing among residents, 90
Leite, Gabriela, 152
Leu, Lorraine, 203n11
Lewis, Oscar, 186–87, 203n23
LGBTQ, 17, 20, 55, 60, 88, 117, 132, 135, 183, 191–92; coming out of closet, 102; liberation politics, as de-radicalized, 18; as political struggle, 87; risk group category, 180–81; untimely deaths, 187
liberal anthropology, *v.* anthropology for liberation, 24, 190
liberal (de)territorialization, 13
liberal heterotopia, 62, 107, 147, 154
liberal humanism, 9–10
liberalism, x, 11, 14–17, 21, 75, 153, 157, 165, 172, 187, 206n64; abolitionist strategy, 10; alternative forms of, 194; and anthropology, 13; as artifact of colonialism, 9; and childhood, 91; as collective mode, 13; colonial apparatus, as fundamental part of, 7–8; and colonialism, 2; decolonization of, xii, 9–10, 188; deterritorialization of, 13; ethnography of, 194; Eurocentric, xi–xii, 9; in favelas, 64; and freedom, 48; and gender, 16; instability, 10; interconnected circuits, 20; and kinship, 193; language, circulation and performance of, 19; as minoritarian existence, 104, 220n11; minoritarian modes of, 7, 12–13, 85, 119; modes of, 69, 98; nation-state, 22, 195; normative, xi–xii; queer experiences of, 65; reconceptualizing of, 5; and religion, 113, 115–16; sex work, 24; and tracing, 19–20; urban centers, association with, 93; as word, xi
liberalization, 151
liberal multiculturalism, 109
liberal normalization: as reproductive futurism, 182
liberated fags, 104–5
liberation theology, 4, 50–51, 132, 203–4n24, 216n27
liberdade, xi–xii, 6, 15–16, 18–20, 23, 32, 100, 109, 111, 196
liberi, 90–91, 100, 103–4
libertarianism, 205n53
libertinism, xii, 14, 23, 43, 68, 75, 131, 158, 206n64; as minoritarian liberalism, 151
liberty, xi–xii, 1, 3, 7, 11, 13–14, 16, 18–21, 23, 48, 54, 58, 65, 67, 76, 83, 91, 94–95, 98, 100, 107, 109, 111, 155, 158, 168, 194, 196, 201n6; negative and positive, concepts of, 208n4; primitive notion of, 103; whiteness, privilege of, 202n11
Liberty Hill, 4. *See also* Morro do Turano
Locke, John, xi, 16, 201–2n6
Loizos, Peter, 14, 206–7n71
London, England, 93
Lula, Luiz Inácio da Silva, 203n20, 209n16
Luz, Marco Aurélio, 135

Macedo, Edir, 126
macumba, 59, 117, 124, 133–34, 210n20, 215n6, 216n33
Mafia, 156, 162–63
Mahmood, Saba, 7–8, 11, 15, 65, 207n73, 212n15
Malinowski, Bronisław, 14, 206n66
Manalansan, Martin, 102–3
Manchester, England, 93
Marabá, Brazil, 84

238

Marcos, João, 110, 184
Marcus, George, 209n17
maroon communities, 2
maroon liberalism, 12, 42
Marrazzo, Piero, 163
Martinslândia, Brazil, 66–69, 77, 79–82, 84–86, 88, 131, 174–75, 177, 179
Marx, Karl, 45, 202n8
matesca, 33, 208n10; travesti, 88
Matos, Rogério, 149
Mattatoio, in Rome, 160–61, 172
mavambo, 58–61
mavula, 60
Mazzarella, William, 9
McFarlane, Colin, 20
Meiu, George Paul, 170, 218n38
Meunier, Jacques, 101
Mexico, 182–83
migrants, 33, 67, 83–84, 156; transport of, 66
migration, 65, 99–100, 161; atavistic migratory instinct, 84–85; oppression, escape from, 85, 92
"Minha Alma" (My soul) (song), 191
minoritarian freedoms, 55, 170, 187, 195
minoritarian liberalisms, 18, 21, 23–24, 101, 108, 141, 154, 181, 183, 187, 190, 193; characteristics of, 13; disidentification, processes of, 11–12; libertinism, 151; peasant liberalism, 84; theory of, 64
minoritarian literature, 12
minoritarian modes of liberalism, 135, 183, 190–91
minoritarian queer freedoms: assemblage of, 107
modernity, 93, 171, 183, 211n27; political, 8; and religion, 140; sex work, 151
modernization, 99–100, 183
Moncorvo Filho, Carlos, 98
Morro do Borel (favela), Residents' Association, 3–4. *See also* Independence Hill
Morro do Turano (favela), 3. *See also* Liberty Hill
motherhood, 213n4; slavery of, 74; subjection of, 74
Muñoz, José Esteban, xii, 12, 205n54

nation-state, 45, 48, 63, 95, 107, 109, 111, 141, 151, 153, 192–93, 196; and liberalism, 22, 195; use of violence against marginalized, 194

necropolitics, 187
neoliberalism, 21, 44, 133, 136, 187, 202n8, 204n38, 204n42; as colonial project of domination, 9; as culture, 8; as governmentality, 8; modes of engagement, 8; neoliberal governance, 5; normative liberalism, as variant of, 11; origins of, 8; as system, 8; as term, 11; as transnational project, 8
Neo-Pentecostal Evangelical churches, 4, 23–24, 126, 132, 138, 143, 192–95; Afro-Brazilian spirits, incorporating of, 124; and devil, 136; and liberalism, 141; liberation services, 117, 127
Netherlands, 48, 151–52
New York, 102
Niemeyer, Oscar, 110
Nigeria, 59
Nightmare on Elm Street, A (film), 218n27
normative freedom, 21, 62; as violent, 48
normative gender binarism, 186
normative liberalism, 7, 11–14, 17–18, 20–22, 24, 43–44, 46, 54, 83–84, 101, 103–4, 108–9, 116, 133–35, 139, 141–42, 153–54, 17, 171–72, 183, 187–88, 190, 193, 214n34; and autonomy, 99; challenging of, 195; colonial effects, 15–16; colonization of liberal possibilities, 191; culture of poverty, 186; elite children, 92; favela dwellers, aggressive toward, 47; individuality, valuing of, 89, 99–100, 151; language, use of, 189; oppressive potential of, 91; of rational city, 98; rule of law, 16, 189; self-care, 180; surveillance, and governmentality, 107; and territorialization, 48; universal rationality, 94
North America, 7–8, 11, 13, 16, 100, 102
Northeast (Brazil), 79, 87, 212n14; peasant liberalism in, 89; poverty, association with, 67; traveling on D-20 flatbed truck, 66, 68–69, 81, 175, 211n4, 211n5, 219n3; "undesirable" migrants, 67

Ogum (Orixá), 124, 216n18
Oksala, Johanna, 18
Olympic Games (2016), 196
Ong, Aihwa, 44, 205n43
Orixá (deity), 216n18
O'Sullivan, Simon, 141
Owner of the Hillside, 62, 64, 138, 197; authority of, 55; fugitives, hosting of, 107;

239

Owner of the Hillside (*cont.*)
  legitimacy of, 54–56; public humiliation of "fags," prohibition of, 102–3

Pacheco de Oliveira, João, 1, 4, 203n22
Pacifying Police Units (UPPs), 196–98
PAFYC group (Young Ladies Crew), 23–24, 91, 95–99, 102, 106, 108, 114, 154–55, 176, 182–86, 193, 213n17; Afro-Brazilian spirits, 136; class privilege, 100; and clothing, 105; coming out of closet, 103; disdain toward, 112; and disidentification, 101; excess of freedom, complaints of, 110, 112; liberation services, 115, 122, 126, 135; as minoritarian, 101; normally accepted freedoms, challenging of, 101; pranks, known for, 104; queerness of, in public, 103; and religion, 116; rules, challenging of, 112
Pai Nelson (spiritual leader), 125
Pajubá (dialect), 58–60, 102, 164
Pandolfi, Dulce, 47
Paraíba, Brazil, 76–77
paramilitary groups, 33
Park, Robert, 94
Parnet, Claire, 205n57
Pastoral of Favelas, 210n13
Pateman, Carole, 16, 62, 151, 153; social contract, 17
Patterson, Orlando, 152
Pavão-Pavãozinho-Cantagalo (PPG), 63–64, 128, 192
peasant cultures, 75; and land, 76; moral order, 76
peasant ideologies, 84
peasant liberalism, 12, 23, 83, 88, 95, 103–4, 154, 171–72; family-based economy, preference for, 89; and homophobia, 89; minoritarian liberalism, 84; modern slavery, prevention of, 89; queer oppression, 89; return to captivity, fear of, 84–85; and transphobia, 89
peasantry, 84
Pereira Passos, Francisco Franco, 2
Perlman, Janice, 210n6
Perlongher, Néstor, 217n7
Perry, Keisha-Khan, 209–10n5
Pina Cabral, João, 212n25
Piscitelli, Adriana, 152–53

Pomba-gira (spirit), 118, 122, 124, 126–27, 130, 132, 135, 143, 195
Portugal, 1, 202n1
possession, 122, 125, 127–28, 140, 194; spirit possession, 134–35, 216n14, 220n19. *See also* devil; exorcism; witchcraft
poverty, 67; and agency, 5; and autonomy, 5; cultural traits of, 203n23; "culture of," 5–6, 186; as entrapment, 5; and oppression, 5; "poverty line," 220n15; and suffering, 91, 101; "unfreedom," source of, 5–6; urban, 5, 186–87; urban land, irrational occupation of, 94; and violence, 45, 47, 203–4n24
Povinelli, Elizabeth, 7–9, 15, 20, 219n15
Proclamation of the Republic, 1–2
prosperity theology, 133
prostitution, 30–31, 80, 120, 127–28, 146, 149, 151, 154–55, 160, 162, 171, 217n7; as binary, 172; as indefensible, 153; as official profession, 152. *See also* sex work
Public Universal Health System (SUS), 159

queer favela dwellers, 10, 153, 170, 188; normative liberalism, problem for, 187; short life span of, 187; social contract, challenging of, 187; witchcraft, as form of minoritarian empowerment, 141–42. *See also* favela dwellers
queer gender, and sexuality, 101
queer identities, 117; and modernization, 100; public identity, 102
queer kinship, 103, 107
queer liberalism, 12, 18, 23, 59, 100, 135, 154, 182; as collective endeavor, 89; expressions of, 104; as form of empowerment, 17; normalization of queer life, 14; sex work, 166–67
queer liberation, 24, 100–101, 108, 111, 142, 182–83; as bodily type of metamorphosis, 105; body elasticity, 105; and clothing, 105; normative liberal conception of, 102; and splits, 105–6
queer life, 95, 182; hierarchies in, 154; queer bodies, 67; queer "care of the self," 171; and risk taking, 181
queerness, 182
queer politics, 89, 181–82
queer sex, and barebacking, 180–81

INDEX

Quimbanda rituals, 118, 124, 143
Quine, Willard Van Orman, 19

racism, 59, 132, 205n58, 211n26
radical liberalism, 92
rationality, 92, 94, 100, 135, 207n75
Red Command (C.V.), 33
Reddy, Chandan, 194
religion, 192; black slave religion, 117; magic, as inseparable from, 117; and modernity, 140; and power, 116; and state, 140–41, 193; underdogs, power to, 119
reproductive futurism, 182–83
reterritorialization, 62
Reviver church, 123, 126–27
Ribeiro, Miguel, 149
Riesman, Paul, 14
Rio das Pedras (favela), 30, 32–33, 52, 177–78, 208n14
Rio de Janeiro, Brazil, 5, 12–13, 15, 19, 23–25, 52, 69, 76–78, 81–82, 86–87, 99–100, 108, 156, 161, 164, 169, 192, 203n11, 217n5, 217n6, 217n8; Barra da Tijuca, 27, 74, 143, 150, 217n4; Black dwellers, targeting of by police, 26; Black population in, 2; celebrities in, 56–57; Copacabana, 63, 128, 137, 217n4; cortiços, 2; drug trafficking, 84; elites in, 27, 44, 46, 48, 92–93; Favela Bairro upgrading program, 95; Favela Hill, 3; "favela problem" in, 96; favelas in, 2–3, 17–18, 27, 44–45, 47, 84, 89, 92, 122, 181, 203n22, 208–9n14, 210n13; formality v. informality, 46; German Complex, occupation of, 196–97; labor market of, as form of slavery, 83–84; Lagoa-Barra Highway, 26–27, 50; liberalism, multiple versions of, 48; as Marvelous City, 22, 32, 47, 68, 88, 95, 141, 146, 149; Morro do Borel, 3; Morro do Turano, 3; No Limite, 27; North Zone, 27, 196; police killings, 210n13; sex work in, 149; soap operas, as portrayed in, 83; South Zone, 30, 49, 186, 217n4; street children in, 98; West Zone, ix, 27, 30, 39, 208–9n143, 217n4. *See also individual favelas*
Rio Gay Pride Parade, 108–9
Rocinha Gay Pride Parade, 198

Rocinha Residents' Association (AMABB), 37, 121, 215n12
Roman Empire, 91, 217n9
Rome, Italy, 24, 133, 160–62, 164, 170, 172
Rose, Nicholas, 220n11
Rousseau, Jean-Jacques, 16, 201–2n6
rule of law, 16, 43, 46–47, 107, 151, 189, 192; Brazilian Rule of Law, 152, 208n7. *See also* laws of the Asphalt
Russia, 14

Salvador, Brazil, 87, 101, 160, 213n31
San Francisco, California, 18
São Conrado (neighborhood), 12, 26–27, 38, 46, 57, 118
São Paulo, Brazil, 118
Scheper-Hughes, Nancy, 203–4n24, 210n14
Scotland, 25, 38–39, 48, 161, 165
secularism, 141, 215n1
self-organized collective action (*mutirões*), 4, 194
Sen, Amartya, 5
sex work, 77, 143, 149–50, 156–58, 172, 186, 195; and "blood" mothers, 219n11; as exploitative, 151; free labor, form of, 152–53; libertine lifestyle, 170; modernity, 151; pimps, protection of, 154; queer liberalism, 166–67; as service transaction, 153; social contract, as form of, 153. *See also* prostitution
Seyferth, Giralda, 84, 212n25
Shange, Savannah, 10
Silva, Vanda, 212n25
Singleton, Michael, 188
slavery, xi, 1, 10, 24, 75, 89, 91, 123, 153, 160–61, 171; abolition of, 2, 202n5; devil worship, 118–19; domestic, 85, 92; labor market, 83–84; liberation from, 132; linguistic heritage from, 59; natal alienation, 152
slums, ix, xi, 2, 5, 10, 22, 24, 38, 45–46, 63, 82, 88, 94–95, 98, 100, 108, 111, 172, 188, 197, 210n13
Smith, Adam, 44
social contract, 17, 46–48, 153, 182–83, 187, 201–2n6
social justice, x, 65
Solomon's Temple, 118
South America: indigenous land, invasion of, 1

Spain, 155, 169, 202n1; Brazil, human trafficking between, 152
Spiritism, 109
spirit possession, 216n14, 220n19; as alterity device, 134; minoritarian mode of liberalism, 135; and otherness, 134. *See also* possession
state power, 22, 27, 48, 94, 119, 139, 177, 193
state violence, 195; against underprivileged populations, 194
Stonewall Riots, as strategic essentialism, 18
Stovall, Tyler, 202n11
street kids, 92, 98, 153–54, 213n7; freedom, valuing of, 101
street life, 214n38; as place of freedom, 75
structural violence, 5–6; invisibility of, 203–4n24
subaltern populations, 12, 15–16
Switzerland, 155

Taussig, Michael, 116, 118–19, 135
territorialization, 13, 56, 64, 92, 99; and elites, 62; as liberation, 95; normative liberalism, and homogenization of difference, 48
Third Command (T.C.), 33
traffickers, 60, 63, 98, 111, 138, 139, 192, 197, 208n2; authority of, 54; "bandits' wives," 211n22; erotic power of, 60–61; hierarchical occupations within, 60; legitimacy of, 54; queer freedom, 23; supportive of community, 55. *See also* drug trafficking; human trafficking
Tranca-Rua (spirit), 122, 127
transgender, 22, 86; sex workers, 30, 172; as term, 30; transgender activism, 18. *See also* travesti
transphobia, 23, 86, 89, 212n22
transsexual, 86, 162–63
travesti, 14, 20, 22, 52, 59–61, 69, 80, 87, 89, 97–99, 102, 109, 144, 151, 157–59, 180–81, 183–84, 190, 208n8, 213n31, 214n37; ability to travel, and freedoms, 67; abuse of, by police, 153–54; bourgeoisie, as impossibility, 39; criminals, treated as, 107; cross-dressing practices, 206n65; exploitation of, 107; favela rights of, 62; in Italy, 160–64, 169; kinship relations, 170–71; and liberdade, 100; older generation of, 104, 111; and pimps, 155–56; police brutality, subject to, 107; in prison, 193; relationality, form of, 104; sex work, 171–72; social norms, challenges to, 88; as term, 30, 206n65; as unruly, 17; work as prostitutes, deriving pleasure from, 167. *See also* transgender
Treaty of Tordesillas, 202n1
trickster divinities, 124
Trouillot, Michel-Rolph, 204n34

Umbanda rituals, 117–18, 124–26, 129, 133, 143, 220n19
United States, 11, 25, 48, 100, 178, 182–83, 194, 202n11; liberalism in, xi; liberty and individual autonomy, 19; neoliberalism in, 8; queer liberalism in, 17–18
Universal Church of the Kingdom of God (UCKG), 108, 117, 133–34, 136–44, 193, 216n24; devil's presence, 130; individual sins, as forms of slavery, 132; liberation services, 114–15, 121–23, 126–28, 135, 194–95; spiritual liberation, focus on, 118; witchcraft, concern with, 123
Universal Declaration of Human Rights (UDHR), 7, 21, 183
universal freedom, 88
Universal Human Rights, 4, 187
universal rights, 88, 109, 183
urbanization, 99; and industrialization, 100–101
urban marginality, 47
urban relegation, 48

Valladares, Licia do Prado, 2, 65, 202n6
Varella, Drauzio, 193
Vargas, Getúlio, 209n15
Varjota, Brazil, 85
Velho, Otávio, 84–85
Viveiros de Castro, Eduardo, 105, 214n36

Wacquant, Loïc, 8, 21, 201n4, 204n42
Wagner, Roy, 208n11
Warner, Michel, 181
West Africa, 59
whiteness, 205n58
Whitt, Mark, 6
Williams, Erica, 167
witchcraft, 59, 115, 120, 122–24, 129, 131, 194, 210n20, 215n11; as leveling force, 135–36; minoritarian empowerment,

as form of, 141–42. *See also* devil; exorcism; possession
Wolf, Eric, 14
Woortmann, Klaas, 76–77
World Cup (2014), 196

Xuxa (TV presenter), 134

Yorubaland, 216n17
Yoruba language, 59–60